PRAEGER LIBRARY OF U.S. GOVERNMENT DEPARTMENTS AND AGENCIES

The Post Office Department

PRAEGER LIBRARY OF U.S. GOVERNMENT DEPARTMENTS
AND AGENCIES

Consulting Editors

ERNEST S. GRIFFITH

Former University Professor and Dean Emeritus, School of International Service, American University; former Director, Legislative Reference Service, Library of Congress; and author of *The American System of Government* and *The Modern Government in Action*

HUGH LANGDON ELSBREE

Former Chairman, Department of Political Science, Dartmouth College; former Managing Editor, *American Political Science Review;* former Director, Legislative Reference Service, Library of Congress

The Post Office Department

Gerald Cullinan

FOREWORD BY
JAMES A. FARLEY

FREDERICK A. PRAEGER, *Publishers*
New York • Washington • London

FREDERICK A. PRAEGER, PUBLISHERS
111 Fourth Avenue, New York, N.Y. 10003, U.S.A.
77-79 Charlotte Street, London W.1, England

Published in the United States of America in 1968
by Frederick A. Praeger, Inc., Publishers

© 1968 by Gerald Cullinan

Library of Congress Catalog Card Number: 67-22288

This book is No. 10 in the series
Praeger Library of U.S. Government Departments and Agencies

Printed in the United States of America

To my wife
BARBARA
who endured the work in progress
with patience and good humor

Charles W. Eliot, president of Harvard College, in collaboration with Woodrow Wilson, once described the Post Office as:

Messenger of Sympathy and Love
Servant of Parted Friends
Consoler of the Lonely
Bond of the Scattered Family
Enlarger of the Common Life
Carrier of News and Knowledge
Instrument of Trade and Industry
Promoter of Mutual Acquaintance
Of Peace and Good Will Among Men and Nations

Foreword

by JAMES A. FARLEY

*Postmaster General
of the United States, 1933-40*

The postal establishment is in many ways the most human of our national institutions. Every person in the United States needs its daily service, and its success or failure depends, basically, on the performance of the human beings who work for it. In recent years, there have been great advances in the development of machines and electronic devices to speed up the task of sorting the mail in post offices, but there will never be a mechanical substitute for the hard-working postmen who walk the streets of the nation and deliver the mail to its front doors.

I found my seven and a half years as Postmaster General one of the most fascinating and rewarding periods of my life. Once the Post Office gets into a man's blood, it stays there. I have never lost my interest in the development of the service, and I still make it a point to attend the annual conventions of the National Association of Postmasters to check up on the well-being of the remaining men and women who became postmasters during my years as Postmaster General.

I hope Gerald Cullinan's book will create a greater interest in the postal service among our citizens. It should. After all, the Post Office touches more people, in a more personal way, and more often, than does any other agency of our government. It is essential to our way of life. Yet, far too many

Americans take it for granted. They shrug it off as a necessary but boring presence in our day-to-day existence.

I think this is a great mistake. Most of the problems that beset the postal service, and have beset it for years, can be attributed to the apathy of the public. If the people of the United States were as interested in superior postal service as, let us say, the people of Great Britain have always been, and if they were just as insistent on the maintenance of excellence, Congress, the Bureau of the Budget, and the Department itself would be far less inclined to make the principle of service subservient to that of economy. Reasonable economy is, of course, necessary in efficient management, but it should always take second place to the requirements of service. I feel confident that many of the service curtailments that have taken place over the years would never have been ordered if the public had exhibited sufficient disapproval.

Over the years, I have developed a great fondness and a deep respect for the men and women who work in the postal establishment. They are fine Americans, hard-working and, for many years, underpaid. There have been times when they have been sorely tried by harsh administrative policies, but even when management has made the achievement of their goal more difficult than it should be, they have always done the best job possible. There has never been a time when they have let the people of this country down.

For example, consider the almost incredible degree of honesty in the postal service. Certainly, there have been cases of corruption at the national headquarters at certain times in our history, but the wonder is that there have not been more. There are numerous persons in the Post Office Department making routine daily decisions that mean millions of dollars to those who do business with the government. The possibilities for graft and bribery are almost limitless. And yet, the reputation of Post Office Department personnel for many years has been one of unparalleled integrity. This is a remarkable phenomenon—and, of course, it holds true for the approximately 34,000 postmasters and hundreds of thousands of postal workers currently employed throughout the nation. The average person has no idea how much money and negotiable paper passes through the hands of postal clerks and letter carriers every working day of the year. The figure runs into the tens of millions. Temptations are constant and great, yet cases of dishonesty are remarkably few.

I am especially pleased that Gerald Cullinan has undertaken the task of writing this book. He is well equipped for the job. A scholar with impressive credentials from the University of Oxford and a writer of wide experience, he knows the Post Office from the point of view of management (having served five and a half years in the top echelon of the Department) and labor (having worked on behalf of postal employees). More than that, he understands thoroughly the political circumstances so important when discussing the postal establishment. He comes by this understanding honestly. I knew his father, the late Eustace Cullinan of San Francisco, for years a leader in the Progressive Republican Party in California. His father's law partner, Thomas W. Hickey, was a particular friend of mine and was one of the most prominent Democrats in San Francisco. I feel this is the kind of bipartisan background necessary for producing a well-balanced history of the Post Office Department.

It is noteworthy that, in 1958, when Cullinan resigned his position in the Post Office Department as a member of a Republican administration, Lyndon B. Johnson, then the Democratic leader in the Senate, saw fit to make a speech on the Senate floor praising him for his ability and his integrity, as well as for his willingness to be helpful to those of either political party who sought his professional or personal assistance.

The history of the postal service is in some ways the history of the nation itself. The reader will find in this book a great deal of information not available anywhere else. He will find much to interest him, much to edify, and much to amuse. He will also learn a great deal about one of the most essential public services our government performs for its citizens.

Preface

There are very few homes in the United States that do not get some kind of communication—a letter, a bill, a government check, an advertising circular, a post card, a magazine, something—every day the nation's postmen are at work.

The postal system is one of the three or four really essential functions that the U.S. Government performs. It is the nation's basic form of communication, the foundation of the exchange of information upon which our free institutions—and, to a great extent, our freedom itself—depend. Without it, we would have social, economic, and political chaos.

Possibly the most significant fact about the Post Office Department is its size. In less than 200 years, it has grown from a small, uncertain operation into one of the industrial giants of the nation. In fiscal year 1965, the Department employed almost 700,000 men and women on a permanent or temporary basis. This figure was surpassed in this country only by American Telephone and Telegraph (including the Bell Telephone System), with some 800,000 employees, and General Motors, with 735,000.

In the same year, the Department's "sales" (i.e., revenues) came to $4.5 billion. This makes it the sixth largest "business" in the United States—larger than such industrial giants as U.S. Steel, Texaco, IBM, and Du Pont. (The similarity stops when it comes to the compensation of top management. The nine top executives in the Post Office Department, in fiscal year 1965, earned a combined salary of $252,000. In the same year, the chairman of the board of General Motors alone was paid $668,750.)

In fiscal year 1965, the Post Office handled 72 billion pieces of mail, roughly equivalent to 1.6 pieces every working day of the year for every man, woman, and child living within our borders. According to U.S. Post Office Department figures, this total is slightly larger than the volume of all the other nations of the world put together.

The Post Office Department is also the fastest-growing big-business operation in the United States. The annual increase in volume averages 2.5 billion pieces, and in fiscal year 1966 the increase was almost 4 billion pieces. As we shall see later on, one of the problems of the postal service is that it is growing far faster than the population is growing. In fiscal year 1965, there was an average of 371 pieces of mail for every person in the country; in 1930, 228; in 1900, 94; in 1890, 64. (In England, the average annual ratio of pieces to people is 208 to 1; in France, it is 133 to 1; in West Germany, 128 to 1; in Spain, 41 to 1.)

Early in 1967, the Postmaster General of the United States, Lawrence F. O'Brien, informed a skeptical appropriations committee of the House of Representatives that the postal establishment is in a constant, close race with catastrophe. Recent crises in the service, particularly in the Midwest in October, 1966, showed that the Post Office is in an alarming state of health, and the Postmaster General, with the best intentions in the world, could not give any positive assurance that, under existing conditions, its chronic illness might be arrested.

The problem is, of course, the size of the service and its rate of growth: how to provide the men, the machines, the facilities, and, most of all, the money to maintain this fundamental service. In short, the postal service is so large and is growing so swiftly that it is in some danger of collapsing under its own weight. In its earliest days, the postal service of the United States suffered from all the diseases of infancy. Today, the disease is acromegaly.

The problem for a writer who attempts to tell the story of the Post Office is also one of coping with size. Obviously, anyone who attempts writing a book as inclusive as this collects an enormous number of debts. I have been dependent upon thousands of individuals who, over the years, have helped to create the history of the Post Office and to record various aspects of it. Some of them are listed in the Bibliography, but, obviously, their contribution deserves more affectionate and respectful notice than is possible in that limited space. My friend and mentor G. B. Harrison, a distinguished maker of books, once said that one of the greatest sins a writer could commit is to be mean about his acknowledgments. I have no intention of committing this sin.

I owe a special debt of gratitude to James A. Farley, not only for his Foreword, but also because he has been so generous in sharing with me his experience and vast knowledge of the postal service.

The present Postmaster General, Lawrence F. O'Brien, and his special assistant, Ira Kapenstein, have been particularly cooperative in extending to me the facilities of the Department, and John D. Swygert, an outstanding career postal professional, was very helpful in supplying vital technical information. Deputy Special Assistant to the Postmaster General D. Jamison Cain and Chief of the Photography Division Carl Patterson were gracious in helping me select illustrations for the book.

I have special affection for the fine little library in the Post Office Department because, during my years in postal management, I was able to play a small part in the broadening of its scope and the extension of its facilities. I am therefore happy to record that the entire staff of the library, from Geneva C.

Chancey down, has given me valuable assistance and that an extraordinary vote of thanks is due Gertrude Enders for her creative and indispensable help. The staff of the Library of Congress has also been very cooperative.

I owe a debt of gratitude to Dr. Richard F. Fenno, Jr., professor of political science at the University of Rochester, who responded generously when asked for advice and direction. No one could have been more knowledgeable or helpful.

Deep thanks are due also to Jerome J. Keating, president, and James H. Rademacher, vice-president, of the National Association of Letter Carriers, who encouraged the work and gave freely of their time in checking the account of the recent years of the postal service against their own experience. E. C. Hallbeck, president of the United Federation of Postal Clerks, and other leaders of that organization have also helped greatly with comments on various aspects of the book.

J. Don Kerlin, one of the nation's experts on the technical aspects of postal legislation, was especially generous in giving assistance and advice. So was Booth Mooney, who had many constructive suggestions to make during the writing of the book.

A special acknowledgment goes to my daughter, Mary Patricia Cullinan, for her editorial help. And, finally, I want to express my gratitude and commiseration to Kathryn Hammersmith, who typed the manuscript and struggled to decipher not only my handwriting but also my typewriting.

To all these and many others, my warmest thanks. They are in no way responsible for the shortcomings of this account, but they deserve to share credit for whatever virtues it may have. The book would not have been possible without them. It is my sincere hope that the result will not be in any way a disappointment to them.

GERALD CULLINAN

Washington, D.C.
October, 1967

Contents

A section of photographs follows page 112.

Part I

MAIL FOR A NEW LAND

I

The Colonial and Revolutionary Posts

On the continent of North America, the first indication of any attempt to regularize the postal service appears in the *Massachusetts General Court Records* for November 5, 1639:

> For preventing the miscarriage of letters . . . it is ordered that notice bee given, that Richard Fairbanks, his house in Boston, is the place appointed for all letters which are brought from beyond the seas, or are to be sent thither . . . are to bee brought unto him and hee is to take care, that they bee delivered, or sent according to their directions and hee is allowed for every such letter 1d. and must answer all miscarriages through his owne neglect in this kind; provided that no man shall be compelled to bring his letters thither except hee please.

For at least the first 120 years, the postal system in the American colonies was primitive, slow, and uncertain. Roads were often no more than foot trails hacked through the forests. (Seymour Dunbar, in his *History of Travel in America,* reports that as late as 1704, a schoolteacher was forced to ride on horseback from Boston to New York because the road did not permit the passage of a stagecoach.) The population was sparse and, for the most part, huddled along the seacoast. Only the most adventuresome trappers penetrated the mountains, and these men were considered beyond the reach of communications—almost as if they had stepped off the edge of the world.

There was little communication between the people of one colony and those of another. Official correspondence among the colonies usually traveled by ship, a slow and uncertain process. The real interest was in maintaining communication with England, the mother country. Subjects of the crown who wished to write to those living beyond the seas were obliged to make private arrangements with ship captains, whose custom it was to hang a leathern postbag on a wall or a post in a local tavern for the receipt of letters, which, for a fixed fee, might eventually be delivered to the addressee. This arrangement was obviously haphazard, not only because of the varying characters of the captains, but also because the postbags were not locked; it was just as easy to remove letters of value as it was to deposit them. There was practically no attempt to extend postal service inland.

In 1766, almost a century and a half after the landing on Plymouth Rock, Benjamin Franklin told the House of Commons, in answer to a question, that no posts went to the inland towns and that a man living inland could direct a friend to pay the postage due on his mail and pick it up for him. It was the only way he could get his letters, unless he went himself.

Private citizens communicating with one another depended upon friends who happened to be traveling in the general direction or upon reliable Indians. (John Endicott, writing to John Winthrop, April 13, 1638, said: "Your kinde lines I receaved by Mascanomet"; and, in a letter written on April 27, 1650: "I resavid yours by the Indian.")

In the Southern colonies, roads were few and almost impassable and the population so sparse that for many years it did not seem worth the effort to try to establish any sort of postal system. In 1657, the Colonial Court of Virginia came up with an interesting attempt at a solution. It passed a law providing for the transmission of letters from one plantation to another. Each planter was required to provide a messenger to carry the dispatches to the next plantation. Failure to comply promptly made the planter liable to a fine of a hogshead of tobacco. But the law applied only to official mail.

LOVELACE'S LETTERS AND PACKETS

There were some farseeing people in the colonies during these early days who could visualize the social, economic, and political advantages in establishing a reliable postal system both within each colony and among the various colonies.

Foremost among these was Francis Lovelace, governor of New York, who, in 1672, managed to establish an intercolonial post with New England. In a letter (dated December 27, 1672) to Governor John Winthrop of Connecticut, he proposed a monthly postal communication between the two colonies "consonant to the commands laid upon us by his sacred majestie, who strictly enjoins all his American subjects to enter into a close correspondence with each other." He added that the person he had chosen to handle the New York end of the business

> I conceaved most proper, being voted active, stout and indefatigable. . . . I have affixt an annuall sallery on him, which, together with the advantage of his letters and other small portable packes, may afford him a handsome livelyhood. . . . I shall only beg of you your furtherance to so universall a good work; that is, to afford him directions where, and to whom to make his application upon his arrival in Boston; as likewise to afford him what letters you can. . . . It would be much advantageous to our designe, if in the intervall you discoursed with some of the most able woodmen, to make out the best and most facile way for a post, which in processe of tyme would be the King's best highway.

Instructions issued "at Ffort James ye 22nd of January 1673" by Governor Lovelace to his original courier included the following:

You are to comport yourself with all sobriety and civility to those that shall entrust you. . . . You are principally to apply yourselfe to the Governors, especially Gov. Winthrop, from whom you shall receave the best direction to forme ye best Post Roade. . . .

You shall do well to provide your selfe to a Spare Horse, good Port Mantels soe neither Letter nor Pacquetts receive any Damage under your hands.

There are some other considerations wch I shall forbear to mention till your return and I receive a further accompt of you, and soe God bless all your honest undertakings.

As if the courier would not be busy enough carrying, picking up, and delivering mail and forming post roads along the way, the governor, in a postscript, instructed him to report any deserting soldiers and runaway servants he might meet.

The "Lovelace Post" did not have a chance of survival. In August, 1673, approximately six months after its institution, with England and Holland at war, a Dutch fleet entered the harbor of New York and retook the colony. Governor Lovelace found his occupation gone—and with it, his dreams of an efficient intercolonial post. The Dutch, in uneasy repossession of New Amsterdam, were not particularly eager to communicate with their English neighbors. When, not long after, through the Treaty of Westminster (February, 1674), the English were ceded New Amsterdam once again, it was a new English governor, Sir Edmund Andros, who accepted the surrender of the city.

Andros, an imperious and ambitious man, was nevertheless an able administrator. He was far too busy consolidating his own position in this doubtful land to worry about reinstituting the Lovelace Post. He was sufficiently occupied trying, unsuccessfully, to annex to New York the Jerseys, the Delaware Territory, and part of New England and—an effort that was to be successful—to create a solid and lasting alliance with the Iroquois. The idea of establishing a useful system of postal communications languished.

NEALE'S PATENT

The first glimmer of a breakthrough occurred on February 17, 1692, when King William and Queen Mary granted Thomas Neale, a favorite of the crown, a twenty-one-year patent empowering him to set up and maintain a postal service in the American colonies. Patents or monopolies such as this were designed to enable royal favorites to enrich themselves with very little effort. The American colonial postal patent, however, was an unlucky one. Instead of enriching Neale, it bankrupted him.

The patent was granted and received in an atmosphere of almost total ignorance of the problems involved. The crown, the postal masters in England, and Neale himself had absolutely no idea of the primitive conditions of transportation prevailing in the colonies. It is probable that they understood but imperfectly either the distances that had to be traversed or the difficulties inherent in the uneven distribution of the population.

In the patent, the monarchs stated the need for an organized postal service in America in this way:

> Whereas our Trusty and wellbeloved servant, Thomas Neale Esquire hath lately humbly represented to us that there never hath bin any post established for the conveying of Letters between Virginia, Maryland, Delaware, New Yorke, New England, East and West Jersey, Pensilvania and Northward as far as our Dominions reach in America. And that the want thereof hath been a great hindrance to the trade of those parts.

Of course, Neale had no intention of ever setting foot in the colonies, and he never did. His responsibility was simply to devise a plan and appoint a deputy who would represent him in America and make the plan work. He could charge such rates of postage as the traffic would bear and keep the profits. He was not required to make an accounting to the English Treasury until twenty of the twenty-one years of the patent had expired. He was expected, however, to keep "fairly written" books, which Treasury officials could look at upon demand.

Neale began well. He appointed as his deputy the governor of the Jerseys, Andrew Hamilton, an able and attractive Scotsman. Hamilton persuaded most of the colonies to cooperate in regard to intercolonial posts, but he ran into great difficulty, especially in Massachusetts and Virginia, in the matter of intracolonial posts. There was a loophole in the patent, and the deputy could do little to force compliance. The colonies were naturally eager to retain the revenues from posts that originated and terminated within their borders.

Since intracolonial mail represented the bulk of the business, the failure of colonies to cooperate in this area doomed the patent to failure. But other problems beset Hamilton: the widely varying value of the coinage in the various colonies made the application of a uniform rate structure impracticable, the lack of usable roads made the transportation of the mail hideously expensive and slow, and the volume never approached the expectations that had prompted the granting of the patent in the first place.

Supervision and policing of the mail system were almost nonexistent. Everyone carried the mail. Important letters were not entrusted to the post. It has been estimated that less than half of the total volume of correspondence went by official post, a situation that naturally deprived the struggling postal service of potential revenue.

In 1698, Neale tried to sell his patent back to the government for a lump sum of £5,000 or £1,000 a year for the rest of his life. The government refused. Neale died bankrupt the next year. His principal creditors, Hamilton and a Robert

West, were awarded proprietorship of the American colonial postal service. In 1703, Hamilton died, and his widow retained control of the monopoly until 1707, when the crown bought back the patent for a reported £1,664. Hamilton's son, John, was retained as Postmaster General for America, a post he held until 1730. With the purchase of the Neale patent, the history of the privately owned post in America came to an end.

THE CROWN TAKES OVER

In 1711, the government of Queen Anne finally decided to do something constructive about creating a proper mail service in the colonies. It was high time. The crown had about 295,-000 subjects living there, with almost half that number located in New England. New York had about 20,000; the Jerseys, Pennsylvania, and Delaware, about 35,000; Maryland, Virginia, and North Carolina, about 100,000. South Carolina, the far frontier, had fewer than 9,000, most of whom were living in and near Charleston. The roads were scarcely any better than they had been sixty years previously. In clement weather, an official letter from Virginia took six weeks to reach New York; in winter, twice as long.

However, the Act of 1711, which established an official colonial post, indicated that the crown was more concerned with raising revenues to pay for England's wars than with improving service. In England, there was still vast ignorance of the physical conditions existing in America and a complacent disregard for the almost insurmountable colonial problems. Rates of postage were set: from London to New York, 1s.; from Charleston to New York, 1s. 6d.; from the West Indies to New York, 4d.; from New York to Philadelphia, 9d.; from New York to Boston, 1s.; from New York to Annapolis, 1s. 3d. As can be seen, the rate structure was capricious, with little bearing on comparative distances or difficulty of transmission. To ensure maximum revenue, the rates between the largest settlements were set high, and the act also attempted to impose a monopoly on private letters.

Although most of the colonies incorporated the Act of 1711 in their own statutes, Virginia refused to do so. The House of Burgesses raised, for the first time, the issue of "taxation without representation" and not only refused to appropriate any money to promote the success of the project, but also passed crippling legislation that made the operation of the parliamentary posts practically impossible within Virginia's borders.

Hamilton was able to use the provisions of the act to improve transportation conditions to a point where, in 1717, according to Jonathan Dickinson of Philadelphia, a post between Williamsburg, Virginia, and Boston could be "completed in four weeks, from March to December, and in double that time in the other months of the year." But lax supervision and the persistent determination of the colonists to avoid paying postage combined to provide deficits rather than the hoped-for profits.

In 1730, Hamilton was succeeded by Alexander Spotswood, former governor of Virginia, who, in a moment of sublime optimism, contracted with the crown to manage the colonial postal system at a fixed salary of £300 a year for ten years plus 10 per cent of the clear profits. He held the position for nine years, during which time, of course, there were no profits, clear or otherwise.

Postmaster General Franklin

Spotswood's most notable act was to appoint, in 1737, Benjamin Franklin deputy postmaster general in Philadelphia. (All local postmasters were called deputy postmasters general.) Franklin's obvious capability caused him to be placed in charge of several other neighboring post offices as comptroller.* In 1753, after two of Spotswood's successors failed to

* This system was followed, in essence, until the Post Office Department decentralized its operations in 1954.

make any improvement in the postal system, Franklin and William Hunter of Williamsburg were appointed co-postmasters general for the colonies.

It should be noted that the postmastership of Philadelphia was a windfall for Franklin, who was a moderately successful publisher at the time of his appointment. Publishers eagerly sought appointment as postmaster in their communities. The laws contained no provision for the introduction of newspapers into the mails, and no rates of postage were established for them. Postmasters could make up their own rules as they went along. If they were also publishers, they could, and did, send their own publications through the mails free of charge and deny the use of the mails to their competitors. Naturally, this gave the publisher-postmaster a considerable advantage.*

Franklin, in his *Autobiography,* says of his appointment to the Philadelphia position: "I accepted it readily and found it to great advantage; for though the salary was small, it facilitated the correspondence that improved my newspaper, increased the number demanded, as well as the advertisements to be inserted, so that it came to afford me a considerable income." To his credit, Franklin, when he became Postmaster General, admitted all newspapers to the mails at a reasonable rate of postage.

Franklin and Hunter performed a miracle of management. They moved swiftly and energetically to reform the demoralized service. Franklin made an extensive tour of inspection, traveling as far south as Virginia; he authorized new surveys of the routes, shortening some and improving those in existence. He persuaded state legislatures to build usable post roads and repair those they already had. In one notable case, he instituted night service between New York and Philadel-

---

* Earlier, tavern keepers were the usual "postmasters" in the colonies. The fact that letters were left in their establishments, to be called for by addressees, attracted potential customers. Also, it was often the custom to pay the innkeeper for his trouble by excusing him from the excise tax on the beverages he sold—permitting him to undersell his opposition.

phia and thus made it possible, in clement weather, to achieve overnight communication between those two cities. The service was improved between New York and Boston so that a citizen could reasonably expect an answer to his letter in three weeks. Before the Franklin regime, the usual time was double that.

Franklin and Hunter cracked down on the dishonest postrider and, by so doing, greatly enhanced the revenues of the service. The practice was for postriders to solicit business on their own. As a result, many postriders carried in their bags only a few letters upon which postage had been paid—and a great many others from which only they derived profits.

Stagecoaches were still sparingly used in the postal system at this time because of the scarcity of roads capable of accommodating them, but the drivers of these vehicles also deprived the Post Office of revenues and profited thereby. The drivers hung the letters they were carrying for their own profit from a pole suspended from the coach so they could swear they were carrying no contraband correspondence inside. Stagecoach drivers and ferrymen also were guilty of delaying the mails by refusing to move until they had a full passenger load. Franklin induced the colonial legislatures to take action against these operators and thus greatly accelerated the service.

Hunter served ably until his death in 1761. He was succeeded as co-Postmaster General by John Foxcroft, a New Yorker, who held the position until the Revolution brought the British colonial postal system to an end.

The miracle of Benjamin Franklin was that he made the colonial postal service pay. After showing a deficit of £943 16s. 1d. for the first four years, during which he was instituting reforms and improvements, he was able to return an annual profit to the British Treasury. For the years 1758–62, he reported a surplus of £1,438 9d. The official records of the British Post Office, laconically noting the receipt of this lastmentioned sum, added: "This is the first remittance ever made of this kind."

In 1765, when Canada and Florida had been added to the possessions of the crown, the American colonial posts consisted of the Northern division (from Quebec to Virginia) and the Southern division (the Carolinas, the Floridas, and the Bahamas). Franklin and Foxcroft retained direction in the North. The Southern division was never a success. Sparse population, totally inadequate roads, and low volume combined to keep it from being anything but a persistent drain on the English Treasury.

During the last half of the 1760's, Foxcroft managed the postal service in the North almost singlehanded. Relations between the colonies and the crown were worsening, and Franklin was sent to England as a "lobbyist" for Massachusetts in an effort to effect the repeal of the Stamp Act. He remained for eleven years. In his absence, Foxcroft carried on well. The postal service prospered. The profit for 1769 was £1,859, and in 1774, the eve of the Revolution, it was £3,000 —a considerable sum in those days.

But despite surface appearances, the postal system of the crown was in serious trouble. By 1766, the rebellious Sons of Liberty were disrupting the postal service in the colonies, calling it a "grievous instrument of taxation." Ship captains were forced to deliver their letters to coffeehouses instead of to the legal post offices, thus depriving the service of revenue. The inland posts, such as they were, became uncertain because postriders were often intercepted by rebels in the performance of their duties.

By December, 1772, Franklin had fallen out of favor with the British authorities to such an extent that, without consulting him, the government appointed Hugh Finlay "Surveyor of Post Offices and Post Roads on the Continent of North America." His job was to report to England the true conditions of the postal service in America and, very possibly, to develop sufficient evidence to support the dismissal of Franklin. (As

Franklin himself wrote in a letter to Foxcroft, February 4, 1772, he had "become a little obnoxious to the Ministry.")

Finlay found much about which to complain. His journal shows that the regulations of the postal service were almost universally disregarded. Postriders and drivers of stagecoaches were stealing business from the post offices that employed them. (In one case, Finlay found a postrider delivering some oxen along his route, having undertaken this assignment for his own enrichment and at considerable detriment to the speed of the posts.)

Worse still, from Finlay's point of view, plans were being laid for the creation of an American postal system independent of and competitive with the established posts of the crown. William Goddard, a Baltimore publisher, was openly advocating a "Constitutional Post Office," which, if permitted to survive, would drive the official postal service out of business. Goddard attacked the existing institution on the grounds that it was illegally taxing the colonists. He also objected that postmasters were being instructed to open and read letters passing through their hands in order to check subversion at its source. Goddard's proposals were receiving favorable response from all over the Northern colonies.

Already Franklin had come in for a considerable amount of criticism in England for his absentee direction of the American posts. On January 3, 1774, the blow fell. It came in a terse note from Anthony Todd, secretary to the British Postmaster General:

> Sir: I have received the command of His Majesty's Postmaster General to signify to you that they find it necessary to dismiss you from being any longer their deputy for America. You will therefore cause your accounts to be made up as soon as you can conveniently. I am, sir, your most obedient servant, etc."

Finlay was appointed in Franklin's place and, with Foxcroft, served nominally until 1782.

Franklin was bitter about his dismissal, claiming it was solely for political reasons. (The phrase has a modern sound.) But the crown, from its point of view, had good and sufficient reason for dismissing him. It would have been madness to retain a man of Franklin's political sympathies in control of the only effective system of communication existing in colonies that were becoming increasingly rebellious.

The colonial post never amounted to much after Franklin was dismissed. It deteriorated steadily, with only occasional spasms of activity. For all practical purposes, the story of the British postal service in America ended on Christmas Day, 1775, when the crown closed the post office in New York City. Officially, it continued until October 18, 1782, when the Continental Congress passed an ordinance establishing its own post offices.

GODDARD'S POST

The peremptory dismissal of so popular a figure as Franklin caused great indignation in the colonies. It also caused concern in those circles in England where he was still highly respected. Franklin remained in England for a year after his removal in the hope that he could be of some service in helping to save what was left of the relationship between the mother country and her American colonies. However, he was in deep disgrace with the court, and conditions continued to deteriorate. He returned to America in March, 1775, a month before Lexington and Concord.

Before Franklin returned, Goddard had moved forward with his idea of a separate post, with the conviction that this would "defeat one Revenue Act and unite all the friends of America in one common bond of alliance and reduce postage of letters one-third, as well as insure the transmission of interesting advice to place of destination." His plan called for the raising of money by subscription for the establishment of a postal system, with the subscribers in each colony appointing local postmasters and setting the rates of postage. Postmasters, who were to be paid a percentage of their revenues, were to make their own contracts with postriders.

"Goddard's Post" was so successful that by May, 1775, Foxcroft's revenues had dwindled until he could no longer pay his New England riders and was forced to dismiss them. By that time, there was a rebel post office in every major community from Boston to Williamsburg—thirty of them in all. Many of the postmasters were "converts" from the crown's postal system.

The Americans made the failure of the British post doubly sure by continually intercepting its riders, intimidating those who did business with it, and even arming their own ships to intercept mail on the high seas.

B. FRANKLIN AGAIN

On July 26, 1775, a committee of the Continental Congress (Franklin, Thomas Lynch, R. H. Lee, Thomas Willing, Samuel Adams, and Philip Livingston) recommended establishment of an official American postal service, with headquarters in Philadelphia. The system was to extend between Falmouth, Massachusetts, and Savannah, Georgia. The Postmaster General was to receive a salary of $1,000 a year and his secretary-comptroller $340. The recommendation was immediately and unanimously adopted, and Franklin was appointed Postmaster General on the same day.

The new service drove what was left of the king's postal service out of business. Franklin appointed his son-in-law, Richard Bache, his secretary-comptroller, overlooking Goddard, who, with considerable justice, felt that he deserved greater consideration. Goddard was made a surveyor, at a salary of $100 a year. He was soon eased out of the service altogether. It was typical of the somewhat flamboyant nature of Franklin that as Postmaster General he changed the wording of his frank from "Free, B. Franklin" to "B Free, Franklin."

In September, 1776, Franklin was given the post of Commissioner to France, and Bache was appointed Postmaster General in his place. When Franklin left for his new diplomatic post in November, he ended his official connection with the postal service.

A SON-IN-LAW TAKES OVER

Bache had a tremendously difficult task, which he performed, on the whole, rather inadequately. The Revolution was in full sway. From an operational point of view, the most important job was to keep efficient lines of communication open between the Continental Congress and the armies in the field. Bache was able to do this reasonably well, despite frequent grumblings by the commanders, including Washington, who felt the service could be improved upon. He also was charged with the responsibility of maintaining effective communications among the states—a task considerably complicated by the vicissitudes of war. At various times, the principal port cities fell into the hands of the British, and the post routes were constantly interrupted.

But Bache's principal difficulties were financial. The Continental Congress granted the privilege of the frank to its own members and to the military, from the generals down to the privates in the ranks, thereby drastically reducing potential revenue. The Congress also hampered the postal system's development by refusing to interfere with posts that states operated within their own borders.

But the real stumbling block in the financial picture was the devaluation of the Continental currency. In January, 1779, Bache complained that the revenues were steadily declining and that it had become necessary to pay postriders eight times as much as had been the case in the first year of the service. He wanted the authority to draw on the Treasury each quarter for as much money as had been needed to operate the postal service during the previous three months. The Continental Congress refused, insisting upon its prerogative of appropriating specific sums in advance.

Postage rates were doubled in 1779. At the same time, the salaries of all postal officials were also doubled. Six months later, as American money became almost valueless, postage rates were increased to twenty times what they had been in 1775. And still the deficits continued to rise.

The morale of the new service suffered greatly. In December, 1779, the Post Office owed $17,666 to the postriders "according to the nearest computation the Comptroller could make." The riders went back to their old habit of carrying letters for their own profit. Ship captains once again bypassed the Post Office and delivered correspondence personally, pocketing the proceeds. Roads in most colonies began to deteriorate, and the colonial legislatures were balky about appropriating money to better them.

In May, 1780, postage rates were again doubled. It did no good. Figures for this period are meaningless. Ebenezer Hazard, the surveyor for the Department, received $40 a day for board and lodging when he was on the road. His expenses actually came to $289 a day—and he was by nature a frugal man.

Finally, in December, 1780, the Continental Congress tried to regulate currency by putting it on a specie basis. Salaries were cut back severely, but it was ordered that they be paid in "specie or other money equivalent." Postriders were promised that the losses they had suffered through the depreciation of the currency would be made up. The postage rates were set at double those that had been charged by the British.

On October 19, 1781, the Post Office Committee of the Continental Congress made several suggestions for the reform

of the postal service. One of the first of these urged the aboli-
tion of the congressional frank. This suggestion was turned
down, but others, including reduction of postage rates and
dismissal of all postriders, were adopted. However, the date
of activation was delayed several times. Before the suggestions
could be acted upon, Ebenezer Hazard, who had been postmaster in New York in the Goddard days, replaced Bache as
Postmaster General (January 18, 1782).

To Bind a Nation

Hazard, an effective man, immediately asked that the Continental Congress start from the beginning and revise the Post
Office law from top to bottom. The request was particularly
timely, since Cornwallis had surrendered in the previous October, and a permanent peacetime postal establishment had to
be built.

George Washington was especially aware of this need. He
insisted upon the necessity of improving the lines of communication among the states and with the settlements on the frontier. "These settlers are on a pivot and the touch of a feather
would turn them away," he wrote. And again: "Let us bind
these people to us with a chain that can never be broken."
When the postal establishment was reorganized, he personally
surveyed some of the proposed post roads.

The Congress responded to Hazard's urgent request with
dispatch and thoroughness. On October 18, 1782, it passed
legislation that pulled together all the regulations concerning
organization, mail routes, postage rates, and penalties for
offenses against the posts. The new act made it clear that the
central government would have sole control of both interstate
and intrastate posts.

The act forbade anyone to carry private letters for hire,
even within the borders of his own state. (This prohibition
became a sore point in several of the states, particularly Mary-

land and Virginia, where the Congress was accused of tyrannical behavior.) It also stipulated that each post office must maintain a service of at least once a week and required all officials and employees of the postal service, regardless of rank, to take an oath of office swearing that they would faithfully fulfill the duties imposed upon them.

The act also established the principle of the sanctity of the mails by providing that, except in time of war, no private letters could be opened or destroyed without a specific order from the President or the Congress.

This important act (with amendments) remained the basic postal law in the new nation for ten years. It reiterated the principle established in the Articles of Confederation (finally ratified the previous year) that the Post Office was a service and was not to be considered merely as a source of revenue. The system was to be self-sustaining, but all profits were to be plowed back into it for the betterment and extension of postal services and facilities. (All funds already advanced to the Post Office by the Treasury were to be repaid out of revenues at an accrued interest of 6 per cent.)

Armed with this new code, Hazard worked industriously to create an efficient service. He finally was able to extend postal lines as far south as Savannah, Georgia. He moved to enforce the postal monopoly and brought suit against stagecoaches that carried mail for private profit in violation of the new law.

Roads were improved. Under the prodding of the Congress, Hazard—who had justifiable doubts on the subject—turned more and more to the stagecoaches for the transportation of mail, at least along the "great post road" south of Boston. In 1785, he arranged (at a contract price of $19,600) that during the next year the mail would be carried by stage from Portsmouth, New Hampshire, to Savannah, Georgia, and from New York City to Albany three times a week in clement weather and twice a week in inclement weather.

Hazard still had difficulty convincing postriders, stagecoach drivers, and ordinary citizens of the importance of the mail. Stage drivers would often leave the mail behind them if they could squeeze in a passenger or two in its place. Ferry captains often refused to set sail until their boats were filled with passengers, whether or not mail was delayed. Cases of abandonment of the mails were common. It took a long period of education and law enforcement for this shortsightedness to be corrected even partially.

Hazard also had the problem of dealing with the individual states, which remained jealous of their rights and powers. Separatism and fear of a too strong central government were still endangering the life of the infant nation. In June, 1786, in the face of great protest, the Postmaster General instructed his postmasters not to accept the paper money of the various states in payment for postage. The Congress supported him. He gained congressional approval of the principle that all post offices, whether or not they were situated on the main post road, were under the jurisdiction of the central government. Hazard also took a significant step in establishing crossposts and developing service inland as far as Pittsburgh and Chambersburg, Pennsylvania.

The Post Office showed a surplus of $5,220 in 1785, of $10,730 in 1786, and of $1,839 in 1787. Despite his fine performance, Hazard ran afoul of some of the most powerful people in America when he tried to reduce, by regulation, the heavy expenses involved in transporting and delivering newspapers. When he terminated the practice of "free exchanges" among publishers of papers, even George Washington (who, apparently, never did care for Hazard very much) complained bitterly, accusing the Postmaster General (in a letter to John Jay, July 18, 1788) of purposely trying to limit the exchange of intelligence "at the instant when the momentous question of a general government was to have come before the people." Washington also censured Hazard, quite unfairly, for taking the mail away from the stagecoaches and giving it to postriders. Hazard had grown disgusted with the unreliability of the stages, and when the riders proposed to perform the same services for a little more than half the price, he accepted the offer. He also claimed that the roads, though improved, were not yet good enough to support reliable stagecoach service.

A POLITICAL DISMISSAL

Printers and stagecoach proprietors were two very important interests in American life, and they were solidly against Hazard. The rumor was started that he was anti-Federalist and was suppressing the circulation of information in order to prevent ratification of the new Constitution. On the other hand, the anti-Federalists claimed that he was discriminating against them. Attacks on the Postmaster General became common in the Continental Congress.

Hazard knew his days as Postmaster General were numbered, and so did others who were desirous of his place. As he wrote in a letter in 1788, he felt he would be replaced by "somebody, I dare say, who never risqued his neck *pro bono publico* as I did in 1776 and afterwards, but sees something in a public station now, and more especially under the new Constitution."

Hazard turned out to be an accurate prophet. The new Constitution was ratified. George Washington was elected President of the new nation and was sworn in on April 30, 1789. Samuel Osgood, who had been serving on the Treasury Board, was appointed Postmaster General to replace Hazard on September 27, 1789. (Franklin's son-in-law, Bache, had wanted his old job back again and never forgave Washington for passing him over. Colonel William Smith, son-in-law of Adams, was another unsuccessful candidate.)

The Post Office of the United States of America began its

life with the unbecoming spectacle of a superior and successful public servant being dismissed for political reasons in
favor of a man of comparatively mediocre talents. It was not
the last time that such a thing was to happen in the conduct
of the postal affairs of the nation.

II

The First Forty Years

When Samuel Osgood took office under the Constitution as the first Postmaster General of the United States, there were, by the most reliable count, seventy-five post offices in the country.* The population had grown to about 3 million, not counting Indians or slaves—an increase of approximately 1,000 per cent since the beginning of the eighteenth century.

The form of the postal system had been set. Although it was to vary greatly in particulars over the years, in general it was much the same in 1789 as it was until the 1940's, or before its operations were decentralized. There were 1,785 miles of post roads, almost all of them lying along the East Coast.

---

* The seventy-five original U.S. post offices were: CONNECTICUT: Hartford, Middletown, New Haven, Fairfield, Norwalk, Stamford, New London, Norwich; DELAWARE: Wilmington, Duck Creek, Dover; GEORGIA: Savannah; MARYLAND: Elkton, Easton, Charlestown, Havre de Grace, Harford, Baltimore, Chester Mills, Warwick, Georgetown Cross Roads, Chestertown; NEW JERSEY: Newark, Elizabeth, Brunswick, Princeton, Trenton; NEW HAMPSHIRE: Portsmouth; NEW YORK: New York; NORTH CAROLINA: Edentown, New Bern, Washington, Wilmington; SOUTH CAROLINA: Georgetown, Charleston; PENNSYLVANIA: Bristol, Philadelphia, Chester, Lancaster, Yorktown, Carlisle, Shippenberg, Chambersburg, Bedford, Pittsburgh; MASSACHUSETTS: Wicassett, Portland, Boston, Ipswich, Newburyport, Salem, Worcester, Springfield; RHODE ISLAND: Newport, Providence, East Greenwich, South Kingston; VIRGINIA: Blandensburg, Georgetown, Alexandria, Colchester, Dumfries, Fredericksburg, Bowling Green, Hanover Court House, Petersburg, Cabin Point, Smithfield, Suffolk, Yorktown, Hampton, Norfolk. (Some of the state lines have been shifted since Osgood's day, and some of the post offices are now in states that did not then exist. Thus, for example, Portland, now in Maine, is listed above as a Massachusetts city.)

Because of the insistence of Congress, stagecoaches, unsatisfactory as they were, had become the principal method of mail transportation, except in the South and on the crossposts. In Osgood's first full year as Postmaster General, there was a reported surplus of $5,796. However, the accounting of the time was so haphazard and unreliable that this figure must be considered an approximation.

This surplus might seem to indicate an auspicious beginning for the new postal establishment, but it should be remembered that the morale of the service was deplorable, thefts by coachmen and postriders were commonplace, and the public grumbled continually about the unsatisfactory service and the high rates of postage. In many parts of the country, citizens preferred to ignore the Post Office and transmit their intelligence by private means. The law of 1782 was widely ignored.

A CLOUDED BEGINNING

The U.S. postal service began under a cloud of controversy. The Act of 1789, which created the Post Office on what amounted to a temporary basis, said nothing whatsoever about the position this new creation should occupy in the executive branch of the government. It stated only that "the Postmaster General shall be subject to the direction of the President of the United States in performing the duties of his office and in forming contracts for the transportation of the mail."

British tradition, which the Americans followed closely, dictated that the Post Office should be an adjunct of the Treasury. To this pattern, Thomas Jefferson entered strenuous objection, not because he saw any illogic in the plan, but because his rival and opponent Alexander Hamilton happened to be Secretary of the Treasury. Jefferson said that "the Department of the Treasury possesses already such an influence as to swallow up the whole executive powers," adding that "future presidents . . . would not be able to make headway against this department."

Jefferson, as Secretary of State, suggested to President Washington that the Post Office be made a subsidiary of his department and that all revenues theretofore turned over to the Treasury be transferred to the State Department. However, Washington refused to accede to Jefferson's request, and the Post Office was annexed, rather loosely, to the Treasury.

The term first used to describe the U.S. postal service was "General Post Office." The term "Post Office Department" was not used in any official sense until 1825, and, in fact, the Post Office was not formally recognized by Congress as an executive department of the government until as late as 1873. The early postmasters general reported to the President through the Secretary of the Treasury. Not until Andrew Jackson became President (1829) was the Postmaster General made a member of the cabinet.

Considering the rather difficult circumstances in which he found himself, it is not surprising that Osgood acted somewhat less than boldly in his capacity as Postmaster General. Timidly, he asked Congress for an allowance of $300 a year for rental of quarters for his office—out of which he said that he would be able to engage a domestic to light the fire.

In his first report to the Secretary of the Treasury, dated January 22, 1790, Osgood complained that existing ordinances for regulating the Post Office had not been put into effect. He also expressed the opinion that if the rates were reduced from thirty-three ninetieths of a dollar to five cents, 500,000 letters would be sent a year, with great benefits accruing to the Treasury because of the increased volume. He pointed to the fact that at least twenty private contractors were illegally carrying the mail in competition with the Post Office, and he asked that a system of rates be set up that would take into consideration the various coinages still existing within the states.

These were sensible suggestions, but they fell on deaf ears. Hamilton, his superior, looked upon the Post Office as a revenue-producing agency that could help him reduce the national debt. Congress was too busy debating constitutional matters to take more than passing interest in the development of the postal service. Indeed, the constitutionality of even having a national postal system was debated in Congress. There were those who felt the posts should be operated by the individual states or by private patent.

Also acrimoniously discussed was the question of who should have the right of creating post roads. The House of Representatives felt that its members, being more conversant with the specific needs of their districts (as well as their own political needs), should determine which post roads should be created, which maintained, and which abandoned. The Senate, on the other hand, felt that such an arrangement would lead to extravagance and chaos and was determined to leave this problem in the hands of the Postmaster General.

Because Congress could not reach agreement on this issue, the Post Office was continued in existence only by annual legislation until 1794, when Congress finally established the postal service permanently and officially. (Congress eventually reserved to itself the right of extending post roads.) Before that time, Osgood had had enough. He resigned after less than two years in office and went into public service in New York.

Osgood was followed in office by Colonel Timothy Pickering of Pennsylvania, a rather more forceful personality, who understood better the art of getting cooperation from Congress. He served from August 12, 1791, to January 2, 1795, and made quite a distinguished record.

THE ACT OF 1792

In the first year of Pickering's administration, Congress passed the very important Act of 1792, the first broad, basic postal legislation in ten years. Its thirty short sections covered the entire business of the Post Office. It fixed rates, designated post roads, and provided for punishment of crimes against the posts. The Postmaster General was given the right to appoint all postmasters and to enter into all contracts for the transportation of mail over the routes designated by Congress, provided the contracts were advertised in advance to encourage competitive bidding.

Congress also insisted that the Post Office be self-supporting. The rates of postage set by the Act of 1792 were lower than those that had prevailed previously, but they were still exorbitant. A single letter (i.e., a single sheet folded over, sealed, and addressed on the back) cost six cents for transmission up to 30 miles, with the rate increasing to a maximum of twenty-five cents for any distance over 450 miles. Two sheets cost double, three sheets treble. For a single sheet enclosed in an envelope, the rate was double.

These high rates remained in effect for the next forty-five years (one year, 1815–16, they were increased by 50 per cent to help defray the costs of the War of 1812) and discouraged widespread use of the mails. In the late eighteenth century, twenty-five cents would buy five dozen eggs, four pounds of butter, or two bushels of potatoes. (As late as 1834, there was a case of a farmer settling an account with his postmaster for thirty-two letters by giving him a "good milch cow" valued at $8.) As a general rule, in those days, the recipient of a letter paid for it. He could but hope that his expensive correspondents had something worthwhile to say.

THE ACT OF 1794

The Act of 1794 officially established the Post Office as a permanent part of the federal government and ended the exasperating situation of the Postmaster General each year having to extract from Congress legislation continuing the service in existence.

It was also in 1794 that the first letter carriers made their appearance in the cities of America. They received no salaries but were permitted to collect two cents for every letter they delivered. Since the addressees had the option of accepting this service or calling at the post office to pick up their mail, the letter carriers of the period had little opportunity to become wealthy.

Like Osgood, Pickering believed that the service should be extended and improved, even if it cost more money than could possibly be realized from revenues. He succeeded in establishing routes farther into the West, saying that "our fellow citizens in the remote parts of the Union seem entitled to some indulgence" even if the mail service connecting them with "the seat of government . . . and the principal commercial towns" could not be self-sustaining in the foreseeable future.

Pickering was responsible for a significant advance when he was able to extend the posts from Pittsburgh, Pennsylvania, to the settlement of Wheeling on the Ohio River, making possible the use of the river during nine months of the year as a means of conveying the mail westward by a fleet of small mail boats that ran from Wheeling to Limestone, Kentucky, in five days. (During winter, the mail to Kentucky still had to be transported over the Wilderness Road—a long and arduous journey.)

When congressional doubts were raised about the practicality of the Ohio River route because of its expense, Rufus Putnam, a postal surveyor general, wrote Pickering from Marietta on the Ohio urging that the service be maintained at all costs. He admitted the expense and the danger resulting from constant attacks by the Indians but added: "Nothing can be more fatal to a Republican Government than ignorance among its citizens. They will be made the easy dupes of designing men, instead of supporting the laws, the reason and the policy of which they are ignorant." As George Washington had predicted years earlier, the postal service had become a principal means by which the people of the United States were bound together in loyalty to the central government.

On January 2, 1795, Pickering left his position to become Washington's Secretary of War. When he resigned, the mileage of the post roads had been increased to 13,207 and the number of post offices to 463.

HABERSHAM'S COACH SERVICE

Pickering's successor, Joseph Habersham, a Georgian who had been a delegate to the Continental Congress, served until 1801—during the rest of the Washington Administration and that of John Adams. The Post Office, as Habersham found it, was still a primitive organization. It consisted of himself, an assistant postmaster general, and three clerks. In 1795, Habersham complained that while the mail volume had increased sevenfold since the institution of the office (by a very rough official estimate of the time, from 265,545 letters a year to 1,365,469, not counting newspapers), only three clerks had been added to the staff. Congress responded cautiously, raising his allowance for clerk hire from an original $2,000 a year to $4,250 and then telling him he could hire as many additional clerks as he wanted, as long as he didn't exceed the appropriation for this purpose. By the time he left office, he had added three more clerks to the headquarters staff.

So small was the operation of the postal service in these years that when the government was moved from Philadelphia to Washington in 1800, all the records, furniture, and supplies of the Post Office made the journey in two wagons. It was not until 1810, during the Madison Administration, that the federal government considered the Post Office sufficiently important to have a headquarters of its own, bought the "Hotel Building" in Washington for $10,000, and transformed it into a headquarters for the Post Office and the Patent Office.

Tired of the difficulties of dealing with stagecoach operators, Habersham risked political suicide by instituting a government-owned coach service between Philadelphia and New York. The mail coaches, which were designed in 1799 according to Habersham's personal specifications, must have been gaudy affairs. Habersham's design called for the following:

The body painted green, colors formed of Prussian blue and yellow ochre; carriage and wheels red, lead mixed to approach vermilion, as near as may be; octagon panel in the back, black; octagon blends, green; elbow piece on rail, front rail and back, red as above; on all doors Roman capitals in patent yellow, "United States Mail Stage," and over these a spread eagle of size and color to suit.

There was no reason for anyone to mistake the U.S. mail coach when it rolled into town.

By the time Habersham left office, he had increased the mileage of post roads to 22,207. The new nation was forcing its way relentlessly into the wilderness. Habersham was able to report, with evident satisfaction, that "cross-roads are now established so extensively that there is scarcely a village, court house, or public place of any consequence but is accommodated with the mail." In view of this considerable achievement, the manner of Habersham's dismissal from office was a little surprising.

Thomas Jefferson, during the years before he was elected to the Presidency, had been extremely critical of the Post Office and all its works. He doubted what he termed the "fidelity" of the establishment and, above all, feared that it would become a vicious political instrument. As he wrote Madison in 1796: "I view it as a source of boundless patronage to the executive, jobbing to Members of Congress and their friends, and a boundless abyss of public money."

Like so many men before and after him, Jefferson altered his public views considerably upon reaching the pinnacle of power. The change was marked in regard to patronage. Once elected President, Jefferson appeared to feel that he could not trust any man in office who had prospered under John Adams. Federalist appointees were proscribed, and Habersham was "permitted to resign" nine months after Jefferson took office.

EXPANSION UNDER GRANGER

Habersham's place was taken by Gideon Granger, a Connecticut lawyer, who served as Postmaster General for twelve years—longer than any other to date in U.S. history. Andrew Jackson is generally credited—or discredited—with having instituted the spoils system in the federal government. However, Thomas Jefferson, though acting in a more genteel way, preceded him by twenty-eight years. He ordered Granger to get rid of all Federalist postmasters and to pay particular attention to those who were also printers and editors of newspapers.

Granger obediently followed orders. As he wrote to one printer-postmaster: "The printer of a newspaper is not the most proper person to discharge the duties of a postmaster. . . . The public interest will be promoted by the appointment of a new postmaster." It need hardly be mentioned that the Jefferson-Granger prejudice against printer-postmasters did not extend to members of their own party.

As Postmaster General, Granger presided over the greatest expansion of the postal service in the nation's history. The Louisiana Purchase, in 1803, added nearly 1 million square miles to the land area of the United States. The approximately 80,000 persons living in the southern area of the Purchase and the uncounted number living to the north and west had no reason to hold any particular allegiance to the United States. Moreover, as soon as the Purchase was made legal, Americans started moving in to settle the newly acquired wilderness. They could quickly have become out of touch with the rest of the

United States had not efficient communications been established between the Louisiana Territory and the center of government, as well as with every other portion of the country. These communications were established, although roads had to be built through almost impenetrable wilderness, much of it inhabited by Indians who had good reason to be hostile toward all white men, whether they were American, French, or Spanish. In little more than a year, by the end of 1805, the postal system of the United States was extended west to St. Louis and south to New Orleans—a prodigious feat.

The reports of the Postmaster General for the years 1805 and 1806 indicate that the road to New Orleans was a rough one. It consisted of a path through the forest, cleared to a width of only four feet. (Granger's surveyors believed that a path of any greater width would only encourage underbrush.) A good part of the journey had to be taken through territory that was not cleared and was impassable when spring thaws filled the swamps. Some of the streams were formidable. A postrider sometimes had to throw a sizable log across a stream to ford it and keep himself and his mail dry, while his horse swam across on the downriver side of the log.

In 1806, an agreement was reached with Spain whereby the mail could pass unimpeded through territory that Spain still claimed to own. (The Louisiana Purchase document was imprecise, the territories involved but vaguely described.) By the end of 1806, the posts could travel from Washington to New Orleans in thirteen days and seven hours in good weather.

An interesting insight into the arduous conditions of the mail service of the period can be gathered from a letter Granger sent to his new agent in Indian territory: "In the selection of riders, you must always take persons of integrity, sound health, firmness, perseverance and high ambition, pride of character. Among these a preference is due to young men, *the less their size the better.*"

Riders were issued lanterns so that they could travel at

night. Their instructions stipulated that "the mail is not to stop except five minutes once in ten miles to breathe the horse and twenty minutes for breakfast and supper, and thirty minutes for dinner."

During this period, road building in much of the existing nation was greatly stimulated. Congress and the states cooperated in a massive effort to create and repair the avenues of communication. General Edward Braddock's old road, from Cumberland, Maryland, to Pittsburgh, Pennsylvania, and the Genesee Road, in New York's Mohawk Valley, were made into permanent and usable highways. Some states even instituted lotteries to pay for the building of roads. The length of the post roads almost doubled in twelve years' time, reaching 41,736 miles in 1814, the year Granger left office. The mail volume had more than quadrupled—from an estimated 1,243,204 pieces in 1801 to 5,112,590 in 1814.

The South still presented a problem to the postal service. The roads, as always, were inadequate, the mail volume low. It was the custom in many parts of the South for Negro slaves to carry the mails. Habersham had not objected to this practice, which reduced the cost of operations. However, Granger, soon after his appointment to office, wrote to Senator James Jackson of Georgia (who was chairman of the Senate Committee on the Post Office) asking that he look into the propriety of using slaves as mail messengers but requesting that the senator's investigations be handled with the greatest discretion, since the situation was far too delicate for public discussion.

Granger's objections to the use of slaves in this capacity were not based on humanitarian reasons. Far from it. His argument was that since only the most intelligent bondsmen were being used for this mail service, they could, in their travels, gain knowledge of the geography of the region and the disposition of the populace and might use this knowledge should the slaves rise up against their masters. Congress was

impressed with Granger's reasoning and, in 1802, decreed
that only free white persons could carry the mails.

Postmaster General Granger was also a great friend of the
stagecoach interests, and they prospered exceedingly during his
term of office. As early as 1802, he wrote to Senator Jackson:
"The transportation of the mail in stage coaches is considered
of such importance as to justify an extra allowance of at least
twenty per cent to aid an infant establishment." Thus, the first
Post Office subsidy of transportation was established.

MADISON, MONROE, AND MEIGS

When James Madison became President of the United
States in 1809, he did not want Jefferson's Postmaster General any more than Jefferson had wanted the Postmaster
General of John Adams. However, Madison was committed
to the ideal of keeping the Post Office out of politics, so he put
up with Granger until 1814, when the Postmaster General
went too far. Following his legal prerogative of having sole
control over the commissioning of postmasters, Granger appointed a certain Dr. Leib as postmaster of Philadelphia in
preference to Madison's own candidate. By this time, Madison
had had enough. He dismissed Granger out of hand and, on
April 11, 1814, appointed the governor of Ohio, Return Jonathan Meigs, Jr., to the office.* Postmaster General Meigs
served through the rest of Madison's second term and through

---

* When he was Postmaster General, James A. Farley became fascinated
with the curious first name of his predecessor Meigs. He investigated the
matter and found that Meigs's grandfather, whose name was Jonathan, had
courted a Quaker girl without notable success. Upon being refused for the
fourth time, he was leaving the Quaker household for what he believed
would be the last time. Just as he was about to slam the gate behind him,
the Quaker girl called out, "Return, Jonathan," and accepted him. Meigs
named his first-born Return Jonathan, and, of course, the first-born grand-
son was named Return Jonathan, Jr. Through a long and happy association
with Postmaster General Farley, the author has learned never to doubt his
word on anything. Besides, it would be foolish to endanger such a charming
story with excessive research.

both of the terms of James Monroe. He left office on July 1, 1823, after being in charge of the Post Office longer than any other man to date, save Granger.

Historians have accused Meigs of being reckless in his extension of the postal service, particularly since, in the latter years of his administration, this extension was accompanied by a sharp falling off in the rate of increase of mail volume. He has also been criticized because of his marked preference for stagecoach transportation over the postrider.

Certainly, the per mile cost of transporting the mails went up sharply during his administration. Under Pickering, Habersham, and Granger, this cost had remained around $6 per mile per year. Under Meigs, it went up to $13 per mile; under his successor, it reverted to $7 per mile. Also, Meigs was the first Postmaster General to report really sizable deficits in postal operations. In 1820, the revenues of the Post Office were $1,111,927 and the expenditures, $1,160,926. The Post Office continued to lose money through 1823, a fact that caused much adverse comment in the press of the time.

But if the Meigs administration suffered some economic embarrassment, the blame must be shared by Congress. Each congressman was eager to open up his own district, and the best way to do so was to extend post roads to rather unlikely places. The post road was the early nineteenth-century equivalent of the "pork barrel."

Congress went on extending post roads by law, leaving it up to the Postmaster General to pay for such extensions as best he could. This practice put Meigs into a difficult situation, since the roads could not produce enough revenue to justify their existence from a strict accounting point of view, and many of the new roads were so remote that the expense of transportation to and over them was ruinously high. During the years 1820–24, postal volume increased only 8 per cent and postal revenues only 3 per cent, while the length of post roads increased 47 per cent and the cost of mail transportation

28 per cent. Under such circumstances, a postal deficit was inevitable.

Meigs's predilection for the expensive stagecoach as a means of mail transportation can also be attributed to a great extent to Congress. The stagecoach interests of the time were very much like the railroad interests of a later day; they dominated the sympathies and the votes of many congressmen. It took exceptional courage to oppose the stagecoaches, and courage such as this often went unrewarded, as Ebenezer Hazard had found out back in the days of the Continental Congress.

But Meigs himself, whose roots lay in the wilderness, also believed that the future of the country depended upon a bold extension of the postal system, even into areas that for many years would be unproductive of significant revenues. Many members of Congress, particularly those from the wilderness area, supported his position completely. Henry Clay of Kentucky was an eloquent advocate for extending and improving the service no matter what the cost to the Treasury. John C. Calhoun of South Carolina was another. He urged that Congress "bind the public together with a perfect system of roads and canals" and, in an outburst that has a familiar ring to twentieth-century ears, cried: "Let us conquer space!" He added: "It is thus that a citizen of the West will read the news of Boston still moist from the press. The mail and the press are the nerves of the body politic."

With support like this in Congress, Meigs was able to extend the service into what was then called the Northwest Area (Illinois and Indiana) and into Arkansas and other distant regions. During the nine years he was in office, the mileage of post roads increased from 41,736 in 1814 to 84,860 in 1823.

During the first year of Meigs's administration, the war with England interfered seriously with the speed and reliability of the posts, particularly in the South. As an example of the low estate to which communications fell during this period,

Congress did not learn about the Battle of New Orleans, fought on January 8, 1815, until February 4.

Although Meigs has been criticized by some historians inclined to judge postmasters general principally in terms of revenues and expenditures, it can reasonably be argued that he knew what was good for the United States at his particular moment in history and that he moved forward boldly and imaginatively to achieve goals that a lesser man would have feared to attempt.

Meigs resigned from his post in the middle of James Monroe's second term and died two years later. He was succeeded by John McLean, another Ohioan—a distinguished lawyer who had served in Congress eleven years before and who came to the Post Office from Ohio's Supreme Court.

McLean's "Department"

McLean had character. He was tough and quite impervious to political pressure. Almost immediately after he took office, he began to crack down on the stagecoach interests, insisting that the mails be carried on horseback except in those areas where the population and the condition of the roads justified the expense of coach service. As he wrote to a friend in 1825:

> I will add, too, the confession of my inability to perceive the propriety, or to comprehend the force, of your objection to the transportation of the mails on horseback. . . . The great city of New Orleans receives its mail from the other Atlantic markets in the same way. The intelligence of more than half the nation is conveyed on horseback.

Like Meigs, he placed considerations of service above those of economy. As he told a Senate committee after he had retired from office: "I say now, as I have always said when speaking on the subject, that I do not consider an efficient administration of the Department is shown by the annual balance in its favor. Its funds should be actively employed in extending the operation of the mail."

Richard Rush, the Secretary of the Treasury and, technically, McLean's superior, concurred in the Postmaster General's philosophy of "service first." He defended McLean's policies, even though they had exhausted the funds "of that extensive and useful establishment," because they were serving "the highest purposes of revenue by contributing to the intercourse and the prosperity of the country."*

McLean began his administration by completely reorganizing the headquarters operation, creating a semblance of order out of chaos and instituting sensible accounting procedures and a reliable system of record-keeping.

Although liberal in other respects, he was a hard man on his employees. On several occasions, he stated that he had no intention of paying those who worked for him a sufficient stipend to sustain them without recourse to other gainful employment. In 1824, he wrote a letter to Henry Clay in which he admitted that the postmasters were the most poorly paid officials of the government but refused to consider an increase in their remuneration because "competent persons to discharge the duties of Postmasters have been willing to serve in every part of the country." If good men could be found to serve at the going rate, he saw no purpose in increasing the salaries.

There is reason to believe that many postmasters accepted their positions, despite the low salary, because of certain perquisites that went with the job, particularly the privilege of sending and receiving letters free. And there is evidence that many postmasters were not above obliging their friends (for a fee) by permitting widespread use of their frank.

A postmaster's frank was especially valuable in areas where lotteries were popular. The postmaster at Canandaigua, New

* No Secretary of the Treasury had taken that position before the time of Richard Rush, and few have since.

York, for example, made a very good thing of running his own lottery while avoiding all postage expenses. In one year, he is known to have sent out 3,080 free letters and to have received 1,397 in his lottery business alone. And Canandaigua was not then nor is it today a large town. In 1827, McLean finally persuaded Congress to pass legislation forbidding postmasters to act as agents for any lottery business or to use their frank to advertise lotteries.

More than any Postmaster General of the United States before him, McLean's forceful personality caught the imagination of the public. He was a very popular official—the most popular postal figure since Benjamin Franklin.

It was typical of the man that he should have instituted, in 1825, the Express Mail, which operated among the principal cities of America and was the prototype on which the more famous Pony Express was modeled thirty-five years later. Express Mail riders used relays of horses stationed approximately fifteen miles apart, and the mail moved, day and night, at an average speed of about ten miles an hour. Express Mail cost three times as much as ordinary mail, but the improvement in the speed of service was spectacular. For example, the time of delivery between New York and New Orleans was cut from sixteen days to seven. Express Mail was particularly popular in the burgeoning West, which found ordinary postal communication from the East very slow and unsatisfactory.

McLean's stalwart approach to business also brought about the recognition of the Post Office as a full-fledged, if unofficial, department of the government. When he first took office, he simply instituted the practice of reporting directly to the President of the United States instead of to the Secretary of the Treasury. He then began to head his correspondence with the words "Post Office Department" instead of the customary "General Post Office." Apparently, nobody objected to the pretensions of the new Postmaster General, and Congress soon grew accustomed to considering the Post Office as a separate department.

John Quincy Adams, who became President in 1825, approved of this arrangement. He wrote in his diary (November 17, 1825):

I desired him [McLean] to make me a report upon the concerns of the Department, which has been usual yearly since he came into the Post Office. It had not heretofore been customary, but the practice was introduced within these few years by Mr. Monroe and appears to be much approved.

Perhaps McLean's greatest show of independence was his absolute refusal to yield any part of his prerogative of commissioning postmasters of his own choice. He declined to take the advice of the President or Congress and did simply what he thought would be best for the service. As he wrote to Edward Everett:

If subserviency to the President . . . shall be the passport to office . . . however objectionable he may be to the people, offices will be filled not with high-minded and patriotic citizens, but by fawning sycophants, loud in their professions, without principle. . . . I would scorn to hold any office, as a creature of any administration.

John Quincy Adams was as "high-minded and patriotic" a citizen as ever graced public life, but understandably he did become irritated when McLean could find the proper qualifications for the position of postmaster only among those citizens who favored the cause of Andrew Jackson. Adams thought seriously of dismissing McLean, but he found that his Postmaster General's popularity and irreproachable administration had made him a political untouchable. McLean stayed on.

It was when Jackson, whom McLean had supported, succeeded Adams in the Presidency in 1829 that the incumbent

Postmaster General really became a problem. The Democratic Party had been swept into office on a program that openly advocated—among many other things—the introduction of the spoils system. Jackson wanted to proscribe all the Adams men in the postal service and replace them with his own people. To his surprise, he found that McLean was just as stubborn with him as he had been with President Adams. He refused to dismiss any postmaster for political reasons. And Jackson knew full well that it would be reckless to fire his popular Postmaster General.

Ben: Perley Poore (as he styled himself), who was the Washington correspondent for the Boston *Journal* for four decades, in his memoirs, published in 1886, described the scene in which Jackson resolved his dilemma. Matters came to a head when McLean told the President that he would not turn out of office all the postmasters who had worked for the re-election of Adams unless he could also turn out, impartially, all those who had worked for the election of Jackson himself. Poore recalled:

> To this General Jackson at first made no reply, but rose from his seat, puffing away at his pipe. After walking up and down the floor two or three times, he stopped in front of his rebellious Postmaster General, and said: "Mr. McLean, will you accept a seat upon the bench of the Supreme Court?"
>
> The judicial position thus tendered was accepted with thanks.

McLean's appointment, on March 7, 1829, to the U.S. Supreme Court, where he served until his death, thirty-two years later, ended an era. When McLean left office, there were 8,050 post offices in the United States, or 107 times the number there had been in 1789. By 1829, the post roads extended 114,780 miles, or approximately 64 times their length forty years previously. The volume in letter mail was recorded as 13,659,344, or 51 times the estimated figure for the first year of operation under the Constitution.

McLean was succeeded by William Taylor Barry of Kentucky, a man whose background was, superficially, very similar. Barry was also a lawyer who had held office in Washington (as a senator) and, like McLean, was a member of the Supreme Court of his home state when appointed Postmaster General. However, Barry was not quite so high-minded as McLean and did not "scorn to hold any office, as a creature of any administration." He was a political animal of the new breed—and precisely the kind of Postmaster General that Andrew Jackson wanted.

III

Birth of a Political Mechanism
1829-61

In making the postmaster-generalship a cabinet office, Andrew Jackson's purpose was not so much to honor the Post Office as to control it. As the result of his action, the entire character of the postal service was changed.

Under Jackson, the Post Office became a political mechanism, the principal patronage-dispensing agency of the party in power. The President claimed the right to appoint (or dismiss) any postmaster receiving $1,000 or more a year in fees, but, in fact, the patronage prerogatives he seized went much deeper than that. Ever since the Jackson Administration, despite numerous reforms over the years, the aroma of politics has emanated from the Post Office more than from any other agency of government.

Since Jackson took office, it has been the custom to change postmasters general with every new Presidential administration. Before that time, a man like John McLean could hold office with reasonable comfort during the terms of men with such divergent views as James Monroe and John Quincy Adams. Since then, even when a President has died in office and been succeeded by his Vice-President, the Postmaster General has usually been changed soon after the transition.

After 1829, the tenure of the average Postmaster General became much shorter. In the first forty years of the Republic, there were but six postmasters general, with an average service of six years, eight months. In the years since, there have been fifty-one, with an average service of two years, nine months. This change has had a profound effect on the development of the policies of the Department. As the terms of the post-masters general grew shorter, so did their chances of making permanent improvements in postal practices. What one man built up, his successor was inclined to destroy—and this tendency was particularly evident during the thirty-two years from McLean's departure to the Supreme Court until 1861. During this time—a period of intense growth in the United States, when the population expanded by 144 per cent and the land area by 70 per cent—the dominant political party changed four times. In that same thirty-two years, there were thirteen postmasters general and almost as many postal policies to match.

Unfortunately, the strong and able lasted in the job no longer than the weak and vacillating. In 1851, Congress, finally tiring of the power vacuum created by the lack of definitive, continuing leadership at the head of this vital agency, set what it hoped would be a permanent postal policy. Various postmasters general have nibbled away at the edges of that policy during the intervening years, but the controlling voice of Congress has been dominant in postal affairs ever since.

Political feelings during the 1830's ran deep and violent. The differences between the Adams faction (or "National" Republicans, as they were beginning to call themselves) and the Jacksonian Democrats were social and geographical as much as they were ideological. Adams represented the Eastern "establishment"; Jackson, the frontier. The Adams followers looked upon their political rivals as uncouth upstarts; the Jacksonians considered the Easterners decadent snobs. There was little liking or mutual respect between the factions and very little friendly communication between leaders of the two groups.

Jackson entered upon the Presidency determined to humiliate the Easterners. He had promised his followers that they would get the spoils of political success, and he lived up to his word.

THE SPOILS SYSTEM AND THE EARLY SCANDALS

During the first year of the Jackson Administration, an estimated 543 postmasters, or about 7 per cent of the more than 8,000 postmasters in the country, were removed for political reasons. This figure may seem comparatively small, but it represents almost all the postmasterships worth bothering about. Most of the changes were made in New York and the New England states, the stronghold of the Eastern establishment. More than sixty years later, the spirit of these times was reflected by William H. Wallace, an original Jackson appointee as postmaster of Hammondville, Ohio, who gleefully recalled in an interview in 1892: "General Jackson succeeded Mr. Adams as President, and the way the Postmaster General, John McLean, and the postmasters of any note had to fly the track was a caution!"

In putting this spoils system into effect, Postmaster General William T. Barry, completely loyal to Jackson, served as an effective hatchet man. But Barry had almost no understanding of the most ordinary business practices and exhibited a lack of leadership both in his own headquarters in Washington and throughout the entire postal service in the field. For a politician, he was extraordinarily tactless in his dealings with the Congress; he had a positive genius for making powerful and implacable enemies on Capitol Hill.

Jackson was determined to develop the postal service so that his fellow Westerners could keep in touch with the nation's capital. He wanted to give the frontier a postal service at least reasonably comparable to that which the Eastern seaboard took for granted. In his first message to Congress he said:

> In a political point of view, the Post Office Department is chiefly important as a means of diffusing knowledge. It is to the body politic what the veins and arteries are to the natural—carrying, conveying rapidly and regularly to the remotest parts of the system correct information of the operations of the Government, and bringing back to it the wishes and the feelings of the people.

Congress, in 1829, was inclined to agree.

Barry's reflected determination was to extend post routes to every county seat in the nation, without regard for whatever potential receipts the Department was likely to realize from such routes. During the six years he was in office (1829–35), the accounts within the Department were kept in slovenly fashion, but it is nonetheless apparent that the Postmaster General was optimistic to the point of recklessness about the eventual revenues that would accrue as the result of his expansionist policies. The audited deficits of the Department during the four fiscal years for which he was totally responsible amounted to only $411,675—a figure in itself hardly sufficient to account for the congressional wrath that descended upon Barry's head—but the deficits were unrelieved by any surpluses and wiped out the Department's account with the Treasury.

Besides, Barry's conduct as an administrator and a politician was not of a kind to inspire congressional compassion. One senator, during a debate, complained about the manner in which his request for information was treated at postal headquarters. "This new fledged, or rather unfledged head of a recently created department, did not condescend to answer the inquiry of a senator," he said. "I received a note from one of his subordinates which was, in substance, this: 'I am directed by the Postmaster General to inform you that you are not permitted to know, sir.' " Barry made a mortal enemy of

Senator Felix Grundy, the Whig leader, by refusing even to comment on the removal of an important postmaster. "In the discharge of this duty," he wrote, "the legislative branch had no right to interfere or participate."

To add to Barry's troubles, the Eastern Whigs were bitterly opposed to the program of expanding the postal service into the pioneer West and making it more accessible to those who were their political enemies. In 1835, for instance, when a proposal was being considered to extend a post route from Independence, Missouri, to the mouth of the Colorado River, Daniel Webster arose in the Senate to voice eloquent opposition:

> What do we want with this worthless area? This region of savages and wild beasts, of deserts, shifting sands and whirlwinds of dust; of cactus and prairie dogs? To what use can we hope to put these great deserts or those endless mountain ranges? . . . Mr. President, I will never vote one cent from the Public Treasury to place the Pacific Coast one inch nearer to Boston than it now is.

Such Eastern provincialism may sound hopelessly narrow in the twentieth century, but in the 1830's it was sufficiently strong to be troublesome to Jackson's Postmaster General.

Other problems beset Barry. Despite the continuing expenditures, the quality of postal service deteriorated alarmingly, and complaints against it were constant. The wholesale proscription of Whig postmasters had been followed by the too hasty appointment of Jacksonian replacements, many of whom were ill equipped for the job or altogether incompetent. The new breed of postmasters considered their offices primarily as electioneering outposts and had little concern for the efficiency of the mails. Unwarranted delay of the posts was commonplace, and the morale of the service was very low.

Despite the fact that the penalty for robbing the mails was death by hanging, the activity of highwaymen increased, particularly on the less frequented post roads of the South. In his reminiscences, Ben: Perley Poore told a story about a mail robbery that gives an interesting glimpse into Jackson's character. Poore wrote that:

> One night a mail coach was stopped near Philadelphia by three armed men, who ordered the nine passengers to alight and stand in a line. One of the robbers mounted guard while the other two made the terrified passengers deliver up their money and watches, and then rifled the mail. They were soon afterward arrested, tried and convicted. . . . Fortunately for one of the culprits, named Wilson, he had some years previously, at a horse race near Nashville, Tennessee, privately advised General Jackson to withdraw his bets on a horse which he was backing, as the jockey had been ordered to lose the race. The General was very thankful for this information, which enabled him to escape a heavy loss, and he promised his informant that he would befriend him whenever an opportunity should offer. When reminded of this promise, after Wilson had been sentenced to be hanged, Jackson promptly commuted the sentence to ten years' imprisonment in the penitentiary.

(The other two men were hanged.)

The Postmaster General's gravest trouble came from his habit of permitting payment of suspiciously extravagant bonuses to contractors for increasing their services in transporting the mails along the post routes. Often, the improvements thus paid for were not readily discernible; when discernible, they were certainly not proportionate to the expenditures involved. Some of the Jackson Administration's critics in Congress accused Barry of personal dishonesty. (The Postmaster General challenged Representative William Cost Johnson, a Maryland Whig, to a duel for making such a charge on the floor of the House. Bloodshed was avoided when the congressman apologized.) The allegation was almost certainly untrue, but it did become apparent, when both houses of Congress investigated the Department, that a number of Barry's subordinates were taking kickbacks from those with whom they did official business.

The investigations, which were held in 1834 and 1835, also brought out the fact that when appropriations were not forthcoming from Congress, the Postmaster General, quite without authorization but in the name of the Department, had borrowed a great deal of money from private banks. Corruption was common throughout the Department, and the letting of contracts had become an open scandal. As the Senate committee stated:

> [We] . . . found affairs of the department in a state of utter derangement, resulting, as it is believed, from the uncontrolled discretion exercised by its officers over contracts . . . and their habitual evasion, and in some instances, their total disregard of the laws which have been provided for their restraint.

Despite efforts on the part of some members of the Congress to impeach the Postmaster General and institute criminal proceedings against him, Barry emerged with his personal honor in fairly good array but his reputation as an administrator in shreds. On May 21, 1835, he was forced to resign as Postmaster General to accept a post as U.S. Minister to Spain, a position, as a friendly contemporary pointed out, "calling for less financial ability."

Evidently embittered by his experience, he wrote to his friend James Buchanan at the time: "I have agreed to take it [the new position] but do not leave my present office until I receive the Commission in due form—I remember your admonition on this subject." He had learned to trust nobody, not even Jackson. He died in Liverpool en route to his diplomatic assignment.

The United States Magazine and Democratic Review, a journal friendly to the Jackson Administration, summed up

Barry's shortcomings in a retrospective article, published in its issue of September, 1839:

> We are far from defending the laxity of Mr. Barry. . . . Whatever may be the contrariety of opinion as to Major Barry's personal agency in creating the manifold embarrassments in his Department, which called down legislative indignation upon the management of the Post Office, there can be none as to the wretchedness of the condition in which he left it.

AUDITOR TO POSTMASTER GENERAL

Jackson was not the sort of man who repeats a serious mistake. When he chose a successor to Barry, he reached over to the Treasury Department, across the street from the White House, and came up with its fourth auditor, Amos Kendall of Kentucky.

Kendall was a newspaperman of considerable talent and a shrewd politician. He had accepted a minor post in the government in order to remain near the seat of power and all during Jackson's first term had been a powerful member of the so-called kitchen cabinet despite his lack of prestige. Jackson leaned heavily on him for advice. Kendall knew how to make friends—and in which circles. In earlier days, he had been tutor to Henry Clay's children. During his time in Washington, prior to his ascendancy to the postmaster-generalship, he had divined that Martin Van Buren was the coming man in government and had served as Van Buren's campaign manager in his successful race for the Vice-Presidency. Kendall had verve as well as common sense, and he became a truly superior Postmaster General.

He moved into his job with fortitude and dispatch and began by rearranging the Department's sloppy accounting procedures, paying all current accounts out of the funds accruing during the quarter of their performance and transferring the balances due to contractors to a set of accounts entitled

"Arrearages," with the understanding that these would be settled out of future profits. He immediately stopped all extra allowances to contractors, thereby eliminating the principal source of the scandal that had enveloped the Post Office. Perhaps the most damning evidence of the inefficiency of Barry's administration is that by October, 1837, Kendall was able to liquidate a debt of $500,000 and create a surplus of $780,000 without increasing the rates of postage and without significantly impairing service.

Kendall also had the uncanny knack of being right. On December 5, 1836, he warned Congress that the Post Office building in Washington was a firetrap and asked that consideration be given to the construction of larger quarters in which the records of the Department could be kept in greater safety. Ten days later, on the morning of December 15, the building burned down. Almost all the earliest records of the Post Office, as well as the priceless models in the Patent Office, which shared the building, were destroyed in the fire.

Unlike his predecessor, the new Postmaster General knew how to get along with Congress. He persuaded that body, soon after his accession, to pass legislation successfully reorganizing the Department. The Act of July 2, 1836, was an important one. Through it, Congress seized financial control of the postal establishment—which it has never relinquished (see Chapter X). Congress also reduced considerably the Presidential prerogative of appointing postmasters, decreeing that thereafter all postmasters receiving annual fees of $1,000 or more could be placed in office only with the "advice and consent" of the Senate and that all such appointments should be for four years only. The act also created a third assistant postmaster general and made it possible to maintain an adequate staff in the Washington headquarters.

Administratively, Kendall, in effect, closed out the chaotic books of the Department and started a new set of books more or less from scratch. (The fire of December, 1836, gave him an excellent opportunity to do this.) He also improved the financial status of the Department by going after postmasters who had become desultory in returning revenues. A surprising number of the new appointees not only felt they had little obligation to operate their offices efficiently, but also felt no compunction about pocketing a sizable percentage of the revenues that passed through their hands. These practices were stopped, and the supervision over postmasters was greatly tightened.

When Van Buren became President in 1837, Kendall became the dominant figure in the cabinet. Opinions about him varied. The English traveler Harriet Martineau considered him one of the personages of the capital city and called him "undoubtedly a great genius." A Whig contemporary, however, referred to him as "a miserable reptile . . . a wretched printer." In 1837, the *National Intelligencer* called him "the most influential man in the Cabinet." Representative Henry Alexander Wise, a Whig from Virginia, said he was "the President's *thinking* machine!, and his *writing* machine, ay, his *lying* machine!"

During his years in office (1835–40), Kendall presided over tremendous improvements in the transportation of the mails. He tried, briefly, to revive McLean's Express Mail but abandoned it when lack of volume made the experiment too costly to maintain. The most significant event of his administration was the coming of age of the railroad, a development that had a permanent impact on the growth of the postal service.

Barry had been the first Postmaster General to mention the railroad in connection with the transportation of the mails. In his annual report of 1834, he had said: "If provision can be made to secure the regular transportation of the mails upon this [Washington to New York] and other railroads which are constructing . . . it will be of great utility to the public." By 1838, Congress was ready to declare all railroads as post roads and empowered the Postmaster General to convey the mails over them as much as possible, provided that the cost to the Department was not more than 25 per cent "over and above what similar transportation would cost in post coaches."

The language of the act was loose and the interpretation of it imaginative. Kendall complained that "similar transportation" was a meaningless phrase, since the railroads were unique. The term "post coaches" was also too vague, since the mail was being transported by a wide variety of horse-drawn vehicles under greatly differing rate schedules.

This was, of course, several decades before the first anti-monopoly legislation, and the railroads (few of which were in actual competition with one another) openly conspired to make certain the Post Office Department paid maximum prices for the services they provided. The railroads operating between Baltimore and Philadelphia, for example, demanded and got $320 per mile per year for transporting the mails between those two cities. Nonetheless, extravagant as it was, the Post Office Department's increasing use of the rails during this period not only resulted in more efficient mail service but also contributed greatly to the growth of a vital industry that made much of the subsequent development of the nation possible.

The following figures tell the story of the growth of the railroads during these years:

Year	Total U.S. rail mileage	Total rail mileage used by Post Office	Per cent of total rail mileage used by Post Office
1830	23	—	—
1834	633	78	12.3
1838	1,913	1,500	78.4
1840	2,818	2,300	81.6

While Barry was Postmaster General, Congress, in an effort to reduce costs, had cut post-road mileage down to 112,774. Kendall built the figure up to 155,739 miles before he left.

Altogether, Kendall's policies proved so successful that, in 1837, he asked Congress to reduce the rates of postage, which, he said, were so high that they were unnaturally inhibiting the use of the service. But the great business crisis of that year intervened, and Congress would not consider a rate reduction. During that depression period, the banks refused to pay out the funds the Department had deposited in them, causing considerable embarrassment to the Post Office, which had half its funds deposited in private banks. However, Kendall rode out the storm, effecting temporary economies in the service and persuading the contractors to carry the mails, for the time being, for the postage only.

By 1840, the pendulum had swung back. When Amos Kendall resigned his position in May of that year, the Department was in far better condition than it had been when he took office. He left his position to edit the *Extra Globe*, a campaign periodical dedicated to the task of re-electing Martin Van Buren President of the United States. Just before resigning, Kendall sent out to the 13,000 postmasters of the nation, under his own frank, a manifesto urging them to subscribe to the newspaper he was about to edit. He also asked the postmasters to act as subscription agents for the journal, informing them that they could send the money to headquarters under their franks. Most postmasters considered compliance a necessity. Subscriptions poured into the Department at the rate of 400 a day, while the Whigs in Congress bellowed with rage at this blatant abuse of the franking privilege.

At Kendall's suggestion, he was succeeded by John Milton Niles, a Connecticut politician who had once been postmaster of Hartford. Niles served during the few remaining months of Van Buren's term.

ͺ WHIGS AND THE INFLUENCE OF SIR ROWLAND HILL

In November, 1840, the Whigs won the Presidency for the first time with their "Tippecanoe and Tyler too!" campaign. An elderly Indian fighter, General William H. Harrison, turned the tables on Van Buren, who had beaten him easily four years earlier. Harrison appointed Francis Granger of New York as his Postmaster General.

In 1836, Granger had run as a Whig for the Vice-Presidency and had received more electoral votes in that campaign than had Harrison himself. However, he had been an unsuccessful candidate for the second spot on the Whig ticket in 1840, shouldered aside in favor of John Tyler. There was little love lost between Tyler and Granger, and when Harrison died, a month after his inauguration, it was plainly only a matter of time before the Postmaster General would be replaced.

Aside from personal differences, the principal reason for Tyler's antagonism toward Granger was the Postmaster General's insistence on the perpetuation and enlargement of the spoils system. Tyler had expressly stated that he did not want postmasters removed for political reasons. Granger chose to ignore this. Later, after he had been elected to Congress, he boasted on the floor of the House of Representatives that in the seven months he had been Postmaster General, he had removed 1,700 postmasters (out of 13,778) and said that had he remained two more weeks, 3,000 more would have been added to the list.

After Granger resigned, Tyler appointed as Postmaster General Charles A. Wickliffe of Kentucky, a member of a prominent family whose political position was one of implacable opposition to Henry Clay. The new Postmaster General immediately tried to reduce expenditures by curtailing services and cutting salaries. Like so many who followed him, he soon found that these actions accomplished little in the way of economy and served only to irritate Congress and the people.

By 1843, he was ruefully admitting that "it is not always certain that by discontinuing the number of trips on a given route we save in the expense more than we lose by the decrease in postage."

The effects of Wickliffe's three and a half years on the postal establishment were alarming. In 1844, the revenues were only $4,237,288, or about $300,000 less than in 1840. The volume of mail was 1 million pieces less than it had been four years earlier, and, most significantly, the per capita expenditure for postage had fallen drastically from twenty-seven cents a year to twenty-two cents.

The Tyler Administration sputtered out disastrously. When the "accidental President" found he could not possibly gain the Whig nomination for the Presidency in 1844, he tried to transform the postal service into a personal political machine in the hope of retaining his position as an Independent. The Senate rejected most of the men he nominated for postmasterships, and great indignation was aroused when he attempted to assess postal clerks and letter carriers in large offices as much as $20 apiece in order to raise campaign funds. He finally gave up the struggle and retired from the race.

In 1844, Congress, weary of the Postmaster General's bumbling, created a United States Postal Commission in order to establish policy. After hearing many witnesses, the commission reported back to Congress with a ringing statement:

> The United States postal service was created to render the citizen worthy, by proper knowledge and enlightenment, of his important privileges as a sovereign constituent of his government; to diffuse enlightenment and social improvement and national fellowship; elevating our people in the scale of civilization and bringing them together in patriotic affection.

The commission's findings were that the Post Office was a vital public service and should be maintained as such, no matter what the cost in dollars and cents. Congress seized upon this report and immediately set about the task of drafting legislation that reformed the postal service and made it a much more vital force in the life of the nation than it had been in the past.

The Act of March 3, 1845, which took effect on the day before Wickliffe (and Tyler) left office, stemmed in large part from reforms that Sir Rowland Hill had promoted in England, where they had proved very successful. Hill's thesis was simple: if the government made the rates of postage sufficiently low and the service generally attractive and accessible to the public, increased volume would eventually create more revenue than higher rates would produce and, to a considerable extent, would also promote the over-all welfare of the nation. This thesis was to work out as well in practice in the United States as it had in England.

REFORMS OF 1845

The principal item of reform in the Act of 1845 concerned postage rates, which had remained virtually unchanged since the beginning of the Republic. Congress all but eliminated the cumbersome zone system and based new rates on weight rather than on the number of sheets in a letter. All letters weighing half an ounce or less could be sent up to 300 miles for five cents. Anything of that weight sent farther would cost ten cents. In some cases, these rates were only one-fifteenth of what they had been before the act was passed. Within two years, the revenues of the Department were just as high as they had been under the old rates, and the volume, which had been static, leaped ahead.

Congress also reformed the procedures for letting out transportation contracts, insisting on open, legitimate competitive bidding. This change proved so effective that in the first four years of the operation of the law, even though the length of post roads was increased by almost 24,000 miles, the cost of transporting the mails was reduced by $328,000. Included in the act was a provision establishing the star-route system of transporting the mails between post offices by private carrier, as well as a section stiffening the penalties for violating the law against operating private expresses in competition with the Post Office.

Congress, in this legislation, also finally started to make some restrictions on the franking privilege, which had grown very much out of hand. (There had even been a case of a senator who solemnly declared his horse "a public document" and affixed his frank to its bridle so that it could be transported home to Pittsburgh free of charge.)

All in all, the Act of March 3, 1845, was one of the most significant pieces of postal legislation ever to be passed. But it was passed without the active support of the Postmaster General.

CAVE JOHNSON'S POST OFFICE

In the November elections, the Democrats regained the Presidency with James K. Polk of Tennessee. Polk was the first "dark horse" President. He had never expected anything more than the Vice-Presidency, but intraparty dissension over the annexation of Texas more or less pushed him into the campaign for the Presidency. Once elected, he appointed as his Postmaster General the man who had been the manager of all his campaigns since 1825, Representative Cave Johnson, also from Tennessee.

Johnson, who was barely literate, had little interest in the postal service as such. He was principally interested in using the Post Office Department as a base for his political manipulations. He was Polk's closest friend, personally and politically, and the President's liaison man with the Congress. As Postmaster General, he became so much Polk's alter ego that he grew into the habit of using the term "we" when discussing the President's policies with recalcitrant congressmen.

Earlier, as a member of Congress, Johnson had been known as the "watchdog of the Treasury." (An opposition congressman was once heard to remark, "A watchdog? Oh, yes, a cur!") Because of the role he had played in Congress, one of the most interesting interludes in Post Office history came to an end, by curious coincidence, on the day he became Postmaster General.

On May 20 of the preceding year, Samuel F. B. Morse had successfully demonstrated the practicability of his invention, the electric telegraph, by sending the message "What hath God wrought!" from Washington to Baltimore. As a result, Morse had been put in charge of a special division in the Post Office Department to develop his system of communication. Congress, however, had decided that the telegraph should be developed by private enterprise (if at all) and refused funds for further experimentation. Cave Johnson, watchdog of the Treasury, had led the fight against the appropriation. At a vital moment in the debate, he had derisively offered an amendment that would have given half the appropriation to a traveling mountebank named Fiske for the furtherance of his experiments in mesmerism and animal magnetism. The bill failed of passage.

Although the new Postmaster General demonstrably was far more interested in replacing Whig with Democratic postmasters than he was in operating the postal service, Congress once again stepped into the breach and created important policy that was to shape the future course of the Post Office.

THE FIRST ADHESIVE STAMPS

The Act of 1847 authorized, for the first time, the use of adhesive postage stamps in the United States. Such stamps were another of Rowland Hill's ideas. He had persuaded the British Government to adopt this method of assured prepayment of postage in 1840. Unfortunately, the U.S. Congress followed the British model too timidly. It stopped short of making prepayment obligatory. That step did not come until 1855, and the use of adhesive stamps was not made universal until 1856.

However, the cumulative effects of the cheap-postage Act of 1845, coupled with innovations such as adhesive stamps, which made the postal service much more convenient for the average citizen, became dramatically evident during Cave Johnson's tenure as Postmaster General (1845–49). Postal volume more than doubled, from 38 million to 81 million. During fiscal year 1848, postal revenues made an unprecedented leap of $675,000—an increase greater than the total revenues had been just thirty-eight years previously. In that same year, after ten years of declining revenues and increasing deficits, the Post Office showed a profit of $174,751—this despite the fact that mail service had been extended to Texas and California. The Rowland Hill thesis of the economic advantages of low postage rates was paying off prodigiously in America and was instrumental in revivifying a postal service that was showing unmistakable signs of decay.

From a political point of view, President Polk had been a doomed man almost from the day he assumed office. The Democrats were hopelessly split between those who were opposed to extending slave territory (the "Barnburners") and those who favored extensions of national territory regardless of such considerations (the "Hunkers"). A further, horizontal split occurred between the "Old" Democrats and the "Young" Democrats. These differences were intensified rather than settled during the four years that Polk was in office.

In his letter of acceptance in 1844, Polk had stated that he would serve only one term. He decided to abide by that decision, and on May 13, 1848, he wrote a letter to a Tennessee postmaster declaring that he would not be a candidate for re-election. The letter was read to the Democratic Convention the following month, just before balloting.

POLITICAL CHANGES, POSTAL PROGRESS

Once again, the Whigs rolled out a moribund general as their candidate and won handily with him. This time it was Zachary Taylor, the victor of Monterrey in the recently ended war with Mexico. His running mate was Millard Fillmore of New York. They won in a reasonably close election.

Taylor, who was aptly called "Old Rough and Ready," had little interest in politics and little understanding of politicians. When he was being mentioned prominently as a candidate for the Whig nomination for the Presidency, he grew exasperated at the enormous amount of correspondence arriving collect for him at his local post office. With some indignation, he informed his postmaster that he could not afford to pay the postage on unsolicited mail and refused to accept it. The letters piled up. Among them was the official notice from the Whig Convention that he was their nominee for the Presidency of the United States. When he failed to acknowledge the nomination, inquiries were made, and the official letter was eventually found among those accumulating in the crowded post office. Taylor paid the postage on the letter of notification and acknowledged his nomination. (Undoubtedly, the incident strengthened the cause of compulsory prepayment of postage.)

Taylor's cabinet was undistinguished. As Horace Greeley wrote, it was a "horrid mixture, just such as a blind man . . . would probably have picked up, if turned among three or four hundred would-be magnates of the Whig Party and ordered to touch and take." His Postmaster General was an obscure Vermont judge named Jacob Collamer, who had served in Congress and who was known mostly as a raconteur. A friendly contemporary, evidently perplexed over what he could say in behalf of the new Postmaster General, could only come up with the statement that "his talents were of a high order, although not showy," but added that his "private character was most estimable."

Collamer accomplished nothing of value as Postmaster General. Unfortunately for him, he chose to ignore Fillmore in the matter of postmaster appointments, even in the Vice-President's home state of New York.* Fillmore, a touchy man at best, was not the kind of person to forget such a slight. When President Taylor died after sixteen months in office and Fillmore succeeded (July 9, 1850), the cabinet members as a matter of courtesy offered their resignations en masse. To everyone's surprise and chagrin, Fillmore accepted them all, leaving his Postmaster General (according to William Henry Seward) "desponding below any degree of despondency I have ever touched."

Fillmore, presumably after scanning the list of eligibles throughout the country to find a worthy man to serve as Postmaster General, decided that the worthiest candidate in all the land was his own law partner, Nathan Kelsey Hall. Although a man of little political experience on the national level, Hall was Fillmore's closest and most influential political adviser. Like Cave Johnson, he was interested in only the most political aspects of the Department, but either because of his lack of concern for the postal service or in spite of it, during his administration Congress passed one of the most notable of all laws affecting the postal system.

THE ACT OF 1851

The Act of March 3, 1851, reduced the rate on *prepaid* domestic letters of half an ounce or less from five cents to three cents for any distance less than 3,000 miles. (If unpaid beforehand, the rate remained five cents.) The rate was double for letters transported more than 3,000 miles. These regula-

* President Taylor did not wish to proscribe Democratic postmasters who were doing their job well. However, Collamer, urged on by the ineffable Francis Granger, who advised him to be "bloody at all times," managed to replace most of the incumbent postmasters with deserving Whigs. During his short term in office, 3,547 postmasters were removed and 5,383 "resigned" out of a total of 16,582.

tions all but eliminated the zone system on first-class mail. Even more importantly, the act established the principle that the Post Office was a service to all the people of the United States and that it should be operated with that ideal in mind rather than with an undue concern for deficits. It specifically sanctioned postal deficits and forbade the Postmaster General to reduce or curtail postal services. The act provided, in part:

> That no post office now in existence shall be discontinued, nor shall the mail service on any mail route, in consequence of any diminution of the revenues that may result from this Act; and it shall be the duty of the Postmaster General to establish new Post Offices, and place the mail service on any new mail routes established, or that may hereafter be established, in the same manner as though this Act had not passed.

The debates in the Congress prior to the approval of this legislation indicated that many members of both chambers believed that lower rates would eventually provide greatly increased revenues and considered the act a temporary measure to forestall panic curtailments of service on the part of the postal administration. Nonetheless, the act created a permanent policy in favor of service over other considerations. From 1851 to this day, the Post Office Department has been operated at a deficit almost every year except under special wartime conditions, when the military assumes a major share of the cost of transporting the mails.

Fillmore was never popular except in the South, and he was refused the nomination of his party in 1852. He immediately appointed his Postmaster General and former law partner to a lifetime job as a federal district judge. Hall, who had been too ill to attend the Whig Convention, apparently found restorative powers in this judicial appointment and served on the bench for twenty-two years. To replace him, Fillmore appointed a political and postal nonentity from Connecticut named Samuel

Dickinson Hubbard, who served as a "lame duck" Postmaster General without incident until the following March.

THE "KNOW NOTHING" ATTACK

By 1852, the immigrant vote, predominantly Catholic, was becoming an important political factor in the Eastern states. The new Democratic President, Franklin Pierce, was widely suspected of being anti-Catholic because he came from New Hampshire, a state that had reluctantly given Catholics the vote only the year before and still maintained political "tests," that prevented Catholics from holding state office. Pierce tried to counteract this feeling by appointing a Catholic to the cabinet. His choice was James Campbell, a Pennsylvania judge generally thought to have engineered the 9,000-vote majority the Democrats had achieved in his state's elections the year before.

As a political ploy, the appointment was a failure. The anti-Catholic, anti-immigrant "Native Americans"—soon to be called the "Know Nothings"—were whipped into a frenzy of bigotry that plagued the Pierce Administration for four years. And, unfortunately for the cause of ecumenism, James Campbell was not much of a Postmaster General, being of a Merovingian—or do-nothing—bent. The Postmaster General's lack of outstanding competence made him a convenient target. In the congressional elections of 1854, the anti-Catholic Know Nothings carried Pennsylvania and New Hampshire, the home states of Campbell and Pierce, and elected enough representatives to hold the balance of power in both houses, where they aligned themselves with the Whigs.

Nonetheless, through all these vicissitudes, the magic of Rowland Hill's theories was still working wonders with the U.S. postal system. On paper, at least, Campbell's administration of the postal establishment was a resounding success. During his four years as Postmaster General (1851–55), the

Post Office Department spurted ahead with one of the greatest growth periods in its history, as the following figures show:

Year	Post offices	Miles of post roads	Volume (letters)	Population
1845	14,183	143,940	39,958,900	19,878,000
1850	18,417	178,672	69,426,400	23,192,000
1855	24,410	227,908	132,100,000	27,256,000

While Campbell was in office, the postal volume almost doubled, but the population rose by only 12.5 per cent. However, this increase should be credited to the lowering of postage rates and the use of adhesive stamps more than to any particular merit of the Postmaster General, who found his position "a very toilsome & laborious one."

Pierce was an unpopular President in the North, where he was considered to be soft on slavery, and he was rejected by the Democratic Convention in 1856. He withdrew his name after the fifteenth ballot, and James Buchanan, the "Sage of Wheatland," Pennsylvania, was nominated two ballots later.

Buchanan's Postmaster General was Aaron V. Brown of Tennessee, a close friend of Cave Johnson. Brown had been the law partner of former President Polk and had been mentioned as a possibility for the post at least eight years previously.

BUCHANAN'S MAN BROWN

An experienced man who had been a member of the House of Representatives from 1839 to 1845 and governor of his state for the two years following, Brown was blatantly political. The morals that characterized his administration of the Post Office were deplorable. Politics was everything. For instance, a swindling New York postmaster, Isaac Fowler, was permitted to "escape" to Mexico, despite the fact that he had embezzled $155,000 in postal funds, because he was a sterling Democratic politician and Tammany Hall wanted no embarrassments. In the cleanup that had to follow, Aaron Brown's nephew was released from his job in New York's post office when he was found to be receiving $800 a year for doing absolutely nothing. Other instances of embezzlement, fraud, and general dishonesty were common throughout the service.

But despite insensitivity in regard to political morals, Brown had his virtues. He was a competent enough politician to know, essentially, what was good for the country, and he insisted on opening up mail routes to the Pacific Coast even though he was aware that such routes could not be expected to be profitable. He knew (much better than did his President) that a national conflict was imminent, and he was determined to help keep California faithful by improving communications between the two coasts, which formerly had had mail service only by ship. This service was, of course, extremely slow, and the shipowners, who had a monopoly, charged extortionate rates. Brown quickly opened up six routes to the West Coast that cost the postal service $2,184,000 a year while yielding revenues of only $339,000.

Then, on March 3, 1857, at Brown's urging, Congress authorized the Postmaster General to establish a great overland route between the Mississippi and San Francisco. On September 16 of that year, a contract was made with John Butterfield and his associates to transport the mail on a semiweekly basis from St. Louis at an annual compensation of $600,000. In a very short time, this overland system had the greater portion of the mail business to the West Coast, with 100 coaches in operation, 700 drivers, and 1,500 horses and mules. The first run of the Butterfield Overland Mail traveled over the Sonora Road (the Warner Pass) in twenty-three days, twenty-three hours, and forty minutes. Although a great improvement, this service was still expensive. In 1857, postal expenditures were $4 million more than the revenues; in 1858, they were $5 million higher. Both deficits were records for the time.

But Brown's policies had an important political effect. The Democratic Party in California was badly split between the Southerners and the Irish, or, as the saying went in those days, the "Chivalry" and the "Shovelry." In 1854, the Know Nothing Party had swept the state at the congressional and the state legislature levels. The improvement of communications between the two coasts undoubtedly did a great deal to destroy the Know Nothing power in California and, indeed, to keep the state in the Union.

Naturally, Brown's rather cavalier attitude toward federal funds shocked conservatives in the Congress and, even more so, accountants in the career service of the Post Office. D. D. T. Leech, one of the latter, who worked under Brown, was extremely censorious of the Postmaster General when he wrote his book *History of the Post Office Department, 1789–1879.* "He placed under contract many long routes to connect the Western states with the Pacific Coast, which resulted in a financial burden beyond the ability of the Department to sustain without a heavy subsidy from Congress," Leech wrote. *"His financial policy was far from being a safe one."*

Brown died suddenly, in March, 1859. The choice of his successor had its comic aspects.

THE POSTMASTER GENERAL WHO HAD NO HEART

Jacob Thompson, who was Secretary of the Interior at the time, wrote that Buchanan, upon hearing of Brown's death, called an emergency meeting of his advisers to discuss the appointment of a new Postmaster General. "Brown was a good officer," Buchanan is reputed to have said, "but he was too good a man. The Department has suffered much because of his kindheartedness, and we must find a man who has no heart."

According to Thompson's account, the name of Edwin

Stanton immediately sprang to everyone's mind, but the suggestion was ultimately rejected. Secretary Thompson claimed that he himself then said: "Mr. President, I have a man who exactly fills your description. He has not a friend in the wide world that I know of, and he has no heart—no soul. I mean my commissioner of patents—Holt."*

Two days later, Joseph Holt of Kentucky was lifted from obscurity to the postmaster-generalship of the United States. Holt played to the hilt the role the President allegedly wanted. He was taciturn, vindictive, and ill-mannered. In fact, Buchanan later complained that Holt disconcerted even those he appointed to office, because he did so "in such a silent and ungracious manner." To those he turned down, he was, said the President, even worse, since "he never condescended to palliate the refusal by any kind explanations."

The new Postmaster General immediately set about trying to reverse all the policies of his predecessor. In his first annual report, dated less than four months after Brown's death, he announced the new policy:

> The Post Office should be self-sustaining. The transmission of a letter or newspaper or pamphlet for the citizen is no more public business than would be the transportation of his person or his merchandise. It is eminently proper that they, *and they only,* who use the mails, should pay for them, and that such payment should be exactly proportioned to such use.

Holt pulled out all the stops. He publicly scorned the performance of his predecessor and begged the Congress to remedy "the overburdened and sinking position in which the Department had been placed for the last few years." He even deplored the effect of public opinion on postal policies, stating (with doubtful historical authority): "The importunate and unceasing demand for the improvement, as well as the extension of postal facilities, has led the Department away from

* In fairness, it should be added that Holt, in a pamphlet published in 1883, denied these deficiencies.

the principle to which it had previously adhered." In his view, it was proper for the people to sit silently and obediently by while the Postmaster General administered the posts for them.

Congress paid no attention to him. He was able to effect some economies during the first year of his administration, but with the Civil War approaching and with the growing need for swifter communications among all sections of the nation, Congress ignored the protests of the Postmaster General and insisted on extending postal service in every direction.

Like several other postmasters general, Holt made the grave political mistake of taking on Congress in a head-to-head battle. He tried to bully the members into compliance and to bribe them into support through the manipulation of patronage. In such cases, Congress seems to take an almost mischievous pleasure in going beyond normal expectations to frustrate the Postmaster General's desires. Holt demanded that the Post Office Department be restored to that "basis of independence and honor on which it was placed by the founders of the government." Congress, feeling that it had settled that question once and for all in the Act of 1851, responded by establishing 695 new postal routes without providing a single penny for their support. In fiscal year 1860, the postal deficit was $10.6 million—twice as great as it had been during the free and easy days of Aaron Brown.

Holt, though a Southerner, was a strong abolitionist. As the situation in South Carolina worsened alarmingly during the last month of 1860, Buchanan determined to replace his Secretary of War with a man who was more certainly pro-Union. He chose Holt, who, before he assumed his new duties, took a parting shot at those in Congress "whose unscrupulous ambition would use the revenues of this [the Post Office] department as an instrument for political advancement."

To serve for the final month of the Buchanan Administration, Horatio King of Maine was chosen Postmaster General. King was the first career postal employee so honored. He had started out as a $1,000-a-year clerk in the Department under Amos Kendall twenty years before and had worked his way up, becoming first assistant postmaster general in 1854. Naturally, his function as Postmaster General was merely to keep the office open until the Lincoln Administration could take over in January.

THE PONY EXPRESS

Ironically, it had been during Holt's troubled two years that the most romantic episode in the history of the American postal service occurred. In April, 1860, private enterprise instituted the Pony Express as a speedy adjunct to the mail service to the West Coast. The Pony Express was really a development and enlargment of the Express Mail experiments conducted by Postmasters General McLean and Kendall earlier in the century, but it captured the public imagination and has continued to hold it enthralled ever since.

The first run of the Pony Express left St. Joseph, Missouri, the Eastern terminus, on April 3, 1860, and arrived in Sacramento, California, ten days later, or in less than half the time it usually took to transmit the mail between those two points. (The record run occurred in March, 1861, when Lincoln's first inaugural address was transported over the 2,000-mile route in seven days, seventeen hours.)

The devil-may-care atmosphere that pervaded the entire operation can be judged from the following advertisement, which ran in the San Francisco *Bulletin* and other newspapers in March, 1860, when the promoters were trying to recruit riders:

WANTED

Young, skinny, wiry fellows not over 18. Must be expert riders willing to risk death daily. Orphans preferred. Wages $25 per week.

Apply Central Overland Express
Alta Building, Montgomery Street

There was, evidently, no great difficulty in recruiting enough skinny, young daredevil orphans for the work. At its peak, the Pony Express employed eighty riders and owned 400 horses. All were the best obtainable.

The mail carried by the Express bore United States postage plus a surcharge imposed by the company of $5 a half ounce. Each horse carried a load of fifteen pounds. During the eighteen months that the Pony Express was in existence, only one small, relatively unimportant pouch of mail was lost. But, for three major reasons, the Pony Express finally collapsed and went out of business.

First of all, Congress enfolded the venture in its deadly embrace. In March, 1861, legislation was passed that reduced the surcharge from $5 per half ounce to $1 and stipulated further that every rider carry five pounds of government mail free of charge. This stipulation eliminated the possibility of continuing the service on a profitable basis. Secondly, the expenses of running the service were increased enormously when the company found it had to finance a major war against the Indians to keep its routes and stations free from their interference. The *coup de grâce* was delivered when the transcontinental telegraph line was completed to the West Coast on October 22, 1861, thus making the Pony Express no longer indispensable to swift communications with that area. The postal service was never again to be as exciting as it had been during the eighteen months that the Pony Express was in operation.

THE RECORD IN 1861

On March 4, 1861, Abraham Lincoln was inaugurated as President. Five days later, Montgomery Blair, almost certainly the most capable and talented man ever to head the postal establishment, was sworn in as Postmaster General.

During the thirty years that preceded Blair's appointment,

from the Jackson era to the eve of the Civil War, the postal service had shown fantastic growth. While the population was increasing by 144 per cent (from 12.9 million to 31.4 million), the volume of mail had grown by more than 1,300 per cent, from 13.8 million letters to 184.3 million.

During that brief span of three decades, the railroads had come into their own. In 1830, there were just 23 miles of tracks in the United States. By 1860, there were 30,635 miles of track, and 88.5 per cent of this was being used to transport the mails. By 1860, the railroad had finally become the dominant form of postal transportation. In that year, the annual miles of transportation by rail came to 27.6 million as compared with 24.5 million by horseback and sulky and 18.7 million by stagecoach.

In these thirty years, the United States had changed its shape, its form, its character, and its way of life. The postal establishment had grown from a minor agency of the government, affecting few people directly, to a major force in the social, economic, cultural, and political development of the nation.

Part II

GROWTH—AND POLITICS

IV

From Civil War to Civil Service

In 1861, the Blairs were the most influential family in Washington. Francis Preston Blair, father of Lincoln's new Postmaster General, Montgomery Blair, had come to the capital at the request of President Jackson to edit a Democratic newspaper, the *Globe*. In addition, he had become the official printer to Congress and also edited the *Congressional Globe*, predecessor of the *Congressional Record*.

Penniless when he arrived, the elder Blair soon became rich. In 1836, he purchased the famous house across the street from the White House that still bears his name and today is used by official guests of the U.S. Government. He later purchased an immense country estate, Silver Spring, in Maryland, on the outskirts of Washington. (A large portion of Maryland's second most populous city, named for the estate, was built on this property.)

One of his sons, Frank Blair, Jr., became a congressman and a prominent, though controversial, Union officer in the Civil War.* Montgomery, the other son who rose to prominence, was graduated from West Point and then taken under the wing of the famous Senator Thomas Hart Benton of Missouri. Through this auspicious sponsorship, Montgomery Blair became, at different times, U.S. district attorney for Missouri, judge of the Court of Common Pleas of the city of St. Louis,

---

* Frank Blair's statue is in Statuary Hall in the Capitol, representing Missouri.

and mayor of that city. In 1853, he returned to Maryland, building a home (Falkland) near the estate of his father and practicing law. A determined abolitionist, he was one of those who defended Dred Scott all the way to the Supreme Court, and he did what he could to help the fanatical John Brown after the debacle at Harpers Ferry.

In the campaign of 1860, the Blairs supported Lincoln strongly. After the election, it was a foregone conclusion that Montgomery would be a member of the new cabinet. (The Blair family let Lincoln know that was what they wanted, and what the Blairs wanted, they usually got.) There is some evidence that Montgomery Blair would have liked to have been Secretary of War, but he gladly accepted the postmaster-generalship, taking office on March 9, 1861.

Montgomery Blair was an erudite man with an impressive capacity for administration. He became a dominant figure in the cabinet and was thought by many to be the President's most trusted adviser. This fact generated a considerable amount of jealousy among his colleagues, especially since he did not hesitate to interfere in the operation of departments other than his own.* Too much of an autocrat to be bothered with being tactful, he did not suffer fools with any gladness whatsoever.

When he became Postmaster General, Montgomery became the master of Blair House, maintaining it as the social and political center of the capital.

LINCOLN'S PATRONAGE PROBLEMS

The political patronage problems of the Lincoln Administration were prodigious. A brand-new political party had

---

* In particular, he meddled in affairs of the War Department. Blair considered himself far more of an expert in military affairs than the Secretary. Some Union generals, notably Sherman, Butler, and Rosecrans, preferred to make their appeals for additional troops to the Postmaster General rather than to the Secretary of War because they knew Blair would act more decisively.

come into power for the first time, and the faithful were clamoring for a swift distribution of favors. Lincoln and his Postmaster General were mobbed by office seekers and much troubled by their importuning. The newly appointed Ambassador to England, Charles Francis Adams, was shocked when, in his first interview with the President after his appointment, Lincoln discussed with him the postmastership at Chicago rather than matters affecting foreign policy. During the four years of the first Lincoln Administration, almost all the 28,500 postmasters in the country were removed and—in the loyal states—replaced by Republicans.

It was generally conceded that the recommendation of a Republican congressman was the only qualification needed for appointment as postmaster. To relieve pressure on himself, Blair openly recommended that applicants for postmasterships apply directly to their congressmen rather than bother the Post Office Department. The Postmaster General insisted, however, that Republican senators should control the appointment of postmasters in their own home towns. (This courtesy is still extended to senators of the dominant political party, unless they have become *personae non gratae* with the White House.)

Since the quality of the postmasters had not been notably high during the Buchanan Administration, the Lincoln Administration's somewhat haphazard system of appointment did not appreciably affect the service. It did lead to widespread corruption, however, and certain members of Congress made a very good thing out of selling postmasterships to the highest bidders.* As the war wore on, the preference for appointments

* One of the most notorious, reportedly, was Alfred Ely, a Republican congressman from Rochester, New York. Ely, like many other Washingtonians, had journeyed down to Manassas, Virginia, to watch "Johnny Reb" take a licking at the first Battle of Bull Run. When the Confederates turned the tables on the Union troops, the spectators from Washington were thrown into panic, and Ely was one of those captured. He was imprisoned for six months in Richmond but turned this period to profit by selling postmasterships in his district throughout his imprisonment. Gustavus V. Fox, Post-

went to the widows of soldiers and to disabled soldiers—a precedent that became part of the Civil Service Law more than forty years later (June 26, 1906).

BLAIR'S ACHIEVEMENTS

The career of Montgomery Blair as Postmaster General might well serve as a model for how to conduct postal business in wartime. During the greatest military and political crisis the nation has ever experienced, he not only maintained but expanded the service of the Post Office Department and was responsible for more permanent and useful innovations than anyone else who has held that position.

He regularized the payment of postmasters and eliminated the last vestiges of the zone system from first-class postage rates. In addition, he took the first steps toward the forming of the *Union Postale*, the international organization that establishes equitable rates and efficient transportation of international mail throughout the world. His administration also saw the postal deficit dwindle away to almost nothing. Indeed, in fiscal year 1865 (for which he was only partially responsible), the Department showed a surplus of $917,249. However, too much importance should not be placed on this development, since one of Blair's first official tasks was to close down the post offices in the disloyal states. Because the South had perennially been a major drain on postal finances, the closings made the Post Office's fiscal picture look, at least superficially, better than it would have otherwise. Blair did not want to close down the Southern offices. He wanted to keep them open as "the best means to communicate to the people of the South the Judgment which I was confident the civilized world would pronounce against the rebellion, when its real purpose was dis-

---

master General Blair's brother-in-law, claimed that Ely was quite open and aggressive about his business transactions, although he did not explain how necessary communications were maintained.

tinctly seen." Nonetheless, the offices were closed, and the Confederacy eventually established its own postal system.

The greatest innovations of Blair's administration came while the Civil War was at its height, with the creation of the free city delivery system, the money order system, and the railway post office.

Railway Mail Service

The railway mail service, authorized in the Act of March 25, 1864, made it possible for trained clerks to sort letters and other mailable matter en route between cities, thus cutting as much as twenty-four hours from the delivery time. Formerly, mail aboard trains had been delivered "raw" to each city along the way, just as it had been when stagecoaches and postriders were dominant, and still had to be sorted after arrival. Under the new system, the mail traveled in specially fitted cars and arrived sorted and ready for distribution. Since the railway mail service eliminated many clerical jobs in post offices, it cost the Department virtually nothing additional and demonstrably improved the service. Postal clerks were simply recruited into the railway mail program.

Money Orders

The money order system (authorized by the Act of May 17, 1864) was a wartime measure that achieved permanent acceptance. For years, citizens had complained of the hazards of sending currency through the mails. The new system was intended as a means of permitting, for a small fee, relatives and friends of soldiers to forward with confidence sums of money to help alleviate the hardships of war or soldiers to send funds home to their dependents. (See also Chapter VIII.)

Arrival of the Mailman

On July 1, 1863, the day that the Battle of Gettysburg began, the free city delivery service was established. (Development of this service is more fully discussed in Chapter VIII.) On that date, the first letter carriers, 449 of them in all, started trudging the streets of the forty-nine largest cities in the United States.* They revolutionized the postal service and became the walking symbols of it. Their salaries aggregated $300,680 a year, or an average of $670 per man. In 1866, it was estimated that each letter carrier walked twenty-two miles a day on his route, seven days a week, fifty-two weeks a year. It was a rugged job then—and it still is. The city delivery idea worked so well that within three years it was producing ten times as much in revenues as its total annual cost. The introduction of the mailman to the nation was the outstanding achievement of Blair's postal administration.

A RESIGNATION REQUESTED

Despite his eminence as a postal manager, Montgomery Blair was dropped from the cabinet in September, 1864, just before the Presidential election. The reasons for his dismissal were purely political. At the time he was first appointed, Blair was opposed by some people who considered him too intransigent an abolitionist. After his appointment, he was incessantly attacked by the "Radical" Republicans, like Thaddeus Stevens, for being too soft toward the South, although he

* The forty-nine pioneer cities, with the complement of carriers assigned to each were: New York, N.Y. (137); Boston, Mass. (32); Baltimore, Md. (22); Brooklyn, N.Y. (18); Philadelphia, Pa. (119); Cincinnati, Ohio (12); Washington, D.C. (11); St. Louis, Mo. (7); Williamsburg, N.Y. (6); Albany, N.Y. (5); Providence, R.I. (5); Newark, N.J. (7); Newport, R.I. (2); New Haven, Conn. (3); Salem, Mass. (3); Lowell, Mass. (3); Louisville, Ky. (3); Cleveland, Ohio (3); Hartford, Conn. (2); Manchester, N.H. (2); Germantown, Pa. (2); Charlestown, Mass. (3); Lawrence, Mass. (2); New Bedford, Mass. (4); Roxbury, Mass. (2); Pittsburgh, Pa. (3); Troy, N.Y. (2); Paterson, N.J. (2); Jersey City, N.J. (2); Trenton, N.J. (2); Wilmington, Del. (2); Worcester, Mass. (3); Syracuse, N.Y. (1); Utica, N.Y. (1); Nashua, N.H. (1); Reading, Pa. (1); Lancaster, Pa. (1); Norristown, Pa. (1); York, Pa. (1); Newburyport, Mass. (1); Cambridgeport, Mass. (1); Hoboken, N.J. (1); Poughkeepsie, N.Y. (1); Allegheny, Pa. (1); Bath, Me. (1); Frederick, Me. (1); Chelsea, Mass. (1); Marblehead, Mass. (1).

was ruthless against postmasters of secessionist sympathies in the border states and removed them in wholesale lots.

In 1862, he infuriated the Radicals by opposing the timing (not the idea) of the Emancipation Proclamation. The fact that, politically, he was proved right (the Republicans almost lost control of Congress in the ensuing elections) did not soften the anger of his enemies. Blair also supported a humane policy toward the non-slave-owning Southerners, claiming that the savage proposals of Stevens and his supporters would merely substitute white slavery for black slavery in the South.

A military incident brought Blair's unpopularity to a head. In July, 1864, General Jubal Early and his raiders caught the Union Army completely by surprise. They swept down the Shenandoah Valley and invaded Maryland, encamping at Silver Spring, on the outskirts of an almost defenseless Washington.* The Postmaster General's beloved home, Falkland, was burned to the ground before the troops retreated.

Montgomery Blair was furious. He denounced Secretary of War Stanton and Grant's chief of staff, General Henry Halleck, and stated publicly that the War Department was directed and manned by "poltroons and cowards." This indictment caused great indignation throughout the government. John C. Frémont, the powerful "Pathfinder" and former senator, who had been the original Republican Presidential candidate in 1856 and loathed the Blair family, threatened to split the young party in two if Montgomery remained.

Lincoln wanted desperately to be re-elected. He believed it essential to the future of the nation that his moderate policies be continued. But re-election was a very uncertain business.

* Early and his staff made their headquarters in the mansion of the elder Blair. It is a matter of faith in some quarters that the almost inexplicable failure of "Too Late" Early to follow up his advantage and capture the capital was brought about by the discovery in the Blair cellars of quantities of good Bourbon whiskey. The 6th Massachusetts arrived to defend the city, and the Confederate opportunity was lost. Afterward, Early claimed that Lee forbade him to take Washington because he felt the apparent defenselessness of the capital was a trap.

No President since Jackson had been returned for a second term. The four previous Presidents had not even been nominated a second time by their own parties. It was obvious that Lincoln's chances of re-election were being diminished by the continued service of his controversial Postmaster General. On September 23, 1864, the President bowed to the political realities and wrote Blair:

> My Dear Sir: You have generously said to me, more than once, that whenever your resignation could be a relief to me, it was at my disposal. The time has come. . . . In the three years and a half during which you have administered the General Post Office, I remember no single complaint against you in connection therewith.

Blair handed in his resignation immediately, but he was hurt by Lincoln's action. He thought the opposition toward him was dying down. As he wrote his wife on the day of his resignation: "The President has, I think, given himself and me, too, an unnecessary mortification in this matter."

But it is obvious that Lincoln had planned Montgomery Blair's dismissal well in advance and had, in fact, selected his successor beforehand. Immediately upon receiving the resignation, Lincoln wired William Dennison, former governor of Ohio: "Mr. Blair has resigned and I appoint you Postmaster General. Come on immediately." Dennison did. He was sworn in on October 1, 1864.

Dennison was chosen primarily because he was not objectionable to either faction of the Republican Party. He is remembered for two reasons: because he insisted on keeping the mail routes open to California—despite the fact that they were yielding revenues of only $23,900 a year, while costing $760,000 to maintain—and because he persuaded Lincoln to furlough all Pennsylvania soldiers in the Union Army, just before the election, so they could go home and vote "right." Lincoln carried Pennsylvania.

After his re-election, Lincoln refused to have anything to do with political patronage. He had had his fill of it in 1861, and he had more important things to do. However, congressional pressure made many postmasters uneasy, and they had difficulty holding on to their jobs. One way to hold a job was outlined, quite frankly, by First Assistant Postmaster General Alexander W. Randall in a letter to Elisha W. "Boss" Keyes, who was postmaster at Madison, Wisconsin: "In case the *Member* makes a pass at you . . . I send you a prospectus of an oil company in which the Postmaster General takes an interest. You take a little stock. . . . It is a good thing anyway, but I want you to take a little stock in it." Keyes did so and was retained.

When Andrew Johnson succeeded to the Presidency after the assassination of Lincoln (April 15, 1866), Dennison tried, without success, to be the mediator between the unfortunate President and the irreconcilable Radical Republicans, who controlled the Congress. The Postmaster General fell between the two stools, and on July 11, 1866, much to his surprise and chagrin, his resignation was accepted. He was succeeded by Randall, who had been industrious in engineering his downfall.

JOHNSON AND RANDALL

Randall was unwaveringly loyal to Johnson and did his best in behalf of a hopeless cause. Although primarily a politician, he did pull the postal service together after the disruption caused by the war. He used every means at his disposal to encourage the Union Pacific and Central Pacific railroads to complete their transcontinental line, and it was completed on May 10, 1869, shortly after he had left office.

Randall considered the postal service a "great public necessity" and rejected as "erroneous" the theory that the Post Office should be self-sustaining. "There is no appropriation," he wrote, "which brings back directly and indirectly so large a return to the Government and the people as that made in aid of the postal service." In regard to unprofitable mail routes, he said: "They invite settlement and encourage material development, so there come back to the people in real wealth, almost as many millions of dollars as the Government expends thousands in this branch of the service." Not surprisingly, during Randall's term in office, the deficit increased—from $934,-000 in 1866 to just below $4 million in 1867, and hovered around $6.5 million during the next two years.

Ulysses S. Grant won the Presidency easily in 1868. (The Democratic ticket, a weak one, consisted of Horatio Seymour of New York and Frank Blair, Montgomery's elder brother.) There was no room in the new cabinet for Randall. He and Grant were personal enemies. A new Postmaster General, John Angel James Creswell of Maryland, was named.

GRANT, CRESWELL, AND OTHERS

Creswell was shamelessly political in office and made a clean sweep of all the moderate Republican postmasters and postal employees, replacing them with Radical Republicans. He was effective with Congress, however, and persuaded the membership, in the interest of achieving a balanced postal budget, to relinquish the franking privilege. All free mail was discontinued through the Act of January 31, 1873, and the Act of March 3, 1873. (The prohibition lasted for eighteen years.)

Creswell was energetic and imaginative in the pursuit of his duties but, in many instances, years ahead of his time. He strongly urged creation of a postal savings bank, after the British model, more than forty years before its acceptance in this country, and he recommended the purchase by the government of all private telegraph lines so that they could be incorporated into the federal communications system, as had been done in most European countries.

The Penny Post Card

In 1872, Creswell persuaded Congress to authorize the issuance and distribution of "postal cards" with postage stamps impressed at a value of one cent each. This innovation proved vastly popular with the public. In the first year that postal cards were authorized, more than 31 million were issued. The use of this service kept increasing, and it reached a high, in 1951, of more than 4 billion. Rate increases have since lessened the popularity of the postal card, but the average use is still more than 1 billion a year.

Demands for Reform

Creswell's rather brutal approach to political patronage came in for strenuous criticism from such intellectuals as Carl Schurz, who demanded the creation of a civil service system. Some influential newspapers (notably *The New York Times*) took up the campaign for reform. In 1871, a small congressional appropriation was obtained to set up an advisory board that would formulate certain rules for the making of appointments. It was the forerunner of the Civil Service Commission (established in 1883). The rules adopted by Congress in 1871 called for a board of examiners in each department to conduct examinations of applicants for positions and certify the successful ones for appointment. They were put into effect, briefly, in April, 1872. The Post Office Department, the most political of all government agencies, was not greatly affected, since the regulations extended only to appointments in the Department in Washington and in the general post office in New York City.

Creswell, the enthusiastic hatchet man of 1869, became the pious reformer of 1872. He cut down on removals of postmasters (now that his own people were in) and even bucked the party bosses of Philadelphia when they wanted to replace the local postmaster with a political hack.

Although Congress lost its enthusiasm for civil service reform after the elections of 1872, President Grant did not. Congress refused to appropriate any further money for an advisory board, but Grant continued to work, sincerely if ineffectually, to seek its reinstatement.

Creswell left the cabinet suddenly and mysteriously. On June 24, 1874, Grant announced the "resignation" of the Postmaster General. Nobody was more surprised than Creswell himself. He held his peace, however, and confined himself to saying of the postmaster-generalship that "the officer who fills the place acceptably leads a dog's life." He added that he was "worn down and tired of it" and wanted to return to the practice of the law. Nobody believed a word of it. Creswell did not immediately return to private practice but spent some time representing the government in the settlement of the Alabama claims. He did not waver in his devotion to Grant, however, and was a leader in the abortive attempt to nominate the President for a third term.

Charges of Corruption

Perhaps a clue to Creswell's abrupt dismissal can be found in certain financial dealings of his administration that came to light during the 1872 campaign. He was criticized for settling the so-called Chorpenning claims (a mail contractor case) for $443,000, when only $176,000 was actually due the contractor. He excused the added expense by saying it was because of "extra services he [Chorpenning] had performed as mail carrier."

In addition, since the law provided that the Postmaster General had to accept the lowest bid for the carrying of mails, it was the practice of the time for some irresponsible persons to enter ridiculously low bids. When the financial incompetence of the low bidder (who was, of course, working in collusion with the current contract holder) was exposed, the Postmaster General often had to make "temporary" arrangements, often at extortionate rates. A congressional investigation disclosed that Creswell had acted with something less than vigor in attacking the "straw bid" evil, and he emerged with his personal reputation considerably tarnished. Corruption was widespread in the Grant Administration, but the President's personal horror of financial chicanery may well have had something to do with the abrupt dismissal of his Postmaster General.

Postmaster General from St. Petersburg

Certainly, the events that followed indicate that Grant had acted without premeditation. He appointed Eugene Hale, a congressman from Maine and a close friend of Speaker of the House James G. Blaine, as Creswell's successor. Taken by surprise, Hale asked for a short vacation before assuming his office. Grant refused. Hale withdrew his acceptance, and the President cabled Marshall Jewell, U.S. Minister to the Court of St. Petersburg, to return at once and be his Postmaster General. Since Jewell (who was dumbfounded by the change in his condition) could not get back to Washington in less than two months, First Assistant Postmaster General James W. Marshall of New Jersey was appointed (July 7, 1874) to serve until Jewell became available. Jewell took the oath of office on September 1, and Marshall returned to the second spot in the hierarchy.*

The new Postmaster General had been governor of Connecticut and had been in Russia only a year. He turned out to be a good Postmaster General. He used his international experience well, providing for an official departmental representative to attend the initial meetings of the *Union Postale* in Bern, Switzerland, which Montgomery Blair had suggested during the Lincoln Administration. A U.S. delegation has par-

---

* It was against the law to make an interim appointment for more than ten days, so this clumsy arrangement had to be made to keep the position open for the new Postmaster General.

ticipated in its deliberations ever since. He also arranged for beneficial treaties with Canada and several Latin American countries for the more orderly disposal of postal matters.

In 1875, working with the superintendent of the railway mail service, George S. Bangs, Jewell developed the bold concept of running fast trains that would exclusively transport mail between key points, such as New York and Chicago or Washington, D.C. The system proved an instant success, and the transportation of the mail was significantly accelerated. The time for a New York–Chicago run, for instance, was thirty hours and forty minutes. On July 2 of the following year, Congress cut the compensation to the railroads for carrying the mail by 10 per cent. The railroads promptly refused to cooperate with the new program and discontinued the fast mail trains. But public reaction was so unfavorable that Congress found it necessary, in 1877, to appropriate additional funds to provide for the reinstitution of the speedy service.

Like many other postmasters general, Jewell was not popular with the practical politicians, who started plotting to get rid of him almost as soon as he took office. Unfortunately, as Grant began to hope for an unprecedented third term as President, the political spoilsmen gained ascendancy. In July, 1876, Grant peremptorily summoned Jewell to the White House and, without even shaking hands, said: "I would like to receive your resignation." Jewell was not given any explanation and did not seek any. He accepted his dismissal meekly and was replaced by the first assistant, James N. Tyner, a spoilsman of the most blatant type.

THE POST OFFICE UNDER PRESIDENT HAYES

Grant's hopes for a third term were unfounded. Rutherford B. Hayes became the Republican nominee, and he ran against Democrat Samuel J. Tilden on a platform based largely on civil service reform. (Ironically, during the campaign, Postmaster General Tyner saw to it that postal employees made more political contributions than ever before. It was understood throughout the establishment that hefty contributions were necessary for the retention of even the meanest jobs.)

The extremely close election marked the first time the Democratic Party had become a serious factor in Presidential contests since the Civil War. Because of disputes in Florida, Louisiana, Oregon, and South Carolina, the final decision was thrown into the Republican House of Representatives. Hayes was declared the winner by one electoral vote. (The new President wanted Montgomery Blair to join his cabinet, but Blair, characteristically, refused because, he said, Hayes had stolen the election from Tilden and was not the rightfully elected President of the United States.)

Hayes tried to propitiate the South by appointing Senator David McK. Key of Tennessee as Postmaster General. Key was both a Democrat and a former Confederate, and the move proved disastrous. As *The New York Times* said: "The Southern Whites thought no more of the President and less, if possible, of Mr. Key." Northern Republicans were, of course, outraged. In 1880, Hayes gave in and replaced Key with Horace Maynard, a nonentity from Tennessee, who completed the term.

Rutherford Hayes did try to protect postal employees from having their pockets picked by the political spoilsmen and issued an Executive Order (June 22, 1878) forbidding the usual assessments in post offices. But James Tyner, who had been relegated to the first assistant postmaster-generalship, coolly advised party officials to ignore the order.

Despite Hayes's failure to create a permanent climate of political morality in the postal establishment and despite the constant bickering that took place between the Department and Congress, the postal service throve during the four years of his administration. Revenues rose from $27.5 million to $36.8 million, an increase of about 34 per cent, and the deficit was relentlessly driven down from $6.1 million to $2.8 million, a total reduction of 54 per cent. The number of post offices increased from 37,345 to 44,512, and the per capita expenditure on postage rose from fifty-nine cents a year in 1877 to seventy-two cents in 1881. The Department estimated that in 1880 the cost of delivering letters free in the cities of the United States came to only one-fourth of a cent apiece and that the government was making an annual profit of $15 million on this service.

GARFIELD'S POSTMASTER GENERAL

Thomas L. James had been anathema to the spoilsmen when he was postmaster of New York City, and he continued to devil them when he became Postmaster General under Hayes's successor, James A. Garfield. Although the President had little apparent sympathy with reform at first, he became more sympathetic to the idea after his election. James began a crusade against corrupt practices by successfully exposing and prosecuting an organized racket within the star-route system.

It had been the custom of Second Assistant Postmaster General Thomas J. Brady, a Grant appointee, to let bids for carrying the mail to certain favored individuals at a low figure and then to go to Congress for a supplemental appropriation "to expedite the service." As a result, on special routes, a great deal of money was spent for transporting a small amount of mail a short distance. One of the principal beneficiaries of this dishonest system was S. W. Dorsey, secretary of the Republican National Committee. The resultant scandals were an embarrassment to the party and did not enhance James's popularity with the "stalwart" Republican politicians.

James also refused to play politics with postmasterships. He even went so far as to suggest to President Garfield that congressmen first be permitted to nominate candidates for postmasterships and then that a competitive examination be held to select the men most qualified. He recommended that Garfield draft a bill to this effect—one that would also specify the precise causes for which a postmaster could be removed—and that he then go before the nation to arouse public sentiment on its behalf. The news that the President was actually considering this course of action filled the practical politicians with loathing.

Unfortunately, nothing came of the idea. Tragedy intervened. On July 2, 1881, Garfield was shot at the Washington railway station by a man named Charles J. Guiteau, who is invariably described in history books as "a disappointed office seeker." The President died on September 19. He had been conferring with the Postmaster General on reform measures up to nine days before his death.

CIVIL SERVICE COMMISSION ESTABLISHED

Ironically, Garfield's assassination greatly stimulated the public demand for civil service reform. It was pointed out that Garfield had been, indirectly, a martyr of the spoils system. If there had been a proper civil service system, there might have been no "disappointed office seeker." As the public interest rose, Congress began to see the political expediency of regarding civil service with a kindlier eye.

But if Congress paid heed to the swell of public opinion, the new President did not. Chester A. Arthur was not that sort of a man. He was a spoilsman of many years' standing and had no patience with the niceties of political morality. Naturally, he got rid of Postmaster General James as swiftly as he decently could (in fact, a little swifter).

His choice of a successor was a curious one. Timothy O. Howe of Wisconsin, who was sworn in on January 5, 1882, was an elderly political hack who, according to the *Nation,* had the peculiar power "of impressing himself on every administration as a person who must be 'provided for.' " His son-in-law had been the attorney for the defense in the star-route cases, and Howe, while in the Senate, had been a derisive critic of all attempts at civil service reform. He had made a particularly brutal assault on Carl Schurz for his advanced, and "foreign," ideas on political morality. Under Howe's management, it was inevitable that the worst kind of political manipulation should dominate the postal establishment.

However, in the congressional election of 1882, Democrats, waving the banner of civil service reform, made startling inroads on Republican preserves and won control of the House of Representatives. The Republicans in the Senate were impressed. Before the Forty-seventh Congress was disbanded, the members introduced legislation calling for a federal civil service.

The Act of 1883, creating the Civil Service Commission, was by no means a strong one, but it was a beginning. It excluded the 47,000 postmasters in the nation, but it limited their powers by ordering competitive examinations for letter carriers and post office clerks in all offices with fifty or more employees—about half the entire complement of the postal service. It forbade political solicitation in any federal building, prohibited compulsory contributions to political campaigns, and provided for penalties when the law was violated.

Postmaster General Howe died in office, and on April 11, 1883, Judge Walter Quentin Gresham of Indiana was sworn in as his successor. The reformers had high hopes for the new Postmaster General, but he disappointed them. His principal interest was in getting the Republican nomination for President Arthur or, failing that, for himself. He refused to permit the circulation of political circulars on federal premises, but he did permit widespread efforts to secure "voluntary" contributions during the campaign of 1884.

Chester Arthur never had a chance in the 1884 convention. His campaign was badly mishandled by his manager, Frank

Hatton of Iowa, who was also first assistant postmaster general. After the debacle, which saw James G. Blaine of Maine nominated as the Republican candidate, Arthur nonetheless rewarded Hatton by making him Postmaster General for the last few months of his term. In the ensuing election, the Democrats, with Grover Cleveland as their nominee, regained the White House for the first time in twenty-four years.

During the Arthur Administration, postal revenues had wavered rather uncertainly, rising sharply to $45.5 million in 1883 but tailing off to $42.6 million in 1885—still an increase of about 13 per cent in four years. The number of post offices leaped up to 51,252. The deficit was turned into a surplus of $1.2 million in 1882 and $2.1 million in 1883, but the trend was reversed and the audited deficit in 1885 was $7.5 million. Per capita expenditure rose to eighty-five cents a year in 1883 but slipped off to seventy-six cents in 1885.

Also in the Arthur years, owing to the efforts of a remarkable figure in the Congress, Samuel Sullivan "Sunset" Cox, a Democratic representative from New York (who had previously served from Ohio), legislation was passed (June 27, 1884) granting letter carriers a maximum of fifteen days a year paid vacation. (This revolutionary concept was not extended to post office clerks, who for many years thereafter had to work seven days a week, fifty-two weeks a year, for long and uncertain hours.)

THE CLEVELAND YEARS

Although it had been obvious for some years that the Democrats would eventually find their way back to power, Grover Cleveland owed his election, in part, to the "Mugwump" vote —Republicans and independents who looked for sweeping Democratic reforms in government service. Since 75 per cent of all federal employees were in the Post Office Department and since the postal establishment was the most notoriously political of all government agencies, this was the area in which most reform was expected.

As is so often the case when a party has been out of power for a long while, the Democrats in 1885 had difficulty in finding men for the cabinet with national reputations. Cleveland chose as his Postmaster General William Freeman Vilas, a wealthy and respected lawyer from Wisconsin who had been little more than a political hobbyist.

The appointment whipped the most partisan elements of the Republican press into a frenzy of derision. Vilas was described by the New York *Tribune* as a "backwoods Postmaster General," and his social habits were portrayed as if he were a kind of slow-witted Davy Crockett. Actually, Vilas was a man of considerable culture and dignity. The leading citizen of Madison, he turned out to be a reasonably good and courageous Postmaster General. He was Cleveland's closest personal friend during the four years he headed the Post Office Department.

Throughout his term of office, Vilas was an able advocate of the service concept of the postal establishment. "The notion that the postal service is a business carried on by the government, which should be at least self-sustaining, is not a just or wise one," he said. "To so regard it tends to impair its effectiveness and retard its improvement."

The new President and his Postmaster General soon found that all the high-sounding campaign theories about civil service reform would not work in practice. The Democrats had been banished from the patronage trough for twenty-four years—and they were hungry.

On April 28, 1885, Vilas, under intense pressure, issued a naïve "Confidential Circular" to the congressmen in New York, Ohio, Virginia, and Indiana indicating ways to get rid of partisan Republican postmasters. He suggested that members of the Congress pick out "the most obnoxious and offensive partisans in each county" of their districts. He stated:

I will require no more proof of the partisanship in these selections than the affirmation on the part of a Representative or Senator that the Postmaster has been an active editor or proprietor of a Republican newspaper . . . or a stump speaker, or member of a political committee . . . or, that his office has been made the headquarters of political work, or that his clerks have been put into the performance of political duties.

The circular remained about as "confidential" as the front page of *The New York Times*. Reformers reviled it, practical politicians gloated over it. Young Theodore Roosevelt was especially indignant. "Vilas seems to be a perfect ass," he wrote to Henry Cabot Lodge. "His circular was really phenomenal; I should think it would awaken even the grovelling imbecility of the Independent mind to a sense of the true state of affairs." The idea of permitting members of the Congress to be the sole prosecuting attorneys, judges, and juries in determining what postmasters in their district were obnoxious embodied a presumption of purity and high-mindedness on the part of these gentlemen that was not altogether justified and hardly what the reformers had in mind when they had voted for Cleveland.

To make matters worse, a former Illinois congressman, Adlai E. Stevenson, was appointed first assistant postmaster general and given custody of the guillotine for the decapitation of Republican postmasters. In four years, almost 40,000 heads fell. To facilitate the carnage, Congress, in March, 1887, repealed the Tenure of Office Act, which had been imposing at least a little restraint upon the spoilsmen.

But if he went along in the matter of patronage, Vilas, who was a *laissez faire* Democrat, had the courage—or foolhardiness—to make a frontal assault upon the railroads. He claimed that they were robbing the Post Office Department by charging extortionate rates. There is no doubt that the charge was true. The railroads were not compelled by law to transport the mails, and they were essential to the efficient operation of the postal service. Therefore, they dictated their own terms.

Vilas objected to the fact that the railroads were charging excessively high rates for the rental of their antiquated rolling stock and even more exorbitant rates for hauling these cars along their ways. He presented to the Congress a memorandum showing conclusively that it would be far more efficient and economical for the government to build its own mail cars. He pointed out that the Department had paid the railroads $1,881,580 in 1886 to rent decrepit cars, when an expenditure of just $1.6 million by the government would pay the cost of building and equipping sufficient modern cars for the Department's needs. He also berated the railroads for permitting unsafe and unsanitary conditions in their mail cars and argued that if the government owned the cars, the postal employees would be consulted as to their design—a novel idea in 1887.

But the railroads were a potent political force in the nation and had by far the most influential lobby. For many years, they had made it their practice to dominate the legislatures in key states, and since the legislatures elected the U.S. senators, the railroads also controlled the Senate. In the House, few representatives were willing to oppose the railroads, and almost none of them had widespread influence among their colleagues.

Vilas was ingenuous. His memorandum was completely convincing—and completely disregarded. Representative Henry Clay Evans of Tennessee, a member of the House Committee on Post Office and Post Roads, tried to convince his colleagues to provide an appropriation for the government to buy or build its own cars. He confided to Representative Robert M. La Follette of Wisconsin that he couldn't get a single vote in the committee in support of the proposition. La Follette, who was sympathetic, agreed that if Evans had succeeded in getting his proposal to the floor, "there would not have been a corporal's guard to sustain him. The railroad lobby outside and the railroad members inside would have prevented any action."

Late in 1887, Cleveland asked Vilas to move over to the Department of the Interior as Secretary. Vilas was reluctant because, he said, the Post Office Department "has not had a postmaster general long enough in his place to thoroughly comprehend its proper requirements, or invent the desirable remedial measures due to its highest advantage and utility." There was no question, of course, of his refusing to comply with Cleveland's wishes, but he was granted the time to complete his final annual report.

The change was kept secret until all the details were ironed out. Stevenson was ambitious for promotion to the top position, but Cleveland would not have him. On January 16, 1888, the President commissioned Don M. Dickinson, Democratic "boss" of Michigan, as Postmaster General, and Vilas went to the Department of the Interior.

Shortly after Dickinson's accession, a significant bill affecting the labor relations of the Department was enacted. In the days when postal employees had been hired and fired at will according to the turns of the political wheel, Congress had been somewhat solicitous of their welfare, at least while they still held their jobs. But since the passage of the Civil Service Act of 1883, the members had lost almost all interest in postal employees. If the employees could not help Congress, Congress saw no reason to help them. As a result, conditions in post offices had become intolerable. Employees were very poorly paid and worked interminable hours at the whim of their superiors. The exception to the prevailing congressional rule was Representative Samuel Sullivan Cox. In 1884, as already mentioned, he had won the fifteen-day vacation for letter carriers. In 1887–88, he went on a crusade again and finally succeeded in winning for his "favorites" (as he delighted in calling the letter carriers) an eight-hour workday* (Act of May 24, 1888). However, this forward step still did not affect post office clerks, who continued to work under conditions of near peonage.

On balance, although many Mugwumps were disenchanted by the President's policies toward postmasters, the first Cleveland Administration compiled a good record on civil service reform. Postal employees were more secure in their jobs, such as they were, than they had ever been before, and there was a minimum of corruption. Before he left office, Cleveland signed into law a bill, which he had favored, bringing the railway mail clerks into the civil service (Act of December 31, 1888). This breakthrough was a portent of even more significant changes to come.

Despite the fact that he had a plurality in the popular vote, Cleveland lost the election of 1888 to Benjamin Harrison of Indiana. Although the management of the postal establishment during the first Cleveland Administration was far more enlightened than it had been under Chester A. Arthur, the statistics indicate very little change in the Department's rate of growth or development.

When Cleveland left office, there were 58,999 post offices in the nation, and the revenues came to $56.2 million, or $13.6 million more than they had been the year he took office. The deficit was driven down to $3.8 million in 1888, but in 1889 (for which his administration was only partially responsible) it rose to $6.2 million. The per capita use of the mail rose in the four years to ninety-two cents annually. In 1885, Congress had made a drastic reduction in postage rates, dropping the cost from three cents to two cents per letter and raising the weight limitation from half an ounce to a full ounce, thereby

---

* Cox died in 1889, after attending a function in New York City celebrating the foundation of the National Association of Letter Carriers. The letter carriers of the nation raised $10,000 to erect a statue in his honor, and to this day the letter carriers of Brooklyn make an annual pilgrimage to decorate his grave.

increasing the deficit for the following two years. But sharply rising volume and far greater per capita use of the service had soon returned the balance between revenues and expenditures to normal levels. Once again, the policy of making the postal service attractive and accessible to the public had proved its value to the nation.

By this time, the Post Office Department was becoming so large and so essential to the economic and social life of the country that it almost ran under its own momentum, regardless of who was serving as Postmaster General. Policies changed with each administration, of course, and affected the quality of the service, the conditions under which employees worked, and the financial condition of the Department. But the development of a hard core of permanent secondary management, especially after the Civil Service Act of 1883, ensured that the postal establishment would grow and, in its way, prosper no matter who was nominally in charge. Second-echelon career officials were usually unimaginative and resistant to change of any sort, but they were knowledgeable, generally honest, and often dedicated.

Thenceforth, it would take a strong-minded man to make any permanent impression on the character of the Post Office. In the administration of Benjamin Harrison, such a Postmaster General did come on the scene.

V

Big Business: Wanamaker to Will Hays

Benjamin Harrison was not by nature an adventurous politician, yet he made an astonishing choice for Postmaster General—John Wanamaker of Philadelphia, at the time the most
successful merchant prince in the nation. Wanamaker's interest in politics had been peripheral until the Presidential campaign of 1888. However, once he became involved, his
orderly mind was shocked by the unbusinesslike way in which
political parties were organized and operated. He hated inefficiency, and he decided to do something about it. When
Harrison was nominated, Wanamaker had undertaken to raise
campaign funds from the business community of the nation,
reputedly with the understanding that if he and Harrison
were both successful, he would be rewarded with a cabinet
position. (However, Wanamaker said afterward, "The office
never entered my mind.") The finance committee Wanamaker
headed raised $400,000 during the campaign, an enormous
sum for the time. The Democrats were shocked (or, at least,
pretended to be shocked) at the rather ruthless way the Philadelphia millionaire raised the money and even more so at
the way it was spent. There seems to be little doubt that
thousands of votes were bought and sold on election day.

THE MERCHANT PRINCE AND THE POST OFFICE

The new Postmaster General, an ardent Presbyterian churchman, blandly replied to his critics that he had merely used the same methods he had always used for raising money for the establishment of foreign missions. Certainly, the appointment was controversial. Carl Schurz, who might reasonably have been expected to applaud the selection of a non-politician as Postmaster General, was scandalized. "For the first time in the history of the Republic a place in the Cabinet of the President was given for a pecuniary consideration," he wrote. The *Nation* and *The New York Times* were equally bitter about the new Postmaster General. (In fact, the *Times* was so scathing in its remarks that Wanamaker, in retaliation, banned the newspaper from the reading rooms of the Philadelphia YMCA. The *Times* somehow managed to survive the blow. Its editor, unrepentant in the face of the Postmaster General's wrath, wrote: "We shall persevere in our endeavors to get out of Wanamaker as much harmless amusement as possible during his term of office. There is a world of fun in him.")

Wanamaker brought to the Post Office Department the same hard business sense and imagination that had made him so notable a success in the mercantile world. He was accused by the Democrats and by certain elements in the Republican Party of running the establishment with too much cold-blooded efficiency, as if it were his own department store.* He was also accused of being far too interested in self-advertisement.

---

* In his private office in Washington, the Postmaster General kept a direct telegraph line to his store in Philadelphia so that he could maintain control of its activities with one hand while running the postal service with the other. Considerable resentment was aroused when numerous postmasters who sought to gain favor with their chief insisted that their letter carriers purchase their uniforms only through Wanamaker's Philadelphia store. There is no record of any attempts by the Postmaster General to discourage this practice.

There was some truth in both allegations. He was a flamboyant personality, and his flamboyance helped him achieve his goals. There is no disputing that Wanamaker was accustomed to "thinking big" and that the Post Office Department had great need of big thinking when he assumed office.

The Philadelphian became Postmaster General in the centennial year of the U.S. Post Office. The huge operation that he inherited was unrecognizable compared with the country-store establishment of 100 years before. The United States had become one of the biggest and most powerful nations in the world and, after Germany, had the second largest postal system.

When John Wanamaker took office, there were 58,999 post offices in the land, more than twice the number there had been in 1861, when Lincoln appointed Montgomery Blair. The revenues were up to $56.2 million (as opposed to $8.5 million in 1861), and the average American was spending ninety-two cents a year on his mail, almost three and a half times what he had been spending twenty-eight years previously. The Post Office employed 150,000 persons throughout the nation. The city delivery service, now twenty-six years old, had 8,257 letter carriers on the rolls, working in 401 communities. The mail volume in 1889 was estimated at 3.9 billion pieces. Obviously, the Post Office had become big business.

Although he was every inch a businessman, Wanamaker made it perfectly clear from the outset that he considered the Post Office a public service and not a purely mercantile operation. In his first annual report, he wrote: "The post office is not a money-making enterprise. It is not intended to be, and it is a mistake to expect it to be self-sustaining until it is fully perfected." He did not expect the postal service to be perfected during his lifetime, and during his four years in office, he concentrated mightily on improving the service, without too much regard to the costs. The deficits during his administration averaged around $6 million a year—considerably higher than they had been during Cleveland's first Presidency.

The darkest blot on the Wanamaker postal administration was the widespread disregard of the new civil service system throughout the entire postal establishment. The professional Republicans saw to it that the job of first assistant went to James S. Clarkson, former postmaster of Des Moines, Iowa, who was a particularly loyal member of the spoilsman fraternity. Wanamaker all but washed his hands of the patronage problem and did not attempt to interfere with Clarkson, who, making no bones of his intentions, described civil service as "the toy of a child, the trifling thing of hobby riders." Holding that politically appointed postal employees gave the public better service, he said, "If they are taught to consider that there is not only public but personal advantage to be gained, they will work, and for working they will be rewarded."

In the pogrom Clarkson conducted against Democratic appointees, more than half the 2,684 Presidential postmasters and 49,000 non-Presidential postmasters were fired or forced to resign. Moreover, although President Cleveland, just before his departure from the White House, had brought the railway postal clerks in the civil service, the Harrison Administration delayed putting the order into effect until 2,300 of the total of 5,000 clerks had been removed and replaced by the politically faithful. Complaints were widespread that the highly political Inspection Service was making a determined effort to harass Democratic postal employees. In some areas, inspectors used every ruse imaginable to catch postal employees in real or imagined misconduct or inefficiency so that they could effect their dismissal from the service and thus create openings for Republicans.

By 1893, despite civil service, only 2 of the 151 employees of the Baltimore post office were Democrats, and Baltimore was a predominantly Democratic city. In other places, Republican zeal to "purify" the postal service went to ridiculous lengths. In Ilion, New York, for example, the appointment of the new Republican postmaster was held up and almost canceled because it was rumored that he had named his young son Grover, presumably after the Democratic President. When it was established that the boy's name really was Grosvenor, the appointment went through.

Civil Service Commissioner Theodore Roosevelt was publicly shocked by all that was going on, and he waged an effective and bitter battle in the headlines against Wanamaker and his assistant. "Damn Mr. Wanamaker!" he shouted to Carl Schurz's Civil Service Reform League, and accused the Postmaster General, among other things, of having "a sloppy mind."

But aside from these rather sordid political circumstances, Wanamaker compiled a remarkable record in office. More improvements in the postal service were achieved during his four years than during any previous administration since that of Montgomery Blair. In many instances, Wanamaker's thinking was well ahead of his times. He planted the seeds for numerous postal improvements destined to take effect years after he had left the postal scene.

Wanamaker's Improvements

Wanamaker was the real father of the rural delivery service, although it was not authorized until October 1, 1896. He fought the banking interests and gave the impetus that eventually led to the postal savings system (authorized June 25, 1910), and his labors in behalf of parcel post were so generally recognized that he was given the honor of mailing the first package to inaugurate this service (January 1, 1913), twenty years after he had left office. (See Chapter VIII.)

His personal distaste for partisan politics and petty patronage matters left Wanamaker free to concentrate on the business of managing the postal service, and except for his continuing interest in running his Philadelphia department store, he worked at it to the exclusion of everything else. More than any other Postmaster General since Benjamin Franklin, he made a point of touring the country and inspecting post offices in person, observing at first hand the operations and the working conditions, interviewing the men, and often issuing on-the-spot orders for immediate improvements. He continued to astound the postal professionals in the field with his intimate knowledge of the workings of the system. Through his vast experience as a merchant, he was imbued with concern for the postal patrons, and he insisted that service be the overriding interest of everyone who worked for him. (It was his strict rule that all mail arriving at a post office during daylight hours must be delivered within two hours of its arrival.)

During this period, the system of establishing strategically located postal branches and stations in large cities was originated. Wanamaker saw that postal operations were being strangled by overcentralization in the metropolises and sought —and got—appropriations from the Congress to build subsidiary postal installations to help handle the load and relieve congestion in the main post offices. In New York and Philadelphia, he had swift pneumatic tubes installed between stations to facilitate the movement of the mails. (It should be noted that, in 1892, the French and German postal services were proud to announce that letters were being transmitted through pneumatic tubes between Berlin and Paris, a distance of 750 miles, in just thirty minutes.)

During his first year in office, Wanamaker was responsible for instituting fast mail-train service on a transcontinental basis. Beginning November 15, 1889, on, the mail was transported between New York and San Francisco in four days, twelve hours, and forty-five minutes.

One of his most successful campaigns was to kick the enormously powerful, enormously corrupt lottery syndicate out of the postal service. When he moved against the lottery operators, they reacted savagely. The Postmaster General's life was seriously threatened, and congressmen were blackmailed. According to contemporary accounts, it was a common sight to see the lottery lobbyists patrolling the corridors of the Capitol openly jingling bags filled with gold coins for the "edification" of the legislators. But the lobbyists overplayed their hand, and a backlash of revulsion set in. John Wanamaker organized concerned church, civic, and business leaders, whose efforts led to the enactment of legislation (September 19, 1890) that drove the lotteries not only out of the postal system but out of the country as well.

Plight of Postal Employees

In 1889, letter carriers were earning $600 a year at entrance, $800 for their second year, and $1,000 a year thereafter. Thanks to the efforts of "Sunset" Cox, their patron in the Congress, these rates were slightly higher than they had been in 1863, when the city delivery service was instituted. (In the smaller offices, the salary was a flat $850 a year, regardless of service.) Also, thanks to Cox, they were granted fifteen days of leave a year and, nominally, had the privilege of an eight-hour day. However, the law did not set any limits within which the eight hours had to be worked, and many carriers were forced to stay on the job as long as eighteen hours, on a stop-and-go basis, to fulfill their daily obligation. Half the letter carrier force worked in smaller (non-Presidential) offices and were not protected by civil service. Their patronage jobs were emptied and filled at the whim of the dominant political party. In these offices, postmasters often forced the carriers to falsify their timecards so that the eight-hour law would seem not to have been violated. Refusal to comply, of course, could lead to dismissal, and there was no appeal from such decisions.

But as bad as the plight of the letter carriers was, the condition of the post office clerks was much worse. They had no congressional angel to fight for them. They were paid less, their average salary being $700 a year. They were given no vacations, no days off. A national survey taken in 1889 showed that 90 per cent of the clerks worked 365 days a year and that the average workday was fourteen hours. On top of this, their workrooms were filthy; dirty mailbags filled the air with dust. Tuberculosis was the occupational disease, so much so that it was known in the service as the "clerk's sickness."

The railway clerks not only were poorly paid (averaging $997 a year) but worked under extremely hazardous conditions. The antique wooden mail cars (the oldest stock the railroads could have used) were usually placed immediately behind the coal tender. In even minor wrecks, the flimsy cars were inclined to buckle and splinter into bits. In the four years that Wanamaker was Postmaster General, mail trains were involved in 1,118 wrecks, in which 32 railway post office clerks were killed outright, 264 permanently disabled, and 289 less seriously injured. Thus, about 11 per cent of the total work force for an average year were killed, disabled, or injured in a period of four years. A man starting in the service in 1889 had about a 1 to 9 chance of surviving four years without injury.

Wanamaker at least paid lip service to the plight of postal employees. In January, 1891, he said: "The people who do postal labor ought to have fair remuneration. I think it a shame for the Government to make some of our people work their legs and fingers off for bare support. . . . There is no reason why people doing this hard work should not have at least enough to pay for the comfort of their families." He blamed the indifference of Congress for the miserable condition of his employees, but he did very little to arouse congressional interest. In fact, when it was suggested that post office clerks be given Sundays off and perhaps an annual vacation, he turned the proposal down as too expensive. To his credit, he reversed his position before he left office, and the clerks eventually received the same leave considerations as letter carriers.

In 1892, in his final annual report, the Postmaster General suggested that the families of railway post office clerks killed in the performance of their duties be recompensed by a sum not to exceed the dead man's salary for a year. He added that the money could be derived from the fines imposed upon clerks who had been derelict in their duties. Nothing came of the suggestion.

But the world was changing. Labor was beginning to realize its potential strength and its actual power in an increasingly industrial nation. In the 1880's the Ancient and Holy Order of the Knights of Labor emerged from a purely fraternal organization into something considerably more militant. Letter carriers in many cities secretly joined the Knights, and some of them became leaders in their ranks. By 1889, the Knights had an estimated 750,000 members in 6,000 locals throughout the nation—a not inconsiderable force.

The Letter Carriers Organize

Then, in 1889, a Detroit letter carrier named William H. Wood, a Civil War veteran and an able man, devised, with some of his friends, a plan for organizing the letter carriers of the nation. A call went out, and in Milwaukee, under the cover of the annual encampment of the Grand Army of the Republic, approximately 100 mailmen instituted the National Association of Letter Carriers on August 30, 1889.

The action shook postal management to its foundations. Reprisals against members of the infant union were carried out in many cities. In some communities (St. Louis is an example), all the leaders of the local branch were summarily dismissed from the service, and the branch was temporarily disbanded. In other cities, known members were given the least desirable routes and often were made to work their eight hours, on and off, over the entire twenty-four hours of every day.

The vindictiveness of the postal managers did not deter the carriers in their organization, however, and the NALC grew swiftly and steadily. Today, with more than 205,000 members in about 6,500 local branches, it is a powerful institution with a strong influence upon Congress and within the executive branch.

The Post Office Department unwittingly and unwillingly played right into the hands of the new employee organization. First, the postal managers denied any responsibility for the eight-hour-workday law of 1888, claiming that it had been passed as part of an appropriations bill and therefore was applicable only during the fiscal year to which the bill pertained. Congress and the courts rejected this argument outright. Then, the Department lawyers declared that an eight-hour day *really* meant a fifty-six-hour week and that if a carrier worked nine hours a day for six days, he still owed two hours on Sunday. This interpretation of the law was placed in effect throughout the country. Thereupon, the letter carriers sued the federal government for the unpaid overtime they had been forced to work. The case—*Post* v. *U.S.*, 148 U.S. 124 (1893)—was fought all the way up to the Supreme Court, and individual letter carriers were awarded a total of $3.5 million to settle the thousands of claims that had accumulated. In 1893, this was a startling turn of events, and the prestige of the NALC was permanently established.

The Department delayed paying the claims as long as possible, and instructions were issued that thenceforth no overtime of any kind would be allowed. Special agents were hired to make certain that the carriers wasted no time on the route; mailmen accused of doing so were dismissed out of hand, and postmasters who permitted overtime were also fired.*

---

* In another move to speed up the service, Wanamaker authorized the use of mailboxes in residences for the first time, explaining that letter carriers were wasting too much valuable time at each house waiting for the servant to answer the doorbell.

The post office clerks followed the lead of the letter carriers and met for the first time in Washington on February 3, 1890. They had some trouble organizing (only thirty delegates appeared), but after an initial period marred by internal frictions, the National Federation of Post Office Clerks did develop and grow until it now rivals the letter carriers' organization in membership.

Before Harrison left office (January 25, 1893), he issued an executive order, at Theodore Roosevelt's insistence and with Wanamaker's concurrence, including letter carriers and postal clerks in the non-Presidential offices in the civil service. When Grover Cleveland returned to the White House, he grumbled about this move, claiming that it was just a ruse to maintain Republican appointees in office (although he had done the same thing for the railway post office clerks before he had left office after his first term in 1888). His Attorney General, Richard Olney, found a way to hold the order in abeyance until the postal employee force could be "purified" of Republicans. When a clean sweep had been made and Democrats installed in all the jobs, the order was declared to be the law of the land.

The Storekeeper's Record

John Wanamaker left the Post Office with a record of remarkable achievement and progress. He had increased the number of free city delivery offices from 401 to 610. The revenues of the Department had risen to $75.9 million (up $15 million in four years), and the annual per capita expenditure on the mails had jumped to $1.14. The volume of letters rose to more than 5 billion and the number of post offices to 68,403. Above all, the service was better than it had ever been. In many respects, it was never again to be as good as it was when John Wanamaker was Postmaster General.

The City Hotel on Pennsylvania Avenue near the White House, shown here in 1853, was the fourth home of the Post Office Department (1836–41).

This building, sixth of seven different quarters for the Post Office Department (1899–1934), is scheduled for demolition in Washington, D.C.'s plans for the rejuvenation of Pennsylvania Avenue.

Ebenezer Hazard, 1782–89, established the first peacetime postal service.

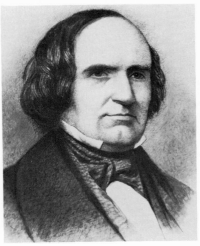

John McLean, 1823–29, named the Post Office Department merely by changing the letterhead on his stationery.

Montgomery Blair, 1861–64, created the free delivery system, the money order system, and the railway post office.

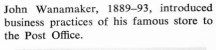

John Wanamaker, 1889–93, introduced business practices of his famous store to the Post Office.

Albert Sidney Burleson, 1913–21, instituted regular air mail service.

Will H. Hayes, 1921–22, headed the Department for "one golden year."

James A. Farley, 1933–40, directed the Department in the turbulent years of the Franklin D. Roosevelt Administration.

Lawrence F. O'Brien, who assumed his post in 1965, has suggested that the Department be replaced by a government-owned, nonprofit corporation.

WANTED

YOUNG, SKINNY

Wiry fellows not over 18.

Must be expert riders, willing to risk death daily. Orphans preferred.

Wages $25.00 per week

Many forms of transportation have been used to carry the mails. "Pony Express" riders were recruited through advertisements such as this one *(above)* in the San Francisco *Bulletin,* 1860. The first steam car to carry U.S. mail *(opposite, top)* is shown here in Michigan. Later, electric cars *(opposite, center)* were used; and, in the early 1900's, the use of trucks was introduced *(opposite, bottom).*

Steam Car
ny U.S. Mail

620

CAPITAL TRACTION COMPANY

UNITED STATES MAIL.

E.R. MILLER

ONE OF THE FIRST

The first airplane mail trip, between Boston and New York, took place on June 11, 1918. William F. Murray, Postmaster of Boston, hands a mail pouch to Pilot Torrey Webb, who has the flight map attached to his leg.

The first coast-to-coast air mail schedule begins at Reno, Nevada, in 1924, as Postmaster Austin Jackson hands Pilot H. W. Huking the mail pouch.

United Air Lines

This satchel cart *(left)* eases the job of mail delivery for the modern carrier, while such improvements as the experimental 24-hour self-service post office in suburban Washington, D.C. *(below)* promises even greater efficiency and ease of operations. The unmanned unit includes a scale, mailing instructions, and vending machines that dispense stamps, envelopes, post cards, and change.

Post Office Department

The first semi-automatic, keyboard-controlled parcel sorter in operation at Biscayne Annex, Miami, Florida. A keyboard code operator reads the address on the parcel and keys the destination number into the system as the parcel is pushed to the synchronized cross-conveyor belt.

Jerome J. Keating, President of the National Association of Letter Carriers *(right),* with his Vice-President, James H. Rademacher *(left),* Postmaster General J. Edward Day, Secretary of Labor W. Willard Wirtz, and Associate Justice of the Supreme Court Arthur J. Goldberg.

YEARS OF DECLINE

For his second term, Cleveland chose as Postmaster General his former law partner and close friend Wilson S. Bissell of Buffalo, an amiable man of remarkable girth who was far more interested in the social life of Washington than he was in managing the postal service. Nothing seemed to work out right for Bissell.

The Spotter System

In 1893, the Post Office Department first initiated the notorious "spotter system," which was to bring it into much disfavor. It hired a band of unqualified political hangers-on, none of them with any postal experience whatsoever, to travel secretly from city to city to spy on letter carriers at work and then submit reports. The idea, of course, was to circumvent the civil service laws and get rid of as many Republican letter carriers as possible.

By the end of the year, approximately one-third of the letter carriers in Chicago, Cleveland, and Philadelphia were up on charges. However, the activities of "special agents," or spotters, were so distasteful and their reports so often malicious that they became completely discredited.* In March, 1896, pressure from responsible newspapers finally forced the appropriations committees of Congress to deny further funds for the employment of special agents, and a very discreditable chapter in the management of the establishment came to an end.

---

* In 1895, a letter carrier on his route in Akron, Ohio, happened to glance through a ground-floor window of a residence and saw a woman and a small child lying on the floor. He gained entrance to the house and found the mother and baby almost asphyxiated by a gas leak. He saved the two lives, but the spotter who happened to be following him recommended his dismissal for "deviation from his route." His punishment was finally reduced to fifteen days' suspension without pay.

Counterfeit Stamps

Whenever Bissell attempted to conserve on expenditures, the quality of the postal service deteriorated, and the public compared his administration unfavorably with that of his predecessor. When he decided to let the contract for printing postage stamps to the Government Printing Office, the press blasted him for permitting the government to compete unfairly with private enterprise. He forced the issue through, but the enterprise turned out to be a fiasco. About 400 million stamps were so poorly printed that they had to be destroyed. Those judged satisfactory proved to be of such a simple design that they were easily counterfeited. The Department lost hundreds of thousands of dollars in potential revenues when a counterfeiting ring made use of the opportunity so unexpectedly offered them.

Finally, in January, 1895, after almost two years of service, Bissell had had enough. He complained to Cleveland that his social life in Washington was costing him $30,000 a year more than his salary as Postmaster General. Cleveland heard his plea and permitted him to return to the less costly pleasures of Buffalo. In his place, the President appointed William L. Wilson, a Democratic congressman from West Virginia. Wilson was responsible for the inception of rural free delivery, which Wanamaker had pushed for earlier, but otherwise accomplished little during the rest of Cleveland's term.

Ineptitude and Corruption

Republican William McKinley, who succeeded Cleveland, had two postmasters general during the four and a half years he was in office. He was most unfortunate in both of them. The first was James A. Gary, a Baltimore businessman. He had no measurable effect on the postal service during the thirteen months he remained in office and resigned in April, 1898, because he opposed U.S. entry into a war with Spain.

Gary was succeeded by Charles Emory Smith, a Philadelphia editor. Smith was an effective politician but a miserable administrator. During his years in office, corruption ran riot in the Post Office Department. However, the scandals did not come to light until after McKinley was dead and Smith safely out of the Department.

Under Smith, the Department used effective subterfuges to circumvent the civil service laws by hiring men outside the protection of the civil service and putting them to work as post office clerks. These were, of course, purely political appointments, and McKinley was accused by the Civil Service Commission and the Civil Service Reform Association of permitting widespread retrogression in the application of existing laws.

In 1900, McKinley was forced to accept as his running mate "that damned cowboy" (Senator Mark Hanna's description) Theodore Roosevelt. On September 6, 1901, an anarchist named Leon Czolgosz shot the President at a public reception in Buffalo, New York. Eight days later, McKinley died and Roosevelt became President of the United States.

Despite the inept leadership in the Department during the McKinley years and the widespread thievery and corruption in postal administration, the Post Office continued to grow and prosper. By 1901, the mail volume had reached 7.4 billion pieces a year. The per capita expenditure on mail was up to $1.44 a year. And the postal deficit, surprisingly enough, was driven down from an all-time high of $11.4 million in 1897 to $4 million in 1901, the lowest it had been since 1888.

THEODORE ROOSEVELT'S POST OFFICE PROBLEMS

Roosevelt was an unpredictable man. Despite his record as one of the most notable civil service reformers in the nation, he selected for his Postmaster General one of the most prominent partisan politicians in the country—the vice-chairman of the Republican National Committee, Henry C. Payne of Wisconsin, who took office on January 15, 1902.

Carl Schurz and his followers were flabbergasted. Schurz said:

> And there is Postmaster General Payne, whose only distinction in public life was that of a lobbyist and a skillful and not over-nice political pipelayer and wirepuller, whose appointment to the control of the great patronage department of the Government, which has the largest field for political dicker, would have fitted the cabinet of a political schemer in the Presidential chair but not the cabinet of the legendary Roosevelt.

Corruption Disclosed

Payne's career in the Post Office was dominated and spoiled by the disclosure of almost unbelievable corruption in the Department. Although the corruption had occurred during the administration of his predecessor, Payne was abused, first, for being slow to realize what was going on and, second, for bending over backward to save the Republican Party from embarrassment.

The charges were only partly true. In 1902, shortly after taking office, Payne received a secret appropriation (with Roosevelt's cooperation) for an extensive investigation of alleged frauds within the postal establishment. Fourth Assistant Postmaster General J. L. Bristow was put in charge of the inquiry. By the time the dust settled, Bristow had uncovered far more chicanery than the administration or Congress had bargained for. Certainly there was evidence that former Postmaster General Smith knew something of what was going on, and there is no doubt that high officials of the Republican Party were deeply involved in the thievery.

Right up to his elbows in all the corruption was James Tyner, who had served as Postmaster General under General Grant and as a particularly vindictive first assistant and spoilsman under President Hayes. Tyner, who was seventy-seven years old, was closing out his career as assistant attorney general for the Post Office Department. When the bombshell burst, Tyner was accused of bribe taking. His wife and her sister made a surreptitious visit to his office in the Department and rifled the safe of all its papers and documents. The Postmaster General, on learning this, pursued them across Washington in his carriage but was refused admission to the house. Tyner was eventually acquitted because of the lack of supporting evidence.

Others were not so fortunate. George W. Beavers, general superintendent of the Division of Salary and Allowances, was sent to the penitentiary for two years. August W. Machen, general superintendent of the Free Delivery System, was given four years and fined $10,000. Two others in the Department were convicted and jailed. There were also several convictions among those accused of offering bribes. Altogether, more than thirty indictments were returned, and the reputation of the Department was in tatters.

Congress did not come out of the mess unscathed. The records showed that 150 members had sought and received illegal favors from Beavers, including unwarranted increases in allowances for rent and clerk hire. At this disclosure, Congress, which had insisted on the investigation in the first place, turned around and attacked Payne savagely for trying to blacken its reputation. The House of Representatives took over the investigation of its own members, and, on March 7, 1904, a special committee of five was appointed. They performed an efficient whitewash job, and the matter was dropped.

All this turbulence was too much for Postmaster General Payne. In September, 1904, he suffered a stroke and on October 4, with President Roosevelt at his bedside, died. He was buried in Milwaukee with full honors, and a detail of uniformed letter carriers bore his body to the grave.

The Gag Rule

During the early years of his administration, Roosevelt also exhibited his unpredictability in regard to his relationships with the postal employees and their organizations. Although he was generally considered very much of a liberal for his times on most issues, he proved himself authoritarian in his dealings with government workers.

When postal employees began to exert pressure on Congress in an effort to achieve a pay raise, numerous bills were introduced to increase wages, create a system of classification, and provide for automatic promotions. At the time, the all-powerful chairman of the House Committee on Post Office and Post Roads was Eugene F. Loud, a San Francisco Republican with antilabor views. Loud not only refused to consider a pay bill but openly advocated reducing postal salaries even further. The subsequent clamoring of the postal employees caused great concern among the conservatives in the government. It was customary for the powers-that-be to put political pressure on postal employees around election time. It was a new and disturbing thing to have that pressure reversed. Conservative leaders in Congress complained to the President, and on January 31, 1902, Roosevelt issued the extraordinary and historic order that has been known ever since as the "Gag Rule." The order forbade all federal and postal employees

> either directly or indirectly, individually or through associations, to solicit an increase of pay or to influence or attempt to influence in their own interest any other legislation whatever, either before Congress or its Committees, or in any way save through the heads of the Departments in or under which they serve, on penalty of dismissal from the Government service.

(This harsh rule remained in effect for ten years, until the passage of the Lloyd–La Follette Act on August 24, 1912. During that decade, it was strictly interpreted and extended in many directions.)

In the election of 1902, the letter carriers struck back. They enlisted the aid of William Randolph Hearst, publisher of the San Francisco *Examiner,* and mounted a campaign against Congressman Loud, who consequently was permanently retired from public life. This strange turn of events alarmed the administration, and the Post Office Department responded accordingly. As a result of the graft investigations in the Department, Fourth Assistant Postmaster General J. L. Bristow had been given powers that made him the dominant man at postal headquarters. Bristow forbade representatives of employee organizations access to the Department and told them flatly that he "did not need, did not want, and would not have" their cooperation in conducting the postal service. He dismissed James C. Keller, president of the National Association of Letter Carriers, from the service because of the part he had played in the defeat of Loud, and the Postmaster General ordered an intensive investigation of the campaign against Loud. Any postal employee who admitted that he had voted for Loud's opponent was closely questioned and threatened with disciplinary action.

Altogether, the postal establishment was in considerable turmoil, when Postmaster General Payne died. Roosevelt decided to let the political pot cool for a while. As Payne's successor, he appointed Robert J. Wynne of Pennsylvania, who had been serving as first assistant postmaster general. Wynne, who was almost completely nonpolitical, remained in office during the November Presidential elections, which Roosevelt won easily, and departed in March, 1905, to become U.S. Consul General in London.

Roosevelt then dealt the civil service reformers another blow by appointing as Postmaster General the chairman of the Republican National Committee, George B. Cortelyou of New York. As long as he was Postmaster General, Cortelyou kept insisting that he was going to resign as chairman of the National Committee as soon as he could clean up some details of his office, but somehow he never got around to doing so. Far more interested in politics than he was in the operation of the Post Office Department, Cortelyou prodded Roosevelt, once the great hope of the civil service reformers, into issuing an executive order that permitted department heads to dismiss employees without notice and without "reasons in writing," which formerly had been legally necessary. This order made the civil service laws considerably less effective as a shield against political persecution.

Under Cortelyou, the Gag Rule was extended to such a degree that postal employees were forbidden, on pain of dismissal, to discuss publicly the conditions under which they were forced to work. Railway postal clerks were prohibited from complaining about the dangerous cars in which they operated on the ground that the railroads were doing business with the government on a contract basis and, therefore, any complaint against them was, in effect, a complaint against the government itself.

In 1906, when the National Federation of Post Office Clerks joined the American Federation of Labor, Cortelyou became seriously alarmed. He announced that he would not tolerate any interference from Samuel Gompers and his organization and that if the AFL tried to circumvent the Gag Rule by representing the clerks on Capital Hill, severe disciplinary action would be taken against the clerks both as an organization and as individuals. He showed he meant business by dismissing the leaders of the clerks' organization in Chicago because they had smuggled members of the Illinois State Commission on Occupational Diseases into the Chicago post office for an investigation of unsanitary conditions there.

Cortelyou left the Post Office after two years to become Secretary of the Treasury. The President followed a curious precedent and reached out to the Court of St. Petersburg to find a successor—George von Lengerke Meyer, a Boston businessman who had been U.S. Ambassador to Russia since 1905.

Meyer was sworn in on March 4, 1907, and served during the remainder of Roosevelt's term.*

It was generally recognized that Meyer's principal task was to achieve the nomination of the Secretary of War, William Howard Taft, for the Presidency, and he used the patronage of the Department extensively for this purpose. The actual operation of the establishment was left to First Assistant Postmaster General Frank H. Hitchcock of Massachusetts.

During his tenure, Meyer presided over several important developments, perhaps the most important of which was the postal pay raise of 1907. The combination of low wages—static since 1888—and oppressive management policies had caused a serious morale problem throughout the postal establishment, and public complaints against the deterioration of the service had become more and more insistent. The turnover in postal employment in major cities reached as high as 20 per cent a year. (In 1906, 550 post office clerks resigned from the Chicago post office alone.) Postal management was finding it almost impossible to retain experienced, competent workers, and even during the depression of 1907, it was difficult to find desirable recruits. The Act of March 2, 1907, raised the wages of post office clerks and letter carriers to a maximum of $1,200 a year, with a starting wage of $600. Substitutes were paid thirty cents an hour.

Growth to 1909

While Roosevelt was President, although the population of the country increased only 17 per cent, the postal volume almost doubled. The per capita postal expenditure also rose dramatically, from $1.44 a year to $2.25. Both Cortelyou and Meyer declared publicly that postal deficits were far less im-

---

* Meyer is one of those credited with persuading Theodore Roosevelt to accept the nomination for Vice-President under McKinley. He is supposed to have said to Roosevelt: "They're trying to bury you, but with your luck, they won't be able to do it."

portant than improvements of the service, and statistics indicate that they meant what they said. Starting from a low of $3 million in 1902, the deficit rose steadily, reaching a new high of $15 million in 1905 and then, after receding somewhat, jumping to $16.9 million in 1908 and $17.5 million in 1909. By fiscal year 1909, there were 27,620 city delivery letter carriers in the service, and the rural free delivery system had grown to a point where 40,997 carriers were traveling very close to 1 million miles every working day of the year.

First Assistant Postmaster General Hitchcock was William Howard Taft's campaign manager in 1908 and was also chairman of the Republican National Committee. He proved efficient in both capacities and, after Taft was inaugurated, was rewarded with the postmaster-generalship.

YEARS OF DISSENSION

There were several improvements in the postal service during Hitchcock's tenure, but they all came after the Democrats had won control of the Congress in 1910, and the Postmaster General was against every one of them. The greatest dissension was in the railway post office service, where conditions were growing worse with each passing month. During the years 1905–10, 98 railway clerks were killed in the cars and 3,640 seriously injured, or about 5 per cent of the total force. Since employees were forbidden to complain to the Congress or to the press, some were so foolhardy as to complain to the Department itself. The attitude of the Department was perhaps summed up best by C. E. Dennison, who headed the Tenth Division of the railway service, in Aberdeen, South Dakota. In response to criticism, Dennison issued the following bulletin (November 5, 1910):

Instructions have been received from the superintendent to inform all clerks in this jurisdiction who are continually making

exaggerated and unfounded reports regarding the physical condition of their cars that *unless the practice is stopped their reports will be referred to the Department with recommendations
not to their liking.*

Hitchcock let it be known that unionism could have no
place in the postal service as long as he was Postmaster General, and all complaints against working conditions were
quashed. A railway postal clerk was fired for showing a newspaper reporter in Houston a dead rat that he had found in
the water cooler of his mail car. When another clerk wrote
to the Department complaining that a close friend and fellow
worker had been killed in the wreck of a railroad car that
had many times been reported as unsafe and antiquated, the
Department replied that it had no control over the construction of mail cars and that men who did not care to assume
the necessary risks had no place in the railway mail service.
Post Office inspectors made a practice of visiting with all clerks
who complained about their working conditions and urging
that they retract their charges. If the clerks refused to do so,
they were dismissed. Under such oppressive conditions, the
postal service naturally degenerated into a shadow of what it
had been when John Wanamaker was in charge. In some cases,
particularly in the Midwest, railway postal employees threatened to resign en masse unless certain conditions were met.
The Post Office Department, realizing that this would mean a
complete breakdown of the mail service in those areas, made
concessions on a local level but refused to extend them na-
tionally.

When the Republicans lost control of Congress in the elections of 1910, the situation changed. The new Congress forced
upon the Department measures that made the postal service
more efficient and considerably improved the condition of
those who worked in it.

The Lloyd–La Follette Act

During the last two years of the Taft Administration, there was practically open warfare between Congress and the Post Office Department. When Senator Robert La Follette of Wisconsin sent out a questionnaire to postal employees on the application of the Gag Rule, employees were forbidden to answer. When thousands of employees ignored this prohibition, La Follette complained that his mail "was subjected to an espionage almost Russian in character." He charged that Post Office inspectors were holding up his mail, opening and reading it, in order to take retaliatory action against employees who were complaining. When William E. Kelly, president of the National Association of Letter Carriers, was invited to testify before the Senate Post Office Committee on pending anti-Gag Rule legislation, he insisted that a subpoena be issued making his appearance mandatory. If he had not been ordered to appear, he would have been dismissed from the service for offering unsolicited testimony.

President Taft himself went on the stump in an unbecoming attempt to preserve the Gag Rule. "Government employees are a privileged class," he said in a speech in Harrisburg, Pennsylvania, on May 14, 1911, "upon whose entry into government service it is entirely reasonable to impose conditions that should not and ought not be imposed upon those who serve private employers."

But on April 18, 1912, the House of Representatives tacked the Lloyd Bill, to rescind the Gag Rule, onto the Post Office Appropriations Bill. It passed with only one dissenting vote, that of the Republican floor leader. Since the Senate was not directly responsible to the electorate, La Follette had considerably more difficulty with the legislation in that body. Many senators felt that any legislation increasing the freedom of federal employees would lead to widespread strikes within the government service. However, when Senator James A.

Reed of Missouri inserted an antistrike amendment, senatorial fears were allayed.

Another beneficial bill, introduced by Representative Thomas L. Reilly of Connecticut, was also tacked onto the appropriations legislation. It specified that postal employees "shall be required to work not more than eight hours a day, provided that the eight hours of service shall not extend over a longer period than ten consecutive hours," and included stipulations for compensatory time off, for pro rata overtime pay, and for the closing of post offices on Sunday. This historic legislation, approved by President Taft on August 24, 1912, to take effect on March 3, 1913, was the first to improve the working conditions of postal employees in twenty-four years.

Although Hitchcock's repressive policies had damaged the postal service in many respects, from an accountant's point of view his program of effecting stringent economies did have some success. The postal deficit was all but eliminated during his four years in office; indeed, in 1911 the Department showed a rare profit of $219,118. Mail volume increased to 18.6 billion pieces in fiscal year 1913, and the per capita expenditure rose to $2.74 a year.

The Lloyd–La Follette Act and the Reilly Law, passed just before the 1912 elections, helped to keep the morale of the employee force from deteriorating altogether. Since the winning Democratic candidate for President, Woodrow Wilson, was generally considered to be more of a liberal than his Republican predecessors, postal employees had reason to look forward to his administration with some optimism. It proved unjustified.

Burleson Versus the Unions

Wilson's campaign manager, "Colonel" Edward Mandell House of Houston, Texas, flooded Washington with Texans. One of them, Albert Sidney Burleson, was made Postmaster General. A congressman of minimal distinction, who had served the preceding two years as chairman of the House Committee on Post Office and Post Roads, Burleson was an almost accidental millionaire, and he had no sympathy with anyone who had been less fortunate than himself. He was a coarse, vain, and excessively arrogant man, and his eight years as Postmaster General are generally conceded to have been the most disastrous in the history of the postal establishment.

Burleson no sooner lowered his right hand after taking the oath of office than he demanded the repeal of the Lloyd–La Follette Act, the Reilly Law, and all other liberal legislation that had been passed by a Democratic Congress and had taken effect the day before he was sworn in. He refused to recognize or to meet with representatives of the postal employee organizations. He called for the dissolution of all unions of postal employees and, to underscore his position, fired from the postal service the president of the Railway Mail Association and the president of the Rural Letter Carriers Association on the same day. He gave the president of the National Association of Letter Carriers the choice of quitting his position or quitting the postal service.

Postal employees reacted to Burleson's policies by flocking into their professional organizations for protection. In addition, the National Association of Letter Carriers, which, before Burleson reached full stride, had voted against affiliation with the American Federation of Labor by a referendum vote of 18,769 to 3,968, decided less than four years later, in 1917, that they needed whatever protection they could get and reversed themselves, voting 23,551 in favor of affiliation and only 1,971 against.

In 1917, the year the United States entered World War I, the cost of living leaped by 20.3 per cent. In 1918, it jumped another 22.4 per cent. A series of smaller increases had already occurred during the years when America was preparing herself for war. The effect on the postal service and on postal employees, whose wages had been set in 1907, was disastrous.

More than one-eighth of the clerical and letter carrier forces left government service for better-paying employment—this in addition to the large numbers who had already left to fight for their country. Unfortunately for the postal service, it was the most experienced and talented employees who left first, and as the quality of the employee declined, the quality of service deteriorated. Moreover, the number of applicants for civil service entrance examinations during the years 1917 and 1918 dropped by 18 per cent, and despite lowered standards, the percentage of successful applicants dropped even further.

Congress, which was receiving constant criticism about deteriorating mail service, as well as complaints from the despairing postal employees who remained, pleaded with the Postmaster General to accede to a substantial pay raise. Burleson was adamant. He merely said (in his annual report of 1917) that post office clerks and letter carriers were receiving three times the wages of soldiers at the front but shared none of their hardship and risk.

Despite his insistence on economy, Burleson did not perform nearly as well as he had hoped. He returned a profit in 1914 of $4.4 million and a deficit in the following year of $11.3 million. In the next four years, the Department showed enormous so-called profits, reaching the staggering sum of $73.7 million in 1919. But in wartime, the Post Office Department always shows a paper profit, since most of the costs of transportation are taken over by the military. Once the war was over, the Burleson record fell apart. In 1920, the deficit sprang back to $17.2 million, and in 1921 (for which Burleson was only partially responsible), it reached the sum of $157.5 million, or about nine times the highest previous figure in the nation's history.

These postwar figures were considerably affected by the fact that Congress, at the urging of the administration, had increased postage rates, through the Act of October 3, 1917, as a wartime measure (first-class letters were raised to three cents an ounce and postal cards to two cents apiece) and, on February 24, 1919, had repealed this temporary increase, thereby contributing greatly to the enormous deficits of fiscal years 1920 and 1921. Congress also passed badly needed pay and retirement bills in 1920, and their effects were felt in 1921.

Advances Despite Burleson

During the eight years of the Burleson postal administration, there were several conspicuous advances, most of which the Postmaster General opposed. The treatment of postal employees and the irritating personality of the Postmaster General had become issues in the congressional elections of 1918, which the Democrats lost to the Republicans. The new Congress defied the administration. Postal pay increases were voted on November 8, 1919, and June 5, 1920. The latter act increased salaries of letter carriers and post office clerks to a range beginning at $1,400 a year, with a maximum of $1,800. In addition, Congress passed laws making annual leave and compensatory time more reasonable for postal employees, and on May 22, 1920, the Civil Service Retirement Act, the first in the history of the U.S. Government, was signed into law. (The letter carriers regarded this law as a triumph of their union, which had campaigned constantly and vociferously for a retirement law since 1889.) Three weeks later, another forward step was taken when the first sick-leave law was approved.

The Arrival of Airmail

Insofar as service was concerned, the most important development during Burleson's postmaster-generalship was the establishment of airmail as a regular part of the mail service (Burleson had supported this idea). On May 15, 1918, the first airmail pilot set off, with the President and Postmaster General wishing him well, on the initial scheduled flight between Washington and New York. The pilot managed to lose his way and never made it, but the flight made history and regular airmail service was soon established.

Permanent airmail service between Cleveland and Chicago began on May 15, 1919, and between New York and Cleveland on July 1, 1919. The Chicago–Omaha run was inaugurated on January 10, 1920, and the Omaha–San Francisco leg of the transcontinental system on September 8, 1920. The flights were made only during daylight hours, with the mail being transferred, on transcontinental journeys, to fast mail trains at night. Congress had set airmail rates at twenty-four cents an ounce. By 1923, this service had become sufficiently efficient to transport mail from New York to San Francisco in 32 hours (as opposed to approximately 100 hours by train). Subsequent improvements in night flying made it possible to inaugurate continuous airmail service across the continent on July 1, 1924. By the last year of Burleson's administration, government planes were flying 653,764 miles a year on airmail service and carrying 526,578 pounds of mail.

Of course, the idea of airmail service had been bandied about for years. As early as 1822, the *Freeman's Journal* of Norristown, Pennsylvania, had urged Postmaster General McLean to consider flying the mails by balloon. When Sam Houston was a senator (1845–59), he introduced legislation that, had it passed, would have secured appropriations to investigate the possibility of balloon mail service. But it was not until the end of World War I that planes were available that could actually carry a load of mail between two fairly distant points with any reasonable hope of consistent success.

THE GOLDEN YEAR

The end of the Wilson Administration was a shambles. The exhausted President was incapable of governing, and much of the business of the White House was being performed by the

President's wife, his physician, and a few aides. In 1921, the Republicans won the Presidency with Warren G. Harding, who conducted his campaign mostly from his own front porch in Marion, Ohio. He won easily.

Harding has been called the worst of the American Presidents. He may have been, but there is serious competition for the title. Some of his cabinet appointments were catastrophes: Harry M. Daugherty, Attorney General; Edwin Denby, Secretary of the Navy; Albert B. Fall, Secretary of the Interior. But others were excellent: Herbert Hoover, Secretary of Commerce; Henry C. Wallace, Secretary of Agriculture; Charles Evans Hughes, Secretary of State; Will H. Hays, Postmaster General. It was a curious cabinet, and its meetings must have been strange, considering the wide disparity in intelligence and integrity among its members.

The new Postmaster General, Will H. Hays, was a man of innate decency as well as a man of intelligence, and he knew precisely what to do with his job. He denounced Burleson and all his works and pomps, reversing the policies of his predecessor as flamboyantly and as completely as possible. In the twelve months that he served, Hays changed the entire direction of postal management and made a name for himself as one of the three or four most successful postmasters general in history.

The success of Hays was based more on what he was than on what he did. There were no dramatic service improvements during his year in office, although the productivity of postal employees increased in proportion to their improved morale. There were no further pay raises and no important legislation affecting the welfare of the workers. The Sixty-seventh Congress was, in fact, a conservative one, and no such action would have been possible during those twelve months.

Oddly enough, very little was expected of Hays when he took office. He was chairman of the Republican National Committee and had been the principal architect of Harding's victory in a remarkably dull campaign. He was from a state that had not previously been outstanding for its production of effective liberals. He was physically rather less than inspiring, and as a platform orator he was somewhat of a bore. His appointment was considered a routine reward for a routinely successful political manager and was greeted by the nation's press with editorial yawns.

But, from the first day he took office, Hays electrified the postal establishment with his ideas and enlightened concept of his office. On March 9, 1921, four days after he was sworn in, the new Postmaster General made the following declaration:

> The postal establishment is not an institution for profit, it is an institution for service, and it is the President's purpose to improve that service.
>
> Every effort shall be exercised to humanize the industry. Labor is not a commodity. That idea was abandoned 1,921 years ago next Easter. There are 300,000 employees. They have the brain and they have the hand to do the job well; and they shall have the heart to do it well.
>
> We purpose to approach this matter so that they shall be partners with us in this business. It is a great human institution touching every individual in the country. It is a great business institution serving every individual in the country.
>
> I know that with 300,000 men and women pledged to serve all the people and honestly discharging that duty, fairly treated and properly appreciated, all partners with us here in this great enterprise, we can do the job. It's going to be done.

The prose style had its deficiencies and the arithmetic concerning the date of Easter Sunday was a little weak, but the heart and the sentiment were there. The idea of the Postmaster General and the postal employees being "partners" caused an emotional upsurge in the postal work force. *The Postal Record* said, in its issue for April, 1921,

When one emerges from a dungeon into the sunlight, one is temporarily blinded and confused. Letter carriers and other postal employees are in a similar situation. They can scarcely realize that the query propounded by the *Literary Digest*—"Are Letter Carriers Human Beings?"—has been answered in the affirmative by their new commander-in-chief, Postmaster General Will H. Hays. . . . The selection of Mr. Hays of the word "humanize" in expressing the Department's attitude toward the men and women workers in the postal establishment was happy. Not in years has such a sentiment been expressed by a head of this Department.

On March 16, Hays invited the leaders of all the employee organizations into his office for an informal colloquy. This was the first time such a confrontation had taken place in eight years and, indeed, one of the few times such a thing had happened at all. The Postmaster General told the leaders that he intended to make such meetings a regular thing and announced an open-door policy for employees who wished to see him and discuss their problems.

The Postmaster General lived up to his promises. In many important policy matters, he decided in favor of the employees. He set up an orderly procedure for the reinstatement, with full seniority, of postal employees who had served in the war and, at the urging of the employee representatives, rejected the prosposal to make retirement of postal workers at sixty-five mandatory.

He brought Dr. Lee K. Frankel of the Metropolitan Life Insurance Company into the Department to head up a "service relations" bureau to study and make recommendations for the betterment of the conditions under which postal employees were working. Frankel went to work with a will and effected significant improvements. Understandably, he was a popular figure throughout the service.

Hays was not an ardent political spoilsman, but he was inexorable in his pursuit of local tyrants who modeled their behavior, at the local level, on that of Burleson. The most notorious of these was Colin M. Selph, postmaster of St. Louis, who made life unbearable for everyone who worked under his direction. Selph had had a military uniform designed for himself and wore it regularly to the office. He exacted military salutes from his subordinates and spent his spare time composing laudatory cheers that the employees were forced to shout in unison whenever the postmaster appeared in their midst. Hays fired Selph early in 1922, when Post Office inspectors had completed an iron-clad case against him.*

On March 4, 1922, after exactly one year in office, Hays resigned as Postmaster General to become "czar" of the movie industry, which, at that time, badly needed a popular hero to furbish its tarnished image. The National Association of Letter Carriers, in an unprecedented gesture of gratitude, made Will Hays an honorary member for life. Hays asked that the word "honorary" be striken out of the citation and that he be permitted to become a regular dues-paying member. Amusingly enough, this request caused a minor embarrassment to the letter carriers, since their constitution did not permit anyone to pay dues into their treasury who had not earned that right through carrying the mail on his back. A hasty exception was made, Hays was gratefully accepted, and he continued to pay his annual dues to the NALC for thirty-two years, until his death in 1954.

* The list of charges that the Post Office inspectors prepared against Selph covered several pages and included many faults of a very serious nature. However, the cheers were something special, and at least one of them, copied verbatim from an inspector's report, should be preserved:

> "1-2-3-4! 3-2-4-1!
> Who for? What for? Who you gonna yell for?
> COLIN M. SELPH!
> Yea, Post! Yea, Master!
> Yea! Yea! Postmaster!"

VI

Between the Wars: Farley's Years

Will Hays was succeeded in office by his first assistant, Dr. Hubert Work of Colorado, a practicing physician turned politician, who was president of the American Medical Association at the time of his appointment. Like Hays, Work served for exactly one year, but his administration was clouded by the new Bureau of the Budget's whittling down of his appropriation request even before it went up to Capitol Hill for congressional scrutiny and by an unexpectedly large increase in mail volume (up to 23 billion pieces in fiscal year 1923), which the Post Office Department simply did not have the funds to handle. The service deteriorated dramatically, and post offices throughout the country, especially in the larger metropolitan areas, were burdened with unmanageable backlogs of mail. The Department was forced to fall back on a policy of "retrenchment," which only added to the confusion of workers and the deterioration of service. Work did succeed in forcing the deficit down to $60.8 million in 1922. In 1923, for which he was only partially responsible, it was sliced to $24 million.

Much to his relief, Work was transferred to the Department of the Interior as Secretary. His successor in the Post Office Department was a lame-duck Indiana senator, Harry Stewart New, who took office under Harding and, after the President's death in August, 1923, continued to serve under Calvin Coolidge for the following six years.

COOLIDGE AND THE POST

In the summer of 1923, when the postal employees began to campaign for a wage increase, both New and Coolidge agreed that their cause was just. The pay legislation of 1920, which had raised the salaries of letter carriers and clerks from $1,400 a year to $1,800, had been barely sufficient to keep them even with the escalating living costs of the early postwar period, and living costs had continued to spiral upward. But the Postmaster General, at the insistence of the President, quite suddenly and unexpectedly reversed himself and told Congress that the increased cost of a pay raise should be covered by a corresponding increase in postage rates.

Representative Clyde Kelly, a Pennsylvania Republican, espoused the cause of the postal employees. He introduced legislation to raise postal salaries by $300 a year. His bill attracted widespread popular support, and, in general, the press backed it. Late in 1924, it was passed by both houses of Congress with stunning majorities (73 to 3 in the Senate and 361 to 6 in the House). This was an election year, and President Coolidge himself was seeking return to the White House. Nonetheless, he vetoed the bill because Congress had failed to raise postage rates in order to cover the cost of the pay increase.

When Congress reassembled after the election, its temper was considerably different. Although the Republicans retained control, their majority had been considerably reduced, and many key figures had been unexpectedly retired from political life. Some of those who had been strong in their support of the postal employees before the elections were now, as lame ducks, dependent upon President Coolidge, who had been triumphantly re-elected, for appointments to positions in the executive branch. They were more interested in retaining the good will of the appointing power than in alleviating the economic conditions of the postal employees. (As William C. Doherty, former president of the letter carriers, has written in his auto-biography *Mailman, U.S.A.:* "They did not love us in December as they did in May.") After a bitter fight, the Senate failed, by a single vote, to override the veto (January 6, 1925).

Clyde Kelly went back to work and came up with a bill retaining the pay provisions of his previous bill but also providing for postage rate increases that could conceivably bring an additional $51 million into the Treasury. The legislation sailed through both the House and the Senate, and President Coolidge, with an obvious lack of enthusiasm, signed the bill into law on February 18, 1925. The postage rate features of the legislation were a failure. They were unpopular with the public, and the deficit climbed to $32 million in fiscal year 1928. Thereupon, Congress, again in an election year, reduced the rates pretty much to where they had been.

The obdurate attitude of Harry New toward the pay raise legislation did a great deal to end the brief honeymoon between the Department and the employee organizations. The open-door policy of Will Hays was retained, but a mutual wariness crept into the intercourse between labor and management.

Airmail Advances

The success story of the Postmaster General New's administration, as far as service was concerned, was the dramatic development of airmail. As already noted, by 1924, airplane engineers had fairly well beaten the problem of night flying, and on July 1 of that year, continuous airmail flights had been started between the two coasts. The planes stopped at Chicago and Omaha en route and were able to negotiate the distance across the continent in about twenty-seven hours.

In these infant days of airmail, the planes were army craft and the aviators army fliers. However, there was growing demand that the federal government get out of competition with private enterprise and start to encourage the new airlines by engaging them to fly the mail on a contract basis. On February 2, 1925, legislation was approved that permitted 80 per cent of the revenues from the mail transported either at airmail or ordinary first-class rates to be paid for private contract service. It was stipulated that the rate for airmail would not be lower than ten cents an ounce. In the following year, airmail contracts were permitted, on the basis of weight rather than postage, at a rate of no more than $3 per pound per 1,000 miles. In July, 1928, the government stopped flying mail planes altogether, and to encourage the use of the service, the postage rate was dropped to five cents for the first ounce of each piece of airmail.

There is no doubt that the lower postage rates and other favorable contract terms with the carriers had an enormous effect on the growth of the airplane and airline industries in the United States. The air transport industry was subsidized, just as shipping and railroads had always been subsidized, in the interest of the growth, development, and protection of the nation. Unfortunately, as in earlier years with the railroad and shipping industries, subsidization of the air transport industry led to shady permissiveness in the letting of contracts and, as we shall see, resulted in national embarrassment and tragedy.

The following tables illustrate how airmail service grew during these important formative years:

GOVERNMENT-OPERATED AIRMAIL SERVICE

Year	Pounds carried	Cost
1918	17,831	$ 13,604
1919	230,251	717,177
1920	526,578	1,264,495
1921	1,120,852	2,653,882
1922	1,224,723	1,418,146
1923	1,696,896	1,897,151
1924	1,500,034	1,498,674
1925	232,513	2,743,750
1926	353,641	2,782,422

PRIVATE CONTRACT AIRMAIL SERVICE

Year	Pounds carried	Cost
1926	3,000	$ 89,754
1927	473,102	1,363,228
1928	1,861,800	4,042,777
1929	5,635,680	11,169,015
1930	7,719,698	14,618,232
1931	8,579,422	16,943,606[a]

[a] By fiscal year 1965, the airlines were carrying mail more than 188.1 million ton miles, at an annual cost to the government of $75.3 million.

THE POST OFFICE UNDER HOOVER

In 1928, Calvin Coolidge chose not to run for re-election as President. Herbert Hoover of California, his successor, appointed as his Postmaster General Walter F. Brown of Ohio, a Harvard-educated lawyer of limited perspective and little popular appeal. Brown inherited the leadership of a postal service that was growing and thriving despite the somewhat undistinguished leadership it had experienced. In 1929, the volume was about 28 billion pieces, and the revenues were $697 million, up $164 million since 1923. The per capita expenditure for postage was up to $5.73 a year. Because of the initial effects of the new rate structure, instituted in 1928, the postal deficit had jumped from $32 million in 1928 to $86.5 million in 1929. But the Hoover Administration, including, of course, the Post Office Department, had only nine months of prosperity to enjoy before the Great Depression struck the nation. Its effects were reflected accurately in the annual statements of the Postmaster General. Postal revenues, which reached an all-time high of $705.5 million in 1930, plummeted 31 per cent in the next three years (to $486.7 million). Mail volume fell from 28 billion pieces in 1930 to 20 billion in 1933. The per capita postage expenditure fell to $4.64, and in 1932 the deficit reached the then astounding figure of $205.5 million.*

The Republican leadership in the Congress was far more advanced in its thinking about postal problems than were the Republican postal administrators at the other end of Pennsylvania Avenue. Congressman Kelly, disturbed by what he considered to be too much concern on the part of the Postmaster General and the Bureau of the Budget for postal economy at the expense of postal service, devised legislation (enacted June 9, 1930) that attempted to segregate in postal accounting the expenses of the Post Office Department for purely postal activities from the expenses incurred in its performance of nonpostal duties that benefit the nation as a whole.

Kelly's statement on the subject, as it appears in his book *United States Postal Policy*, published in 1931, has had a profound influence on postal thinking ever since. He wrote:

During the entire history of the service under the Constitution, from 1789 up to and including 1930, the entire excess of reported expenditures over receipts has amounted to $731 million.† For each of those 142 years there has been an average expenditure for free and nonpostal activities, such as subsidies, amounting to $6 million, or a total of $852 million. Even those who emphasize the money balance may be assured that there has never been a loss in actual postal activities. Those who see

* In the depth of these troubled times, Postmaster General Brown ordered a special official limousine constructed, with sufficient height to permit him to get in and out without knocking off the top hat he liked to wear. The request for the special limousine was buried in his over-all appropriation request. An independent Republican, Congressman Melvin J. Maas of Minnesota, detected the item and challenged Brown on it. As a result, Brown paid out of his own pocket the difference between a limousine with an ordinary body and one built to his own specifications. Charles Michelson, publicity man for the Democratic National Committee, fell upon the Postmaster General's aberration with undisguised exultation, and "High Hat" Brown became a symbol of Republican plutocracy.

† During the 1950's and 1960's, this total deficit for 142 years would have been considered reasonably normal for a single year.

this institution as a great service enterprise may be sure that it has been one of the mightiest factors in American progress, paying dividends in enlightenment and mutual understanding beyond the power of money to express. It has been the nation's most *profitable* institution, inspiring fraternity of feeling and community of interest, and furnishing the surest guarantee of the stability and security of the Republic. . . .

The money from the Treasury which is sometimes needed to supplement postal receipts in furnishing a complete and comprehensive service is not a liability but an *investment,* the dividends being just as substantial as though they were paid in cash. There is not a business in America whose income is not due in considerable measure to the postal service. . . . The Post Office has been a part of their business and no injustice is done when a small part of their income taxes are used to extend postal facilities to every American. It is simply distributing the cost in a manner which will be the least injurious.

The Kelly Law, as it was popularly known, only authorized the Postmaster General to segregate nonpostal from postal costs; it did not direct him to do this—and Postmaster General Brown was not the sort of administrator to avail himself of such authorization. His successor, James A. Farley (1933–40), was quite a different type of executive, and he did avail himself of the provisions of the Kelly Law in his annual reports. By this time, the Kelly Law had lost its impact on the public mind. Farley's claims of operating the postal service on a virtual break-even basis were ignored or attacked by a hostile Republican press as political propaganda. It was conveniently forgotten that Kelly was a Republican and the Congress that approved his philosophy was also Republican.

POSTMASTER GENERAL FARLEY

A highly successful businessman, Farley proved to be one of the most skillful professional politicians in the nation's history. As chairman of the Democratic National Committee, he was, more than anyone else, responsible for Franklin D. Roosevelt's nomination for the Presidency and for his subsequent election.

If one were to play a word-association game with almost any knowledgeable person in the country over the age of forty and were to mention the term "Postmaster General," the almost automatic response would be "Farley." He dominated the office and the service during the seven and a half years he served more than anyone before or since his time.

The postal service was in desperate condition when Farley took office. During the early days of the Great Depression, postal employees were doing better financially than they had ever done before or have done since. The average pay of a letter carrier or postal clerk was $2,064 a year. In 1928, this had been a mediocre wage; by 1930, it had become relatively magnificent. And in a nation with 12 million unemployed, the job security afforded by civil service was especially attractive.

During these years, the Post Office, uniquely in its history, was able to recruit the cream of the labor market. Men who in better times would have gone into the professions were glad to compete for postal jobs. In subsequent years, these recruits rose to positions that enabled them to hold the postal service together despite the antiservice policies of many postal managers. In this respect, the postal establishment was one of the few institutions in the United States to benefit from the Depression.

In the two years before Farley became Postmaster General, postal revenues declined by $127 million, and the volume dropped by 3.6 billion pieces. In fiscal year 1933, for which the Hoover Administration was primarily responsible, the volume nose-dived by 4.5 billion pieces and was at its lowest level in twenty years. Brown had panicked in the face of this downward trend and ordered postmasters to give their employees, on a rotating basis, a month's unpaid "furlough" each year—a move that amounted to an 8.3 per cent cut in wages.

He also urged wholesale reductions in the postal work force, but Congress refused to accede to his request.

These developments, coupled with a threat to reduce postal salaries by another 11 per cent, had seriously impaired the morale of the postal employees. The new Postmaster General was faced with the problem of repairing the confidence of the employees in postal management as well as that of the general public in the postal service itself. He succeeded on both fronts.

Farley was blamed by his opponents for being too practical a politician, and it may be that he erred somewhat, from a tactical point of view, in being too honest and straightforward in expressing his political philosophy. He believed firmly in the patronage system, maintaining that any administration, Democratic or Republican, had the right to make certain that everyone holding a position of responsibility in the government was loyal to its leaders and its policies.

Patronage in a Depression Economy

Few postmasters general in history have had to deal with problems as difficult or as complex as those with which Farley was faced. The Democrats had been out of power for twelve years, and Farley, both as Democratic National chairman and as Postmaster General, was charged with dispensing patronage in a country that had 13 million unemployed out of a population of 125 million men, women, and children. The demand for federal employment was clamorous.

No sooner did the new Postmaster General sit down in his office in the neo-Gothic architectural monstrosity* that served

---

* The old Post Office Department building (erected in 1897) is located at the southeast corner of Twelfth Street and Pennsylvania Avenue and is one of the most distinguished eyesores in Washington. A plan to tear it down has been approved, but its clock tower will remain a landmark, not because it is beautiful but because it is almost indestructible. In 1934, the Department moved to its present quarters, across the street, at the southwest corner of the intersection. The Republicans built the building, but they did not get to occupy it for twenty years.

as postal headquarters at that time than he was almost over-whelmed by an army of office seekers—all of them, by their own claim, lifelong Democrats and personally responsible for having carried their section of the country for the Roosevelt-Garner ticket. It was little short of a miracle that Farley was able to find the time to make important improvements in the postal service while still taking care of the oppressive patron-age problems of the new administration.

Much has been written about "Farleyism" in the postal service, the term connoting ruthless partisanship in matters of patronage at all levels. The figures present a picture very little different from that which accompanied almost every preceding change in Presidential administrations. The Postmaster Gen-eral viewed postmasters in Presidential offices as political ap-pointees and political leaders and saw no reason why these positions should be held by Republicans. During his first year, approximately 1,600 postmasters were removed.* It was rare during the Farley years for Republicans, regardless of in-dividual merit, to be promoted to supervisory positions in post offices. But, again, this was no departure from accepted practice during other administrations. Farley did not violate either the spirit or the letter of the civil service laws by inter-fering with the jobs of rank-and-file employees in the field service, and he made few inquiries into the political beliefs and practices of lesser employees in the Department itself.

* Sometimes the methods of removal were rather primitive. One former Post Office inspector, now dead, once told the author this story, illustrating his technique of creating vacancies in post offices: "In the 1928 campaign, Postmaster General Brown wrote a letter to all postmasters requesting donations to the Hoover campaign. When the new administration came in, I went my rounds asking the postmasters what they had done about the Postmaster General's letter. If they said they had made the donations, I filed charges for political activity. If they said they hadn't, I filed charges for insubordination. I got thirty-two of them that way in one month." Ironically, the man was at the time in the process of being removed from a high policy position in the Post Office Department during the Eisenhower Administration and was very bitter about being forced to retire "for political reasons."

As a politician and as an administrator, Farley was consistent. He realized the political potential of the postmaster in each community, and once he had filled the positions with loyal Democrats, he revivified the dormant National Association of Postmasters—a potentially strong political organization. In 1938, when the Ramspeck-O'Mahoney Act (which was to do away with the traditional four-year term of postmasters and bring these functionaries into the career postal service) was being discussed in Congress, Farley went on record as not favoring the legislation, since he believed that any administration, even a Republican one, should have the right of choosing who should be postmaster in each city in the nation.

Employee Cutbacks

Perhaps no administration ever took office under more dramatic circumstances than did that of Roosevelt in 1933. The morale of the nation was shattered. Its economy tottered on the brink of disaster. The banking institutions of the country were generally threatened with collapse. A sizable portion of the populace was disillusioned with democratic institutions and resentful of the national leadership. A new and overwhelmingly Democratic Congress came to Washington, cowed by the ominous unrest in the country and subservient to Franklin Delano Roosevelt, on whose coattails most of them had ridden into office.

Postal employees barely had time to congratulate themselves on having avoided Postmaster General Brown's attacks on their livelihood before their optimism was dimmed by the policy statements of the new administration. In his inaugural address on March 4, 1933, Roosevelt announced that he would "recommend measures that a stricken nation in the midst of a stricken world may require." He added that extensive government economy would be one of those measures. On the following day, he ordered Congress to convene in a special session.

Roosevelt had campaigned for the Presidency on a platform of government economy. In the heat of the campaign, he had actually accused Hoover of being a spendthrift President who had built up within the federal government a monstrous, proliferating bureaucracy. He had promised to cut government spending to the bone and to balance the national budget. On March 10, the new President delivered a special message to the new Congress. He asked for wide and unprecedented discretionary powers, including the fixing of federal salaries in accordance with the economy legislation he was recommending, saying:

> I request also the enactment of legislation relating to the salaries of civil and military employees of the Government. This would repeal the existing furlough plan, substituting therefor a general principle and authorizing the Executive to make application of this principle. The proper legislative function is to fix the amount of expenditure, the means by which it is to be raised and the general principles under which the expenditures are to be made. The details of expenditure, particularly in view of the great present emergency, can be more wisely and equitably administered through the Executive.

Later that day, Representative John McDuffie of Alabama, after careful briefing, introduced a bill in the House "to maintain the credit of the United States." On the same day, Senator Joseph T. Robinson, the majority leader, introduced an identical bill in the Senate. The next day, without hearings, the House passed the bill by a vote of 266 to 138. The Senate held a hearing of just one hour and on March 15 passed the bill by a vote of 65 to 13. President Roosevelt signed the legislation into law on March 20.

The Economy Act, as it was called, gave the President, among other unprecedented prerogatives, the authority to determine an index figure for the cost of living during a "base period," using the first six months of 1928. He was also "directed" to produce an index of the cost of living during the last six months of 1932 and every six months thereafter. If the President found that the current cost of living was substantially lower than that of the base period, he was authorized to cut the wages of employees accordingly, provided that such reductions did not exceed 15 per cent. Of course, the President had all the figures at hand, and as soon as he had the authorization, he ordered a sweeping 15 per cent reduction in all federal salaries.

It was during the Roosevelt Administration that the Bureau of the Budget became, by Presidential fiat, a dominant force in the making of federal policy. This development was to have a profound effect on the postal service. (See Chapter XI.)

On June 16, 1933, at the insistence of Bureau of the Budget director Lewis W. Douglas, Congress passed legislation that not only ordered compulsory retirement of federal and postal employees after thirty years of service but also placed in effect a "rotative furlough" program that would lay off employees for nine days during the September quarter without pay. Despite the promises about the furlough system he had made in his March 10 message to Congress, Roosevelt signed the bill into law on the same day it was passed. Understandably, postal employees were dismayed to find their wages reduced to the point where they had been in 1916, during the Burleson days. Naturally, the postal employee organizations protested. Congress wanted to do away with the salary reductions and the furloughs, but Roosevelt would have none of it.

However, the administration worked itself into an impossible position. On June 16, 1933, the National Industrial Recovery Act was approved. This act (declared unconstitutional on May 27, 1935) put enormous pressure upon civilian employers to maintain high wages and shorten working hours so as to prime the economic pump. Then, Roosevelt's timing, usually exquisite, went awry. On January 9, 1934, the President announced that he intended to continue the 15 per cent cut in the salaries of postal workers until June 30, 1934. On March 2, the Postmaster General felt compelled to issue an order calling for compulsory four-day payless furloughs for all postal employees, to take place before June 30. On March 5, the President said: "The thing to do is to get more people to work. Every examination I make, and all the information I receive, leads me to the inescapable conclusion that we must now [give] immediate consideration to secure increases in wages and shortening of hours." This statement was followed by an announcement that more than 26,000 postal employees had already been cut from the federal payroll.

Congress, urged on by the postal employee organizations, was in a rebellious mood. The administration unwisely tried to place a gag on debate on the appropriations bill, and this attempt served to intensify irritation on Capitol Hill. Congress proceeded to pass legislation that immediately restored 5 per cent of the postal employees' salaries (retroactive to February 1), with another 5 per cent to be added at the beginning of the new fiscal year (July 1). It also provided for the resumption of automatic promotions (authorized by law) within the postal establishment and urged the President to restore the original salaries as soon as the cost of living reached the proper level.

On March 27, the day after passage of the bill, Roosevelt issued a rather bad-tempered veto message. Within twenty-four hours, Congress, showing unexpected obstinacy, which was to persist until the November elections, voted overwhelmingly to override the veto. On April 14, Postmaster General Farley, noting an upswing in the postal business and a tendency in the economy toward recovery, rescinded his order imposing the additional four-day furloughs.

Airmail: Tragedy and Progress

Perhaps the most unfortunate episode in the early years of the Farley regime involved cancellation of airmail contracts.

Clearly a case in which the Postmaster General acted in the best of faith and for the national good but was victimized by circumstances beyond his control, the cancellation resulted from evidence gathered by a Senate investigating committee in 1933 that revealed that domestic airmail contracts had been let in May, 1930, without competitive bidding as stipulated by law. Postmaster General Brown, according to Post Office Department files, had merely called the representatives of a few large air transport companies to a meeting (May 19, 1930) and had entered into agreements about how much and whom the Department should pay for the transportation of airmail. The companies that were frozen out of the conference were naturally indignant at this highhanded procedure.

Farley's position was that the contracts were illegal and, even allowing for the usual subsidy paid to essential elements in the transportation system, excessively expensive to the Department. The Postmaster General consulted with Attorney General Homer S. Cummings, who agreed with him. Together, they went to President Roosevelt with the recommendation that the contracts be cancelled, pending renegotiation, but that the air transport companies be permitted to continue flying the mail until a settlement could be reached. Roosevelt thought otherwise. He agreed that the contracts were illegal, but he refused to permit the airlines to continue flying the mail during the negotiations. He had been assured by the War Department that the aviators of the Army Air Corps were completely equipped to fly the mail over the most important routes and could provide uninterrupted service. After all, the Air Corps had been the pioneer fliers of the mail, and Roosevelt assumed that advances in training, aircraft design, and equipment would produce an orderly and safe operation.

On February 9, 1934, Farley declared the contracts canceled, the order to be effective ten days later. He said:

> I do not believe Congress intended that the air-mail appropriation should be expended for the benefit of a few favored cor-

porations, which could use the funds as the basis of wild stock promotion resulting in profits of tens of millions of dollars to promoters who invested little or no capital. Nor was it intended to be used by great corporations to force competitors out of business and into bankruptcy. Nor should appropriations and contracts be given to a few favored corporations by connivance.

Roosevelt's confidence that the Army Air Corps could do the job adequately was tragically ill-founded. A combination of almost unprecedented bad weather and an excess of zeal and adventuresomeness on the part of the pilots brought about a major disaster. Several shocking plane crashes ensued, and in a period of less than three weeks, ten army pilots lost their lives either flying the mail or training to fly the mail. The public uproar was directed not against the illegal contracts but against the administration that had terminated them. Although Roosevelt was solely responsible for the decision to let the army fly the mail on an interim basis, he did not see fit to come to the defense of his Postmaster General when things went wrong. That was simply not his style.

Eventually, after competitive bidding, new contracts were let that were far more favorable to the taxpayer. By 1937, two and a half times more airmail was being transported than in 1932, and the total cost to the government was $7 million a year less. What happened to the airmail service during the Farley years can be seen from this table:

Year	Miles flown	Cost of service	Average cost per mile
1932	32,202,170	$19,938,123	$0.62
1933	35,909,811	19,400,265	0.54
1934	29,111,474	12,129,960	0.42
1935	31,147,875	8,814,296	0.28
1936	38,700,643	12,104,797	0.31
1937	39,958,771	13,088,358	0.33
1938	46,166,192	14,666,154	0.32
1939	52,193,772	16,625,474	0.32

Postmaster General Farley estimated that in the three and a half years ending December 31, 1933, the policies of his predecessor, Postmaster General Brown, had resulted in over-payments to the air transport companies of about $46.8 million. No evidence was unearthed by which actual dishonesty on the part of the Republican postal officials could be proved, although, naturally enough, suspicions were cast in that direction. The general consensus among informed sources was that the Department, in the matter of these contracts, had been guilty of gross laxity born of favoritism for certain of the largest air transport companies at the expense of those not so large. In any case, during a time of national economic depression, the taxpayer had been unnecessarily damaged.

Efficient Postal Management

It is demonstrable that during the Farley years, the taxpayer was not severely damaged by any part of the postal operation, although some postal employees felt that the economies of the early years of the New Deal were more or less sweated out of their hides.

As has been stated earlier, Farley took full advantage of provisions of the Kelly Law, which authorized the Postmaster General to differentiate between a gross deficit and a net deficit by segregating in his accounting such nonpostal expenses of national importance as air and ship transportation subsidies, free mail for government agencies, Congress, and the blind, free-in-county delivery of newspapers, the sale of migratory-bird stamps, and the conduct of unemployment censuses. Still, by any conceivable yardstick, the figures of Farley's postal administration prove that the service was operated far more efficiently than it had been operated during the days of Brown, New, and Work:

FARLEY'S RECORD

(In millions)

Year	Volume	Expenditures	Revenues	Gross deficit	Net deficit	Revenue per capita
1932	24,307	$794	$588	$206	$152	$4.71
1933	19,868	700	588	112	48	4.67
1934	20,626	631	487	144	+12	4.64
1935	22,332	697	631	66	+ 5	4.94
1936	23,571	754	665	89	16	5.18
1937	25,801	773	726	47	+13	5.62
1938	26,042	772	729	43	+ 4	5.58
1939	26,445	785	746	39	+15	5.69
1940	27,749	808	767	41	+19	5.81

In 1932 (Act of June 6), postage rates on first-class letters were raised from two cents to three cents. The added penny apparently had a depressive effect on the mail volume during fiscal year 1933, although the revenues remained about the same. (How much the drop in volume was due to the rate increase and how much to the ravages of the Depression is, of course, uncertain.) In 1933 (Act of June 16), Congress modified the postage rates so that the three-cent schedule would apply only to out-of-town mail (about 80 per cent of the total). Local first-class mail reverted to the two-cent rate. This change created a considerable nuisance to the public and an administrative headache for postal officials, but it was probably the cause of the upward swing in volume in fiscal year 1934 and almost certainly the cause of the $100 million decline in revenues in that year.

Farley himself attributed the comparatively disappointing showing in fiscal year 1936 to the forty-hour work week for postal employees (enacted August 14, 1935), which he supported wholeheartedly after some original misgivings. Another factor doubtless was the program of building new post offices, the cost of which was charged, for the first time, to the postal budget rather than to the Treasury. The program resulted in the erection of hundreds of badly needed new postal facilities, many of which are still in operation today. It also put thousands of desperate Americans to work. The efficiency of the Farley regime may be judged by the fact that in fiscal year 1939 the Post Office Department was handling two billion more pieces of mail than it was handling in 1932 and was doing it for less money.

In 1936, Roosevelt had defeated Governor Alfred M. Landon of Kansas in a landslide of such proportions that the Republican Party was almost eliminated as a serious factor on the American political scene. The electoral vote was 523 to 8, the largest margin in history. The Democrats also swept overwhelming majorities into Congress. When the votes were counted, the Senate had: 75 Democrats, 17 Republicans, 2 Farmer-Laborites, 1 Progressive, and 1 Independent. In the House, the count was: 330 Democrats, 88 Republicans, 7 Progressives, and 4 Farmer-Laborites. Once again, Postmaster General Farley had been the architect of victory. The campaign he managed with such consummate skill has since been recognized as the most nearly flawless in American political history.

The Departure of Farley

Although cordial on the surface, the relationship between Roosevelt and Farley deteriorated, particularly during the last year of the President's second term. There were many reasons for this change, some personal, some political. (It is not uncommon for successful politicians to dislike being reminded, even indirectly, that they have not achieved their eminence solely through their own efforts. The newspapers delighted in referring to Farley as "Warwick the King Maker"—a phrase that undoubtedly irritated the Roosevelt ego.)

There was also the matter of the third term. Like his friend Vice-President John Nance Garner, Farley was against it. He sincerely thought it would be bad for the nation and for his party to break the traditional limitation of two Presidential terms. He expressed his point of view to Roosevelt and was not thanked for it. In fact, Roosevelt acted with a distinct lack of frankness and permitted Farley to be boomed in some quarters as a Presidential candidate, while he himself was quietly planning, with his inner circle of friends, to capture the nomination for himself by "acclamation." The Postmaster General was placed in an impossible situation.

But above all, Farley felt he had made as much of a monetary sacrifice during his seven and a half years as Postmaster General as he could afford. His children were approaching college age, and he felt he owed it to them to accept a very favorable offer from private industry. After months of rumors predicting his resignation, he finally did resign, effective on August 7, 1940. His letter of resignation summed up with considerable pride the accomplishments of his administration:

> We have succeeded in placing the postal establishment on a self-sustaining basis with respect to that part of the service that is rendered to the public for hire; we have reduced the hours of labor from 44 to 40 hours a week; we have extended the air mail service by thousands of miles, including the inauguration of the transatlantic and transpacific services; we have supervised the erection of hundreds of new post office buildings in every State and Congressional District in the Nation; we have reduced postal expenditures by several millions of dollars while at the same time doing a record business in both volume and receipts; . . . we have provided new and increased services and have likewise performed several outstanding services for other government agencies.

The "Dear Jim" letter from President Roosevelt, accepting the resignation, was on the cool side. Roosevelt was never very good at saying thank you.

Farley resigned the chairmanship of the Democratic National Committee at the same time. He felt he could not in good conscience direct a political campaign with which he fundamentally disagreed. He did retain the chairmanship of the New York State Committee, however, and when Roosevelt received the nomination for the third term, he went along like a good soldier. He placed his close friend and trusted assistant Vincent Dailey in charge of the campaign in New York, and Roosevelt carried the state over Wendell Willkie by 250,000 votes. Farley left the national political scene with his honor fully intact.

During his years of service, James A. Farley imprinted his personality on the postal service to an extent seldom, if ever, approached in its history. Even those who disagreed with him, politically or philosophically, admired him as a leader who was never afraid to lead, a man who never ducked an issue and who did not hesitate to say and do unpopular things when he felt the good of the nation was involved.

VII

Closing the Circle

By 1940, mainly because of the industrial upsurge created by the nation's efforts to arm itself, the Depression was over. The population of the nation had reached 132 million, although during the previous decade, because of the Depression, the population had risen only 7.2 per cent—less than half the percentage in any other comparable time period. The mail volume had worked its way back up to 28 billion pieces, or just about where it had been in 1929. The postal employee force, which had reached 339,603 in 1929 and had dropped as low as 308,802 in 1935, was up to 353,157 and still rising. And the postal service, which had been through perilous times, was, by the time Frank C. Walker succeeded Farley, relatively thriving.

POSTAL SERVICE IN WORLD WAR II

During the war years that followed, the normal civilian mail service underwent a minimum of disruption, despite the fact that more than 56,000 regular postal employees entered the armed services and were almost irreplaceable. Normal transportation was also considerably curtailed by the war, adding greatly to the burden of moving the mails.

In addition, of course, the mail service had to be enormously expanded and extended to meet the needs of 12 million American servicemen stationed all over the world. This tremendous task was accomplished brilliantly, even though the postal service was not given the priority it should have been given as a major element of defense and morale. Soldiers complained constantly, of course, about the slowness and uncertainty of the mails, just as George Washington's troops had complained during the Revolution, but most of the mail did arrive expeditiously.

The Post Office always shows a false profit during wartime because, as mentioned earlier in these pages, the military assumes most of the financial burden of transporting the mails. Thus, the Walker years showed substantial paper surpluses:

WALKER'S RECORD

(In millions)

Year	Volume	Expenditures	Revenues	Deficit or surplus	Revenue per capita
1941	29,235	$ 837	$ 813	$— 24	$6.11
1942	30,118	874	860	— 14	6.39
1943	32,818	953	966	+ 14	7.08
1944	34,931	1,069	1,113	+ 44	8.06
1945	37,912	1,145	1,314	+169	9.41

It is noteworthy that in 1944, the Post Office Department, for the first time, surpassed the $1-billion mark in both expenses and revenues. By the Act of February 25, 1944, Congress had raised the rate of local first-class mail to three cents, making it equal to the rate on out-of-town mail. This rate raise had no major effect on either the volume or the revenues.

Walker abandoned the Kelly Law computation that had served his predecessor so well. It was felt that segregation of the cost of the nonpostal services the Department was performing would swell the paper surplus to such proportions that it would create agitation for a decrease in postage rates. It was also believed that the publication of such abnormal (and artificial) profits would increase congressional demands for pay increases for postal employees.

The financial plight of the postal workers during World War II became serious. They had not received a raise in pay since 1925, and the inflated cost of living had reduced the purchasing power of their wages to almost half of what it had been eighteen years previously. Letter carriers and post office clerks were receiving wages on a scale that ran from $1,700 a year to $2,100. Workers in shipyards and other war industries were making two to three times as much money. The job that had become enviable during the early 1930's once again had become undesirable. Postmasters found it difficult to retain their most valued employees and impossible to attract talented recruits.

The influence of postal employees on Congress and the nation's press grew steadily during these years. Certainly the postal organizations were becoming more aggressive in their attitudes. The newly elected president of the National Association of Letter Carriers, William C. Doherty of Cincinnati, brought an original and modern concept of trade-union leadership into the postal establishment. (Doherty dominated the postal labor scene from his election in 1941 until his voluntary retirement in 1962 to become the first U.S. Ambassador to Jamaica. He and his capable successor, Jerome J. Keating of Minneapolis, who served as vice-president of the NALC for many years before his accession, have been called the most effective lobbyists in the nation's capital.)

Postmaster General Walker recognized the labor crisis within the establishment, and on September 24, 1942, he made a speech recommending 15 per cent across-the-board raises in postal salaries. However, Walker was not the kind of man who could push his view forward with his chief. The Postmaster General was appalled by the weight of the wartime burden on the Presidency and hesitated to add to it by presenting too forcefully the case for a pay raise for his employees. And Roosevelt, for all his virtues as a President, had never shown any particular interest in or sympathy with the postal workers. His interest in postal matters seemed to begin and end with his passion for philately.

During 1942, the letter carriers and the post office clerks began to put pressure on Congress to approve at least a temporary wartime "bonus" pay increase of $300 a year. Representative George D. O'Brien of Michigan and Senator James M. Mead of New York introduced the necessary legislation in Congress. As the bill was being discussed in the House of Representatives, reports emanated from the White House to the effect that if passed, the bill would almost certainly be vetoed. The tactic backfired, and Congress approved the legislation by an overwhelming vote. On April 9, 1943, Roosevelt signed the bill into law. The pay raise, temporary to June 30, 1945, did a great deal to save the postal service from disintegration. It was not a lavish increase, but it was sufficient to slow down the exodus of experienced employees from the post offices of the nation.

On April 12, 1945, President Roosevelt died, and Harry S Truman became President of the United States. Truman, like most Presidents, wanted his own men around him, and on July 1, 1945, Robert E. Hannegan of Missouri, a long-time friend and associate, became Postmaster General. Hannegan, who had succeeded Walker as chairman of the Democratic National Committee, was a very useful party politician but had little interest in the actual operation of the Post Office. He served for thirty months, retiring because of ill health.

Just before Walker resigned, the postal employees—quoting the President's Committee on the Cost of Living, which had announced that such costs had risen 43.5 per cent since January 1, 1941—successfully concluded a long and arduous campaign to have the temporary bonus of $300 a year made permanent, along with an added $100. President Truman signed the bill on July 6, 1945, and the letter carriers almost immediately embarked on another campaign to gain a further pay increase of $400 a year. Hannegan supported the new proposal, and Congress, at long last finding time to direct its attentions to domestic matters of a peaceful nature, agreed. The bill sailed through both houses, and President Truman approved it on May 21, 1946. The top salary of a carrier or a clerk in the Post Office thus became $3,100 a year, or exactly $1,000 a year more than it had been three years earlier. Naturally enough, the two sweeping pay raises were reflected in postal accounting by oversize deficits in the following two years:

HANNEGAN'S RECORD

(In millions)

Year	Volume	Expenditures	Revenues	Deficit	Revenue per capita
1946	36,318	$1,354	$1,225	$129	$8.69
1947	37,427	1,505	1,299	206	9.02

POSTWAR PROBLEMS

There was considerable public dissatisfaction with the postal service during Hannegan's administration. Practically the only sign of progress in the operation of the service was the introduction of helicopters (1947) to transport mail in some cities from the airport to the main post office. The Postmaster General was too blatantly political and too obviously willing to let his subordinates run the postal establishment without his help or direction. The Post Office Department, rightly or wrongly, was generally charged with being a haven for political hacks, and as the quality of service deteriorated, so did the prestige of the institution. Congress, which was again in Republican hands, investigated the Department thoroughly and was highly critical of Hannegan's management of postal affairs.

In an effort to correct this situation, Truman appointed as Postmaster General a career postal employee of long experience, Jesse M. Donaldson of Illinois. Donaldson had begun as a letter carrier and had spent many years as a Post Office inspector. He had worked his way up to be first assistant postmaster general, and when he took office on December 16, 1947, his was the first bona fide career appointment to the top position since that of Horatio King, who had served briefly in 1861. But despite hopes to the contrary, during the five years that Donaldson served (December, 1947–January, 1953), the postal service suffered dramatic deterioration, and the atmosphere within the Department was hardly less political than it had been previously.

Donaldson turned out to be resistant to change and almost totally incapable of sharing authority with his colleagues. In 1947, he opposed wholeheartedly the recommendation of the Hoover Commission to decentralize operations. (See Chapter IX.) No politician, he did not get along well on Capitol Hill and was inclined to lecture the committees before which he appeared as a witness. He was also highly suspicious of the employee organizations and had very little contact with them. As a result, the employee organizations learned to depend almost exclusively upon Congress for solution of their problems.

During the Donaldson years, Congress passed sixteen laws favorable to postal workers. Three of the bills involved increases in pay, and each was passed after a colorful legislative campaign and over administration opposition.* In 1948, all postal salaries were increased by $450; in 1949, there was an increase of $120; in 1951, another of $400. During this period of activity, the wages of letter carriers and post office clerks were increased so that the scale ranged from $3,270 minimum to a maximum of $4,370. Despite cost-of-living increases dur-

* In 1949, the letter carriers revived the almost forgotten legislative technique of the "discharge petition" to get a pay bill out of a reluctant committee. They have used the technique five times since then, always with success. In the entire history of Congress, there have been only thirty-one successful discharge petitions, and the letter carriers have been responsible for the initiation of six of them.

ing the Truman Presidency and despite the opposition of the Post Office Department, the postal employees, through their organizations and through a sympathetic Congress, managed to gain comparative economic respectability. By 1952, a Post Office job had once again become reasonably desirable.

But, like so many other men who have come up in the career civil service, Donaldson, overly diffident in budgetary matters, hesitated to fight for his proper share of the federal dollar. He accepted, with unwarranted docility, cuts made in his appropriation requests` by the Bureau of the Budget and Congress, and this timidity invited the incident of April 18, 1950, that has been called "The Rape of the Mail Service."

Donaldson Curtails Deliveries

When Congress refused the Post Office Department sufficient funds to operate efficiently, Donaldson scorned to enlist the aid of the powerful postal organizations to effect a restoration in the appropriations. He shrank from employing the techniques that heads of executive departments customarily use in such situations. Instead, without consulting with anyone in advance, he issued an order reducing mail deliveries in residential areas to one a day and in most business areas to two a day. He also severely cut the regularity of street collections, curtailed window service in post offices, and eliminated by half the deliveries of parcel post to business firms. On the majority of city delivery routes, he completely eliminated service on certain selected days.

The order had a calamitous effect on the postal system. Before Congress could pass legislation ordering the restoration of these services, the Korean War broke out (June, 1950), and civilian needs were shunted aside in favor of military requirements. Even so, a bill to rescind the order was passed in the House by a vote of 264 to 108 and was defeated in the Senate by only a single vote.

The issue has never been seriously revived in Congress. Today, millions of letters are delayed daily by a full twenty-four hours because of Donaldson's restrictive order. Letters that arrive at a post office even minutes too late to be sorted before the letter carrier sets out on his route are permitted to lie idle until the next day. Donaldson claimed that the reductions in service would save the Department $80 million a year. However, the figures for his administration do not reflect any great savings:

DONALDSON'S RECORD

(In millions)

Year	Volume	Expenditures	Revenues	Deficit	Revenue per capita
1948	40,280	$1,688	$1,411	$277	$ 9.62
1949	43,555	2,149	1,572	577	10.53
1950	45,064	2,223	1,677	546	11.05
1951	46,908	2,341	1,777	564	11.51
1952	49,905	2,667	1,947	721	12.40

The three pay raises for postal employees added considerably to the expenditures of the Department, since the work force of the establishment was approaching the 500,000 mark, but scarcely accounted for the deficit in Donaldson's final year, which was greater than the total revenues of the Department in any year previous to 1937.

Donaldson's almost fanatical insistence on centralization of authority and his resistance to modern methods of business and finance were costing the taxpayer a great deal of money. The Department was engaged almost exclusively in solving problems that had already occurred instead of planning to prevent their occurrence. For example, significant deteriorations in transportation patterns would not usually come to the attention of the authorities in Washington until serious breakdowns in service were inevitable. The solution of these problems was almost always expensive, and many of the problems could have been avoided by intelligent management on the spot. Postmasters, learning that a sudden increase in volume was imminent, would have to seek permission from Washington to increase their work force in order to handle the load. The request was usually refused because headquarters personnel often knew nothing of local conditions and had no practical knowledge of postal operations. Conditions such as these could only result in a steady decline in the quality of the service and in steadily rising deficits.

THE SUMMERFIELD STORY

The Republicans were singularly blessed in the 1952 Presidential campaign with having, in Dwight D. Eisenhower, an obviously unbeatable candidate. Eisenhower's campaign manager was Arthur E. Summerfield of Flint, Michigan, chairman of the Republican National Committee. The son of a pioneer rural letter carrier, Summerfield was appointed Postmaster General, assuming office on January 21, 1953, and serving the full eight years of Eisenhower's occupation of the White House.

Summerfield must be considered one of the most interesting and most controversial of all postmasters general. During the first eighteen months of his administration, even those who disapproved of his policies admit that he performed wonders in reorganizing the postal establishment and instituting modern business methods. In many ways, Arthur Summerfield was like John Wanamaker. He had the same businesslike approach to the task ahead, the same courage and disdain for the inefficient, traditional practices of the past. Unfortunately, he carried the similarity too far—he also shared Wanamaker's attitude toward labor. He was insensitive to the needs and rights of those who worked under him, and his belligerent opposition to the demands of the employee organizations tarnished his reputation as an administrator. In addition, particularly in the latter years, he infuriated Congress with his persistent assumption that the legislative branch of the government was inferior to, and should therefore be subservient to, the executive branch.* His cavalier treatment of congressmen, including those of his own party, combined with his hostility to the postal organizations, eventually brought to ruin most of his dreams of emerging as the greatest of all postmasters general.

Reorganization

Summerfield made a brilliant beginning. Before he took office, he set an example by resigning the chairmanship of the Republican National Committee, and he proceeded to surround himself with experienced business leaders who had proved their value in the private sector. The Post Office Department had never been overburdened with top-flight talent among its first-rank executives. Too often, it had been used for the convenient disposition of the party faithful who could not be conveniently placed elsewhere. Summerfield startled everybody by seeking out and securing a team that was the most talented not only in the history of the Post Office but, possibly, in the entire government at the time. These businessmen turned postal officials went through a period of shock when they embarked upon their tasks. They found postal procedures so encrusted with antiquity that progress was almost impossible without a complete overhaul of the operation.

At his first staff meeting, the new Postmaster General said that it would perhaps be wise to start with a consideration of the latest financial statement of the Department. He was informed that financial statements ran, on the average, eighteen

---

* One prominent Republican legislator, when told that Summerfield was really his own worst enemy, is known to have growled, "Not while I'm alive, he isn't!"

months behind actual events and traditionally were used only as historical documents, not as management tools. It can be imagined what effect this announcement had on him and on a staff consisting of a former vice-president of Congoleum-Nairn, a former vice-president of the Chesapeake & Ohio Railroad, the former general traffic manager of Sears, Roebuck, the former executive vice-president of Iowa's largest bank, and a leading industrial real estate broker from New Jersey.

Other grave administrative deficiencies soon became apparent. The transportation patterns of the postal service had not been seriously examined in the past twenty-five years— although the Department was spending $600 million for transportation every year. Congress had not appropriated any money for new postal facilities in fifteen years, and the average post office was more than fifty years old. (At some post offices, parcel post was being sorted on the sidewalk because there was no room inside.) There had been little thought given to the development and adaptation of new machines to sort mail electronically. (On the organization chart, the Division of Research and Engineering was placed one step below the Employees' Suggestion Program.) The accounting procedures of the Department were at least fifty years behind the times; they were almost hopelessly inadequate and gave management too little useful information far too late to prevent the occurrence of expensive problems. Above all, every important decision was being made at the headquarters level, far removed from the location where the problems existed.

A great deal was done in a short while. The accounting processes were revolutionized and modernized under the leadership of Maurice H. Stans, one of the outstanding certified public accountants in the country, who was later to become deputy postmaster general and, still later, director of the Bureau of the Budget. The system was centralized and mechanized. Monthly financial statements were issued, containing far more useful information than had previously been available. Within a year, the cost of keeping the Department's accounts was reduced by an estimated $15 million a year.*

In 1953 (Act of July 23), Summerfield received permission from Congress for the creation of a full-fledged Bureau of Personnel, with an assistant postmaster general at its head. (See Chapter IX.) Mail transportation patterns were dramatically reorganized, with a resulting improvement in service and a saving of about $40 million a year in costs. In July, 1955, an experiment was started by which regular first-class mail was flown between certain selected points on a space-available basis. The experiment proved so successful that the system became permanent, despite the vigorous opposition of the railroads. In a year's time, more than 90 per cent of the first-class mail between, for example, New York and Chicago was being flown at very little extra cost to the Department and with great effect upon the speed of transmission.

The new postal administration also received permission from Congress to segregate the hidden subsidies in its budget and charge them to the branches and departments of Government responsible for them. Each department was charged with the costs for its "free" mail, and Congress assumed the responsibility for its own franking privileges† (Act of August 15, 1953). The subsidies to certain airlines were assigned to the proper agency. This not only decreased the postal deficit on paper by $310 million a year but also reduced the total cost of these subsidies to the government. Once the agencies involved found that they would be charged with these ex-

---

* Until 1953, Post Office accounts were kept down to the last cent. Expenditures for a given year were meticulously listed as, for example, $1,504,804,841.23. The recommendation to round off all such sums to the nearest dollar was met with scandalized opposition by Department accountants. However, newer ways prevailed and whole-dollar accounting was adopted, with significant savings in time and manpower.

† See Appendix B for a list of all legislation affecting free mail.

penses, they became surprisingly cautious about incurring them.*

Under Summerfield, the Department, still finding Congress reluctant to appropriate funds for the construction of new facilities, developed means of inducing private enterprise to build and lease them to the Post Office Department. This system has proved to be expensive to the government, but it has provided desperately needed facilities that would not otherwise have been made available.

The most significant achievement of Summerfield's administration was the decentralization of postal operations, started in 1954, which finally broke the massive bottleneck that was making the efficient operation of the establishment an administrative impossibility. (This important development is discussed in Chapter IX.)

Politics Played Down

Although he was brought up in the most partisan school of politics, Summerfield showed an admirable tolerance toward Democratic postmasters. As a businessman, he reasoned that it was impossible to operate the most important industry in the nation without stable management in the field.† To the dismay of the spoilsmen within his own party, he announced soon after he took office that no postmaster need fear for his job as long as he was performing it satisfactorily. He lived up to this promise.

* The cost to the Post Office Department of congressional franking has been greatly exaggerated by the public. In 1953, departmental accountants estimated that free congressional mail was costing about $1.1 million a year. This was a minor item in the postal budget. The cost of handling the "penalty" mail of other departments and agencies free of charge was another matter. It was estimated at about $135 million a year.

† It is interesting to contemplate what would happen to General Motors, let us say, if every district manager were changed whenever a new chairman of the board appeared.

True, the Ramspeck-O'Mahoney Act of 1938 had made every Presidential postmaster a career civil servant, but the efficacy of this protection had never been tested by a change in administration. Republicans in Congress and in responsible positions in the party considered the Ramspeck-O'Mahoney Act merely a political trick to perpetuate Democratic postmasters in power. Certainly it was possible, under the rules, for a politically inspired postal inspector to find enough fault in any reasonably large post office in the country to "justify" a case against the postmaster.

But Summerfield, to his credit, did live up to the letter and the spirit of the law. During his first year in office, the Republicans, who had been denied access to the patronage lists for twenty years, were howling for Democratic heads. Under such circumstances, it was unheard of that the postmasters of such large cities as Philadelphia, Boston, San Francisco, St. Louis, New Orleans, Dallas, Houston, Miami, and Pittsburgh should be undisturbed. But Summerfield did not disturb them and stood up to the importuning of the spoilsmen. In that first year, only 155 postmasters were dismissed from the service (out of a total of 40,609), and almost all these dismissals were for serious deficiencies in job performance. In eight years, fewer than 1,000 postmasters altogether were removed from office. Summerfield's good sense in this area set an example that subsequent administrations have followed. There has been even less bloodletting among postmasters since 1961.

Opposition Develops

Most of the major improvements in the Post Office came during the first two years of Summerfield's administration. After that time, congressional opposition combined with an over-all deterioration in leadership to blunt the edge of postal reform.

Summerfield (once again, like John Wanamaker) was exceedingly publicity conscious. He was almost ruthless in his desire for the limelight and, in achieving it, not overly nice about whose toes he trod upon. There were those who claimed that he hoped to get the nomination for Vice-President in either 1956 or 1960. Whether or not this was true, he did manage to make numerous enemies through his aggressive pursuit of headlines.

In 1953, he called a press conference and, in the most public manner, returned to the Treasury $51.7 million of the money appropriated to his Department for the fiscal year. The implication was that the Bureau of the Budget and the appropriations committees of Congress had been careless of public funds and that he, through his superior business methods and thrift, had saved the public pocket from being picked. Naturally, this implication irritated the Budget Bureau and Congress, but since the appropriations had been made by Democrats under a Democratic administration, his action was shrugged off as rugged but effective politics. However, in 1954, he did the same thing, and this time it was a Republican administration and a Republican Congress. The amount returned was $104.4 million. And in 1955, he returned another $42.5 million.

What was particularly irritating to the Bureau of the Budget and Congress was the fact that Summerfield did not trouble to emphasize that most of the "savings" resulted from his being able to transfer out of the postal budget such items as airline subsidies and the responsibility for the "free" mail of various government agencies. By 1957, many people in the Budget Bureau and on the congressional appropriations committees had vowed not to be humiliated again. They cut the Summerfield appropriation request to the bone, removing not only the fat but a great deal of the lean as well. The Postmaster General had to threaten to close down all post offices on Saturdays (and actually did so for one Saturday) before he could get enough funds restored with which to operate the establishment.*

In subsequent years, Summerfield could never again get the funds he wanted and needed to mechanize the postal service or to develop the electronic devices necessary to modernize the mails. As a result, his administration, which had started out at a dead run, ended up limping.

But Summerfield's reputation was most adversely and permanently affected by his stubborn opposition to the attempts of the postal employees to get raises in pay commensurate with the constantly rising cost of living. He was determined to be the first Postmaster General in history to operate the postal establishment at a profit without benefit of wartime conditions or the bookkeeping assistance of the Kelly Law. He was far more interested in raising postage rates than he was in raising postal salaries, and he enlisted President Eisenhower's complete support in this program.

Between the years 1953–61, Eisenhower vetoed four postal pay bills. Only once before in history had a President vetoed even one. (That was Coolidge, in 1924. In 1934, Roosevelt vetoed a bill to restore the cuts he had already made in postal salaries, but this was not, in the strict sense, a pay bill.) Congress overrode the 1960 veto—one of 2 out of 169 Eisenhower vetoes to be overridden in eight years.

It was always Summerfield's assertion that any increase in the pay of postal employees would only add to the nation's monetary inflation. When the employees responded that they were not the causes but the victims of inflation, the Postmaster

---

* Ironically, the letter carriers, who were by this time feuding bitterly with Summerfield, were instrumental in getting him the necessary money. Jerome J. Keating, then vice-president of their organization, made it clear to the committee members that his members were being caught in the squeeze and were the innocent victims of this battle between the executive and the legislative branches. Congress relented, not so much because they wanted to extricate the Postmaster General from his budgetary problems, but because they did not want to injure postal employees.

General turned a deaf ear. To balance the postal budget, Summerfield had to take two courses simultaneously. The first was to keep postal salaries as low as possible. Since salaries comprised 80 per cent of the postal expenses and since, theoretically, these could be controlled by congressional indifference or, failing that, by executive veto, he followed this course instinctively from the beginning. The other was to raise the rates of postage. He also followed this course.

If Summerfield's neolithic approach to labor-management relations caused resentment among postal employees, his monolithic approach to postage rates created something very much like fury among the nation's publishers and large commercial users of the mails.

The Battle Over Postage Rates

Just three months after he had taken office, Summerfield stormed up to Capitol Hill to demand that the rates on non-local first-class mail be increased from three cents to four cents and that second-class (mainly magazines and newspapers) and third-class (mainly advertising matter) rates be substantially raised.

The committees of Congress included many wise old birds who had been wrestling with the postage rate problem for years. They took a dim view of a Chevrolet dealer recently turned Postmaster General lecturing them about the "immorality" of second- and third-class rates as if nobody in the entire history of the government had ever thought about this subject before. Summerfield consistently underrated the importance, intelligence, integrity, and experience of Congress, and therein lay a great part of the ultimate frustration of his administration. He persisted in approaching the committees of Congress as if he were the chairman of a particularly dim-witted board of a minor subsidiary company. His neglect of the rituals of subordination that congressional committees expect from cabinet officers did not win him friends on Capitol Hill.

The Cost Ascertainment Division on the Post Office Department claimed that the service was losing $240.3 million a year on second-class mail because of low rates. The Department was paying, according to Cost Ascertainment, about 20 per cent of the total cost, the other 80 per cent being carried by the taxpayer. Cost Ascertainment also charged that third-class mail was costing the Department $191.9 million a year. Summerfield was sternly rebuffed by Congress when he made his first attempt to raise the rates, in 1953. He kept coming back with new proposals every year, and the battle between the Postmaster General and the large users of the mails became more and more acrimonious.

In 1958, the Postmaster General finally got his four-cent stamp (and a seven-cent airmail stamp), plus substantial rate increases for second- and third-class mail, but at the expense of a much delayed postal pay bill. The Act of May 27, 1958, also enunciated as congressional policy that the Post Office Department was a service and not, as Summerfield claimed, a business enterprise or a public utility. The act instructed the Postmaster General to segregate the purely post office expenses from the public service expenses in his accounting but did not put down any guidelines for him to follow in doing this. The Post Office committees in Congress and the large users of the mails estimated the extracurricular costs of the Department at a figure more than ten times as high as that estimated by the Postmaster General (see page 203). Summerfield obeyed the law but kept to the low figure when segregating the costs.

As soon as the postage rate campaign was over, the Postmaster General embarked on another one, this time for a five-cent stamp, an eight-cent airmail stamp, and further increases in second- and third-class mail. He fought this battle for two years but could never again reach the ear of Congress. Instead, over his strenuous opposition and despite a veto by President

Eisenhower, Congress gave another pay raise to the postal employees (Act of July 1, 1960), while refusing to adjust the rates.

The fiscal story of Summerfield's administration follows:

SUMMERFIELD'S RECORD

(In millions)

Year	Volume	Expenditures	Revenues	Gross deficit	Net deficit	Revenue per capita
1953	50,948	$2,742	$2,092	$650		$13.12
1954	52,213	2,668	2,269	399		13.99
1955	55,234	2,712	2,349	363		14.23
1956	56,441	2,883	2,419	464		14.40
1957	59,078	3,044	2,497	547		14.64
1958	60,130	3,441	2,550	891		14.71
1959	61,247	3,640	3,035	632	605[a]	17.22
1960	63,675	3,874	3,277	637	597	18.31

[a] Includes concessions for nonpostal services authorized by the Postal Policy Act of 1958 (PL 84-426).

The sharp decline in expenditures and in the gross deficit for fiscal year 1954 was in part attributable to improved management techniques but in far greater part to the removal from the postal budget of items that became chargeable to other agencies of government. The sudden increase in revenues and in per capita expenditure in 1959 (as well as the decline in the gross deficit) must be chiefly attributed to the rate increase in 1958.

In 1944, the Post Office Department had seen, for the first time, its revenues and expenditures pass the $1 billion mark. The expenditures passed the $2 billion mark in 1949, when Donaldson was Postmaster General. In 1953, revenues reached that point under Summerfield; by 1959, the Post Office Department was a $3 billion enterprise in both revenues and expenditures. This rate of growth was unequaled by any business of comparable size in the private sector.

The Case of Lady Chatterley's Lover

In his latter years as Postmaster General, Arthur Summerfield embarked on a much publicized crusade to clean up the mails. As was so often the case with him, his lack of restraint in pursuing his objective spoiled his chances of success. In 1953, he made the mistake of taking official action against an obscure Oklahoma rancher who had distributed a rude but hardly obscene postcard attacking the policies of the Eisenhower Administration through the use of a simple-minded *double-entendre.* The courts failed to see anything very shocking in this primitive form of barnyard humor and refused to take action, and the case made a local hero out of the rancher and caused him to be elected as the Democratic lieutenant governor of the state.

Learning very little from this discouraging skirmish, Summerfield, in 1958, made a frontal assault against D. H. Lawrence's *Lady Chatterley's Lover* and sought to have it banned from the mails. When his judicial officer, whose official function was to be objective in legal matters, advised the Postmaster General that he did not believe the courts would permit the book to be banned, Summerfield dismissed him. Action was brought against *Lady Chatterley's Lover* (which had, after all, been in circulation more or less openly in the United States for more than a quarter of a century), and the courts, as predicted, refused to declare it obscene. The case caused such a stir that the book became an overnight best seller, and people who had never heard of D. H. Lawrence flocked to buy it.

In his eagerness to justify himself, the Postmaster General then raised a number of quizzical eyebrows throughout the country by assembling, in a room directly across the corridor from his office, a chamber of horrors consisting of the most sensational hard-core pornography that the Postal Inspection Service had captured over the years. For months, he invited congressmen, labor leaders, and newspapermen into the Department to view the exhibit and to watch a collection of contraband erotic motion pictures.

The gambit backfired. Anyone in his right mind would agree, after the most cursory glance, that most of the material exhibited should never have been permitted in the mails, but it had very little to do with a book like *Lady Chatterley's Lover*. The exhibit created more derision than it did indignation and, among the coarser spirits of the nation's capital, gained the reputation of being the most torrid stag show in Washington. The Post Office Department became, in short, one of the few places in town where a man could dabble in such depravity without fear of the police. One of the first actions of Postmaster General Summerfield's successor, after he took office, was to close down this unseemly peep show and order the exhibits returned to the archives, where they are kept under lock and key.

Summerfield had many virtues as a Postmaster General, but he had no subtlety. His only way of approaching an objective was through a frontal assault. His intransigence was unabated even after the Democrats swept back into power, with John Fitzgerald Kennedy, in the election of 1960. Summerfield made a futile, ill-timed attempt to bring the Republican regional directors (whom he had once called "little postmasters general") into the career civil service. These positions were never intended to be part of the civil service, being strictly policy-making jobs with strong political overtones. His political ploy was easily frustrated by the new administration, bringing to a sad end the story of a Postmaster General who might have been a great postal leader.

MR. DAY'S APPOINTED ROUND

President John Fitzgerald Kennedy's first Postmaster General was J. Edward Day of California, a very competent Harvard-trained lawyer and insurance executive. The appointment came out of a blue sky and caught official Washington completely by surprise. Day's only public experience had been as a crusading insurance commissioner for the state of Illinois when Adlai Stevenson III was governor. Nobody in Washington knew who he was, and when they found out, they wondered why the selection had fallen so mysteriously upon him. This thought had occurred to Day himself. The new Postmaster General was, in many ways, a distinguished man, but he had not achieved a national reputation and was an innocent in the political jungles of Washington. His troubles, which were immediate, stemmed partially from the difference in the way the national committees of the Republican and Democratic parties operate.

When Summerfield became Postmaster General, he selected his own subordinates—none of them for purely political reasons. They were simply the men Summerfield wanted to fill the jobs, and he achieved clearance from the Republican National Committee for each man after he had chosen him. Postmaster General Day was not consulted in the selection of his principal subordinates. Indeed, his deputy had been selected long before Day himself. Since the deputy was one who, under other circumstances, might well have been chosen for the top position—and was more than ordinarily aware of that fact—the relationships at the highest level of the Department were never easy. Many of the appointees were beholden to the deputy for their jobs rather than to the Postmaster General.

J. Edward Day, who served 929 days (by his own count) as Postmaster General, brought to the position a style and a wit that had never before been particularly conspicuous in his office. Unfortunately, the spectacle of an urbane Postmaster General created an undue sensation among elements of the Washington press corps. The way of the sprightly mind in Washington can be thorny, and the Post Office Department is in the foremost rank of those institutions in which a man can rise solely by his own gravity and sink solely by his own levity. Although he refused to take himself seriously, Day was far from being a lightweight Postmaster General. He was a humane administrator who tried his level best, under very difficult circumstances, to be effective, and much was accomplished under his leadership.* In 1962 (Act of October 11), he was able to get a further increase in postage rates (including a five-cent first-class stamp and an eight-cent airmail stamp) with a minimum of legislative scuffling. The law set out a formula for segregating nonpostal expenses in the postal budget, providing for a clear differentiation between the gross deficit and the net deficit. The same act increased the wages of postal employees by an average of 11 per cent and established the principle of "comparability," which, theoretically, would allow the wages of postal employees to keep pace with rising scales in comparable jobs in private industry.

One of the principal developments of the Day regime was the issuance by President Kennedy of Executive Order 10988 (January 17, 1962), which, for the first time, made management recognition of postal unions mandatory. This was something that the postal employees had been seeking for many years, either through legislation or through administrative action, and it opened the door to limited collective bargaining, at both the local and the national levels.

As is often the case in government, the apparatus implementing Executive Order 10988 became almost grotesquely complicated, involving a cumbersome procedure that takes up the time of more than 100 individuals in both the Department and the employee organizations and produces less in the way

---

* In some ways, J. Edward Day was reminiscent of "a certain Mr. Edwards" who told Samuel Johnson that he had always wanted to be a philosopher but, "somehow, cheerfulness was always breaking in." When he left the postmaster-generalship, Day wrote an amusing book about his experiences (*My Appointed Round,* Holt, Rinehart and Winston, 1965) that was later turned into a musical comedy. It has never occurred to anyone to set the reminiscences of any other Postmaster General to music.

of progress than had been anticipated. Nonetheless, the principle of collective bargaining in certain strictly defined areas was instituted in the postal establishment for the first time.

In the early 1960's, the Post Office Department began to show a predilection for verbal furbelows. New programs became known by their acronyms (NIMS, ZIP, etc.) and were given a great deal of publicity—far out of proportion to their demonstrable effectiveness in moving the mails.*

Mr. Day resigned in September, 1963, in order to resume the practice of the law, and subsequently served as president of the prestigious National Civil Service League (the organization Carl Schurz headed in the latter part of the nineteenth century).

Gronouski's Postmaster-generalship

The second Postmaster General appointed by President Kennedy was John A. Gronouski of Wisconsin, the first citizen of Polish descent ever to be made a cabinet officer.† Two months after Postmaster General Gronouski took office, President John Fitzgerald Kennedy was assassinated in Dallas, Texas. However, the new President, Lyndon B. Johnson, did not disturb the Postmaster General appointed by his predecessor until twenty-one months later. Gronouski was then named U.S. Ambassador to Poland.

During his period in office, Gronouski proved himself to be a liberal-minded administrator, but he was much hampered

---

* The most promising of these, the ZIP Code (Zone Improvement Plan), represents a refinement on the numbered-zone program, which Postmaster General Walker introduced in 1943. Its full benefit will be derived when the Post Office Department has the electronic machines to "read" the coding and distribute the coded pieces mechanically.

† So much was made of Gronouski's Polish origin that Polish-American groups took it for granted he spoke the language of his forefathers. To his embarrassment, the Postmaster General could speak no Polish whatsoever and found it necessary, in addition to running the postal establishment, to take a crash course in the language.

by the Bureau of the Budget, which forced him, in the name of economy, to curtail services, to restrict the delivery of parcel post to five days a week, and to limit the window hours in post offices, much to the discomfiture and annoyance of postal patrons. Understandably, he was somewhat ineffective in fighting off these inroads upon the integrity of the service. He was not an experienced Washington hand, and he lacked the expertise necessary for successful combat against the professional budget parers. It is perhaps also true that the fact that he was not President Johnson's appointee made him less than aggressive in pushing his ideas forward at the White House.

Two pay raise bills were passed during Gronouski's short stay in office, but both were small because of pressures put upon Congress by the President and the Bureau of the Budget. In an attempt to deal with inflation, President Johnson and his advisers devised artificial guidelines within which all wage increases, in both the private and the public sector, should be contained. These guidelines proved all but untenable in the private sector and, in every major labor dispute, were widely exceeded. They were observed only in the public sector.

O'BRIEN TAKES OVER

On November 2, 1965, Lawrence F. O'Brien of Massachusetts became Postmaster General of the United States. His appointment had been announced in August, but his installation was delayed so that he could continue to work full time on Capitol Hill as the President's personal lobbyist. The delay caused a serious power vacuum in the Department.

O'Brien, a personable and respected political professional, had been one of the principal organizers of the successful Kennedy campaign in 1960. He was Kennedy's man on Capitol Hill until the death of the President in 1963 and was retained in the same position by President Johnson. Probably no man in official Washington is more personally popular than

O'Brien. He speaks the language the political professionals of both parties understand, and he is genuinely liked by both Democrats and Republicans in Congress.

From a postal point of view, O'Brien's popularity has drawbacks. The President has continued to lean heavily upon him both as an adviser and as a lobbyist on Capitol Hill for administration programs. It is generally felt that he has not been permitted to devote his full time and talents to running the postal establishment, thus depriving the Department of the kind of tough, consistent leadership it needs.

In the autumn of 1966, one of the worst mail crises in the history of the Post Office Department took place. Almost every major post office in the country suddenly reported a vast backlog of mail, far more than the work force could possibly handle. In Chicago alone, more than 1 million pounds of mail was backlogged, with no available way of moving it. (An assistant postmaster general rushed to the scene and ordered all the third-class mail in Chicago burned and the postage returned to the senders. No such action was taken, but many people were understandably shocked by this suggestion.) Several cities reported that they were eight to ten days behind in handling third-class mail. In the Chicago area, even first-class letters were delayed by as much as three weeks in arriving at their destination. The entire postal service appeared to be on the verge of collapse. Worst of all, this backup occurred in what should have been a normal period—certainly long before the Christmas rush, which usually produces a kind of organized chaos in the nation's post offices.

This crisis was the culmination of a steady process of deterioration that had been in progress for a number of years. Shortsighted "economies" forced on the Department by the Bureau of the Budget, the White House, and the appropriations committees of Congress had produced, finally, a multi-million-dollar catastrophe. An unprecedented increase of 15 per cent in mail volume in some areas had come on the heels of appropriations granted in anticipation of an increase of less than 3 per cent. Compounding the problem, in an ill-advised effort at economy, the Department had severely limited the use of overtime for regular, experienced career employees. This restriction put the burden of moving the mails onto the inadequate shoulders of temporary workers hired at random off the streets.

In the crisis, Postmaster General O'Brien moved swiftly and effectively. He secured $30 million from the Bureau of the Budget to clean up the postal mess. (That is, he received permission to "borrow" that sum from the appropriations for the fourth quarter of the fiscal year, with the understanding that a supplementary appropriation would be granted in the Ninetieth Congress.) He relaxed the unrealistic overtime regulations and arranged to "promote" 26,000 career substitute employees to regulars. He also hired 150,000 temporary workers, beginning November 1, 1966, in anticipation of the Christmas rush.

These were commendable emergency measures. However, in many informed circles, the belief remains that the postal crisis of 1966 would never have reached disaster proportions if the capable Postmaster General had been allowed to devote more of his energies to the postal service and less to the promotion of nonpostal administration programs on Capitol Hill.

Where the Mail Is in the 1960's

Throughout the 1960's, postal volume and postal expenditures continued to rise, as the table on page 182 reveals.

The Post Office today is the product of its past. Its achievements have been considerable, but they have been produced by men working under great difficulties imposed by legislative and bureaucratic restrictions. Its current problems are legacies of past errors, interminably compounded, and of outmoded

THE POSTAL RECORD IN THE 1960'S

(In millions)

Year	Volume	Expendi-tures	Revenues	Gross deficit	Net deficit	Revenue per capita
1961	64,933	$4,249	$3,423	$875	$826	$18.81
1962	66,493	4,332	3,557	837	775	19.19
1963	67,853	4,699	3,879	819	407[a]	20.63
1964	69,676	4,928	4,276	652	204	22.45
1965	71,873	5,275	4,483	792	281	23.35
1966	75,607	5,727	4,784	743	400	24.43

[a] Public Law 87-793 (October 11, 1962) established the formula for excluding nonpostal public services from the postal deficit. The formula was considerably more generous to the Post Office Department than had been the Policy Act of 1958.

and encumbering traditions. Postal managers are prevented by law from performing the ordinary functions of management. The authority of the Postmaster General over the policies of the establishment he heads is slight. Congress dictates what the Post Office shall charge for its services, what it shall pay its employees, and how much money it can spend in any given year. Too often, congressmen determine where post offices shall be located and who the postmasters and regional managers shall be. Except under very restrictive conditions, the Postmaster General cannot even enter into contracts for transportation that he thinks will be beneficial to the service.

As a result, the position of Postmaster General is one of the most frustrating jobs in Washington. Whenever the service suffers a failure, the Postmaster General, the postmasters, and the postal employees get the blame. Rarely does the blame fall on the Congress, the Bureau of the Budget, or the Civil Service Commission, although any or all of them may have imposed the conditions that made the failure inevitable in the first place.

By mid-1967, the postal service was plainly in a state of disrepair. Its prestige was the lowest it had been since the early days of the Jackson Administration. Americans were growing more and more apprehensive about entrusting letters or packages to the mails. As Postmaster General O'Brien has said: "We are in a constant race with catastrophe, and it is a race that we well may lose."

Meanwhile, the Post Office Department continued to demand more and more self-service from its patrons. Early in 1966, for instance, the Department issued an order that all houses in new developments throughout the country would have to place their mailboxes at the curbside and that door-to-door delivery would no longer be provided in such areas. The order affected approximately 7 million Americans, most of them living in suburbs. Protests were loud enough to cause the House Appropriations Committee to grant sufficient funds to permit a partial modification of the order.

In an interview in the Scripps-Howard newspapers (December 9, 1966), Postmaster General O'Brien was quoted as saying that the greatest improvement in the mail service would come when "we achieve widespread acceptance of the ZIP Code." He added that, at the time, only 53 per cent of the population was using it. Soon after, on January 1, 1967, bulk users of the mail were forced to employ ZIP Code addresses on mailed periodicals, thereby necessitating abandonment of old "addressograph" plates.*

In March, 1967, the House Appropriations Committee reduced O'Brien's budget request for fiscal year 1968 by approximately $100 million, claiming that the Postmaster General was overestimating the volume increase for the coming year. This was a surprising decision in view of the runaway

---

* One trade magazine, with a mailing list of 190,000, paid $40,000 to make this change-over. The cost for larger users of the mails has been proportionately higher.

volume increase in fiscal year 1967. The Post Office Department has often made mistakes in the almost impossible business of predicting future volumes, but its errors in estimation have usually been on the conservative side.

1967: The Postmaster General's Proposal

On April 3, 1967, in a speech delivered to a group of publishers in Washington, D.C., Postmaster General O'Brien virtually admitted that it had become almost impossible to administer the postal establishment under current conditions, citing the frustrating division of authority and the proliferating laws and regulations, many of them contradictory, that Congress has set around the Post Office during the years. He suggested that the Post Office Department be abolished. In its place, O'Brien proposed creation of a government-owned nonprofit corporation along the lines of the Federal Deposit Insurance Corporation or the Tennessee Valley Authority. The establishment would be governed by a board of directors appointed by the President and an executive officer appointed by the board. The influence and interference of Congress in postal matters would be eliminated, except to the extent that funds would be appropriated each year to cover the nonpostal costs that the establishment incurs in performing services of social value for the people as a whole. Congress would set the formula for postage rates for each class of mail and would then leave its administration to the corporation. Rates would be adjusted automatically as costs rose or fell.

The reaction of Congress to the Postmaster General's proposal has so far been respectful but noncommittal. There is no sign of enthusiasm, even though the President seems to have given it his tacit approval. Many questions are, of course, being raised.

In 1859, a bill to abolish the postal establishment actually was considered by the House Post Office Committee, but in a report dated January 21, it was rejected as "inexpedient." Seventy years before that, in 1789, there was strong doubt among the founding fathers about the wisdom of having a government-operated postal system. In 1967, the Postmaster General on the job felt the same way. For the moment, at least, the U.S. Post Office seemed to have come full circle.

Part III

POSTAL OPERATIONS TODAY

VIII

Functions of the Department

In its formative years, the functions of the Post Office Department were few and simple: to make provisions within the post offices for the collection of outgoing letters and packets, to transport mail between post offices, and to make incoming mail available for the patrons to pick up. The postage was usually collected upon delivery, from the recipient, although it was possible to pay in advance, whereupon the postmaster in the dispatching office would write "Paid" on the outside of the letter.

Letter carriers were available in the larger post offices, but they were not paid by the government. As described earlier in this book, they depended for their livelihood upon their fees, which were set at two cents for every letter they delivered. Most citizens avoided this expense, preferring to make the journey to the local post office to collect their mail.

On August 2, 1858, the Post Office extended its service to the public by authorizing, in New York City, the use of mailboxes into which patrons could deposit their letters and have them collected by post office personnel rather than having to go to a post office to dispatch a letter. The experiment proved popular and was soon placed in effect in several large cities.

In 1863, when Montgomery Blair was Postmaster General, Congress, at his urging, authorized the institution of free delivery service; from July 1 of that year, city patrons were able to

have their mail delivered to their door by salaried letter carriers. This innovation was an important development in what
remains today the basic function of the Post Office: to move a
letter as safely and as quickly as possible from sender to recipient.

How a Letter Goes Through the Mails

The principal way that the Post Office Department can
make its operation more economical is to cut down the number of handlings that a letter must undergo on its journey
from one person to another. Fewer handlings, of course, mean
fewer employees and also represent savings in time. At one
time, it was estimated that an average letter underwent as
many as forty-five handlings before it reached its ultimate destination. Improvements in techniques and in machinery have
gradually whittled that figure down. In January, 1967, the
Post Office Department estimated that—in cases where a letter
was sent between two cities with the most modern and most
highly mechanized facilities—the number of handlings might
be as low as twenty-two.

The following tells the story of what happens to a letter
mailed under such ideal (but rare) conditions:

1. Letter is deposited in street mailbox.
2. Letter is removed by collection-route driver at next col-
   tion time indicated on box.
3. Driver delivers sack of collection mail to receiving
   platform at post office and deposits sack on preferen-
   tial-mail conveyor belt running under platform.
4. Belt delivers mail to preferential slide in mail-prepara-
   tion area of workroom floor.
5. Sack is removed from slide and emptied into hopper
   of culling belt, where oversize and extraneous matter
   from collection mail is removed.

6. Letter proceeds to edger-stacker machine and automatically feeds through facer-canceler.

7. Trayed letters from canceler are placed on tray conveyor and moved to sorting area, where trayed mail is introduced into the electronic presorter, which segregates addresses readable by machine from those that are not.

8. Assuming address can be read by machine, letter is then passed automatically before the optical-scanning unit, which refers address information to a memory system that in turn indexes the letter-sorting machine to deposit the letter in one of the 279 destination sorting bins.

9. When a light signal indicates the bin is full, a clerk removes the stack of sorted letters, ties them on a tying machine, and places the bundle on a belt for transport to the pouch rack, where another clerk deposits them in a pouch labeled for the city of destination.

10. Immediately prior to the departure of transportation to the place of destination, the pouch is closed and moved to the dispatch platform by conveyor belt.

11. Pouch is transported to destination by railroad, star-route truck, or airplane as appropriate.

12. At place of destination, inbound pouch is received on preferential conveyor belt and over preferential pouch slide.

13. Pouch is emptied into hopper of conveyor belt, and the bundles are cut, trayed, and placed in feed line of multiposition letter sorter.

14. Letter is fed automatically before an operator who reads address and, by actuating keyboard, keys letter to sorting bin corresponding with zone or carrier station of delivery.

15. All letters for each delivery station are similarly

processed and sorted for the appropriate letter carrier.

16. Letters for the delivery route are removed from the sorter bin, tied, and deposited in a sack labeled for a specific route.

17. All sacks for the delivery stations are dropped on a conveyor, transported to the station dispatch platform, loaded on a designated truck, and taken to the carrier station.

18. The sack of letters for a given route is left at the distribution case of the particular carrier who will make delivery.

19. The carrier manually sorts all letters for his route to correspond with the sequence of delivery.

20. After all mail has been sorted, the carrier removes the letters from the case, ties the mail in large bundles, places them in a transport cart, and moves them to the parking area.

21. The carrier places the letter bundles in the vehicle assigned to him.

22. The carrier proceeds to the beginning of his route and successively delivers all letters to their addressed destination.

It should be stressed that the foregoing describes an almost fully automated system that is not yet in wide use. At some older facilities and at installations where volumes do not warrant use of conveyor systems for preferential mail, letters for processing and dispatch are transported on regular industrial trucks. Even at the Post Office Department's most up-to-date facility (in Detroit), the presorter and optical-scanning units are on limited test assignment. The multiposition letter-sorting machines are customarily employed only for the distribution of originating letter mail. The operators of these machines can distribute letters to 279 destinations (see point 8 above). Some residual mail must be manually redistributed to the destination office or sectional center.

By fiscal year 1965, there were 6,091 post offices in the nation with city delivery, about 138,000 regular career letter carriers, and approximately 45,000 career substitutes.

SPECIAL DELIVERY

On March 3, 1885, Congress added to the regular handling of letters another service: special delivery. Through it, upon payment of an additional fee, the user of the mails could be assured that his letter would be delivered almost immediately after its arrival in a post office, no matter what time of day or night. For many years, special delivery was treated as something sacrosanct in the postal service. When John Wanamaker was Postmaster General, for example, he decreed that if there were no carriers in a post office when special delivery mail arrived, the postmaster should get in a hack and deliver the letter in person. Wanamaker also ordered an investigation when he found that it took ten hours for a special delivery letter mailed in Philadelphia to be delivered to an address in New York City.

By 1951, this service had grown to its high point; that year, 124,594,148 letters were handled in special delivery. Since then, unfortunately, the Department has raised the fees and decreased its concern for special delivery, and today the service is of little value except for getting a letter or a package delivered outside of normal working hours. Special delivery letters are too often dispatched with the routine post and are delivered just like any other mail. When special handling is given to special delivery, the letter will usually arrive after the ordinary mail has been delivered. Under these circumstances, it is not surprising that by 1965, special delivery dwindled to 90,100,471 pieces. In other words, in a period when the over-all volume of the mail was increasing by 51 per cent, special delivery volume decreased by 28 per cent.

RURAL FREE DELIVERY

John Wanamaker is generally given the credit for being the father of three important functions of the Post Office, although all three came into being after he left office. The first of these was rural free delivery. Decades before the federal government became concerned about the problem, Wanamaker foresaw the difficulties that would ensue from the concentration of U.S. population in big cities. He sought to develop ways of making life more attractive in the rural areas of the nation, and one important way of doing this, he thought, was to give rural people the same mail service their compatriots in the cities were getting. He continually urged Congress to institute free delivery to rural patrons, to relieve them of the necessity of traveling long distances to a post office every time they wanted to pick up or send off mail.

Congress responded to his prodding cautiously. The politically powerful small-town postmasters were fighting the program, since the development of free delivery in rural areas would inevitably mean the shutting down of thousands of small post offices throughout the country. During the last two years of Wanamaker's administration, the House of Representatives was under the control of hostile Democrats, and he had no chance to put his idea into practice.

Finally, on March 3, 1893, the day that Wanamaker left office, Senator Thomas E. Watson of Georgia was able to get Congress to appropriate $10,000 for experimental rural delivery. However, the succeeding Postmaster General, Wilson S. Bissell, a Democrat who was more than a little jealous and resentful of Wanamaker's reputation as an administrator, did everything he could to undo what his predecessor had accomplished. He was especially scornful of the rural free delivery idea and refused to implement it even when Congress appropriated another $20,000 to finance the project (July 16, 1894).

Two years later, after Bissell had left the scene, Congress added still another $10,000 to the fund (October 1, 1896), and the Postmaster General of the time, William L. Wilson, decided to experiment with five rural routes in his home state of West Virginia. The experiment was such a success that within nine months there were eighty-two routes in operation, involving forty-three post offices. The average route extended twenty-one miles and served 258 persons.

During the early years of the present century, rural carriers greatly outnumbered city carriers (in 1915, the ratio was 43,718 to 33,062). But as the population trend moved toward the cities and as the automobile replaced the old horse-drawn delivery wagon and roads improved in quality, it became increasingly possible to consolidate routes and increase the distance each carrier traveled. Consequently, their numbers were reduced. In fiscal year 1965, there were 30,981 rural routes, extending 1,890,953 miles, or an average of about 61 miles per route.

The small-town postmasters had been correct in their prediction about what the growth of the rural service would do to their ranks. In 1901, there were 76,945 post offices in the country; in fiscal year 1965, only 33,624.*

PARCEL POST

In 1912, Congress passed legislation establishing the parcel post service. Of all the Wanamaker ideas, this had been met

---

* Even today, some of the country post offices are almost incredibly small. In 1953, in the mountains of West Virginia, an office was discovered in which the postmistress's only patrons were her husband and their young daughter. She was being paid a government salary for receiving and distributing mail for her immediate family. Her post office was, of course, shut down and replaced by rural service. A postmistress in a small mountain office in Kentucky recently told me that she could shout from her front porch and be answered by three postmasters in three different offices.

with the most determined opposition. The conservatives attacked the proposal because they considered it socialistic—unwarranted government competition with private enterprise. The railroads and express companies opposed it because it would interfere with their lucrative, and often extortionate, monopoly. Local merchants fought it because they felt they would be losing business to the big mail-order houses. The only ones who wanted parcel post, it seems, were the people—and it took them a long time to prevail.

Even so, from the very beginning, parcel post has been loaded down with such crippling restrictions and fussy regulations that it has always operated at a disadvantage. The principal impediments to its successful operation are the regulations limiting size and weight and the stipulation that parcel post must operate within 4 per cent of a break-even point financially. Whenever it fails to do so, the rates must be increased.

In 1966, because of high rates and sometimes infuriating technical regulations, parcel post was on the verge of extinction. Legislation was enacted to alleviate the situation, but at this writing, it appears doubtful that the 1966 law will have the salutary effect that its sponsors had hoped for.

Over the years, parcel post laws have been written and amended in a very haphazard fashion, and many abuses of the service have taken place. In 1916, for example, the citizens of Vernal, Utah, decided to build a bank of their own. The bricks had to be shipped from Salt Lake City, 150 miles away. When it was discovered that the parcel post rates were less than half the freight rates between the two communities, the bricks were sent from Salt Lake City to Vernal, two or three bricks at a time, by parcel post. The influx of brick parcels strained the facilities of the Vernal post office and reduced the local letter carriers to a state of exhaustion, but the bank still stands—two stories high, covering most of a city block. While Vernal was building its bank, farmers in Utah caught the idea and started sending their produce to market by parcel post. In desperation, the Post Office Department, without even consulting Congress, hurriedly issued a regulation putting a limit of 200 pounds on the weight of parcel post that one individual could send another in a single day.

POSTAL SAVINGS

Another of Postmaster General Wanamaker's desires had been to put the Post Office into the banking business. The postal savings idea originated in England during the 1840's but was long opposed in the United States by powerful banking interests. In every year from 1877 to 1886, legislation was introduced in Congress to add this service to Post Office functions, but none of the bills ever reached the floor for a vote. At the time, there was great need for such a service. Banks were few and far between and had little interest in the small depositor. Small-town banks were usually unprotected by insurance and, in many cases, capriciously operated. In addition, millions of immigrants, particularly from central Europe, had brought with them to the United States a deep-seated distrust of banks and would have nothing whatever to do with them. As a result, many citizens were hoarding their money in unlikely and unsafe places, and millions of dollars were lying idle, not working for anyone.

Wanamaker campaigned vigorously for a postal savings system on the English model, one that would enable citizens to deposit their money in a local post office with the assurance of the protection of the federal government and the satisfaction that their deposits would be earning 2.5 per cent interest every year. The opposition was too strong for him to see his idea adopted during his term of office, but the way was cleared for eventual acceptance by his aggressive campaigning.

The bank failures of 1907 brought the postal savings plan back into focus, and finally, on June 25, 1910, Congress approved legislation enabling the Post Office to assume a major function that was not in any way connected with the business of communication. During the Great Depression, when the banks once again began to fail, postal savings became immensely popular. For a time, the Department found itself operating, as a sideline, one of the largest deposit banks in the nation. The figures for the Depression years tell the story:

Year	Number of depositors	Amount of money deposited	Average principal per depositor
1929	416,584	$ 153,644,529	$368.82
1930	466,401	175,271,686	375.80
1931	770,859	347,416,870	450.69
1932	1,545,190	784,820,623	507.91
1933	2,342,133	1,187,186,208	506.88
1934	2,562,082	1,197,920,188	467.56

The postal savings system reached its height in 1947, when 4,196,517 Americans had $3,392,773,461 on deposit, for an average balance of $808.47. However, by that time, the usefulness of the system had already diminished. The Federal Deposit Insurance Corporation had made most banks safe for depositors, and the banks themselves had become far more friendly toward the small depositor. Postal savings depositories were almost all concentrated in the larger cities, where dependable banks existed, so there was no longer the factor of greater accessibility. The reasons for the federal government operating its own banking system in competition with private enterprise had disappeared.*

* In 1953, investigation disclosed that the postal savings system was being used for strange and frivolous purposes. At some East Coast beaches, people who didn't want to pay for renting a locker would deposit their cash in the local post office, change their clothes on the beach, and, after swimming, return to draw their "deposits" out. Horseplayers guarded against being stranded at race tracks by depositing just enough money in local post offices to pay their fare home. Obviously, such practices were not what John Wanamaker had had in mind.

On March 28, 1966, the postal savings system was officially discontinued by an act of Congress. On that date, approximately $60 million in unclaimed postal savings deposits held by more than 600,000 depositors was turned over to the Treasury Department. The deposits will be held in a trust fund by the Treasury until liquidated. Postmasters were expected to continue for at least a year to assist depositors in submitting their claims to the Treasury for payment. They were also authorized to furnish lists of names of persons who still had funds on deposit in the postal savings system to newspapers and other organizations in order to help accelerate withdrawals.

POSTAL MONEY ORDERS

During the Civil War, Postmaster General Blair was responsible for an innovation that extended the functions of the Post Office in another direction and also proved to be a tremendous success. While the fighting was in progress, citizens complained bitterly about the uncertainty of sending currency through the mails, particularly to relatives and friends in the military service. At the Postmaster General's behest (May 17, 1864), Congress approved the establishment of the money order system, through which patrons, for a small fee, could, with confidence, forward limited sums of money anywhere within the United States (at first the limit was $30, later it was raised to $50).

The money order system was a godsend in wartime and became even more popular during the years of peace. The figures for the first decade of its existence, given on page 200, indicate that it filled a great need in American life.

It should be remembered that banks were scarce during this period—relatively unapproachable for the poor—and were used by only a small portion of the populace. But even when banks did become more accessible, the system flourished.

Year	Number of post offices issuing money orders	Amount of money orders issued
1865	419	$ 1,360,122
1866	766	3,977,259
1867	1,224	9,228,327
1868	1,468	16,197,858
1869	1,466	24,848,058
1870	1,694	34,054,184
1871	2,076	42,164,118
1872	2,452	48,515,532
1873	2,775	57,516,216
1874	3,069	74,424,854

The highest level of acceptance of the money order system was reached in fiscal year 1953, when transactions came to $6.6 billion. There has been a considerable diminution in the use of the system in recent years because of higher fees charged for the service. Nonetheless, in 1965, $4.5 billion worth of money orders were issued in 44,586 post offices, stations, and branches.

NONPOSTAL FUNCTIONS

During World War I, the Post Office, because of its ubiquitous role in American life, was called upon to perform a bewildering number of nonpostal functions *pro bono publico*. Characteristically, the wartime Postmaster General, Albert Sidney Burleson, regretted and resented each and every one of them because they upset his accounting and cost the Department money. But these were services that the Post Office, alone among the institutions of the U.S. Government, was equipped to perform, and there was no way the Postmaster General could avoid the responsibility of their performance. The postal establishment sold Liberty bonds and war savings certificates. Post offices registered enemy aliens. They handled, without charge, millions of tons of government mail, such as draft questionnaires and appeals for food conservation. Every third- and fourth-class postmaster was automatically made a recruiting officer, and every post office, by law, became an employment agency for war industries. These functions were performed with commendable efficiency, despite the fact that post offices were generally shorthanded during these years.

Another function assigned to the Post Office during World War I was that of censorship. At the urging of President Wilson, Congress passed legislation providing for partial censorship of the mails (Act of June 15, 1917). The law (which, in this case, did not go as far as the Postmaster General wanted) was aimed mostly at printed matter and limited the opening of first-class letters to the Dead Letter Office of the Post Office Department and to postal inspectors who had search warrants. (Wilson also proposed censorship of the press, but Congress, on June 1, 1917, turned him down.) On October 6, 1917, Congress passed the Trading with the Enemy Act, which permitted censorship of foreign mail and required foreign-language publishers to supply translations to postmasters of all articles dealing with the government or with the conduct of the war. On May 16, 1918, the censorship laws were toughened and extended even further.

Burleson interpreted the censorship laws far more broadly than Congress had intended. He hired a corps of 1,700 censors, and, on the average, 125,000 pieces of mail were opened by the Post Office every day.* For the most part, the World War I censors performed their duties with great arrogance and became extremely unpopular with the public. As soon as possi-

* The Postmaster General capriciously determined what should or should not be declared mailable. He was vigorous in banning from the mail all material he considered in any way "socialistic," including many union publications that were merely liberal. Books describing the horrors of war were arbitrarily banned from the mails. So was all material criticizing Great Britain's policies in India and Ireland. Thorstein Veblen's *Imperial Germany and the Industrial Revolution* was declared nonmailable at the very time that the government's Committee on Public Information was trying to arrange for its publication serially in the daily press as part of the official propaganda program.

ble after the armistice was signed, Congress voted to take the
Post Office Department out of the censorship business.

During World War II, the Post Office once again assumed
the burden of numerous extracurricular functions. However,
it was not entrusted, except to a very minor degree, with the
responsibility of censoring the mails.*

Over the years, in addition to major nonpostal functions
assigned to the Post Office in wartime or emergency functions
assumed during major national crises, there has been a steady
accretion of minor federal functions that have been made the
responsibility of the Department, mainly because, in most
communities, the post office is the only federal office in town
and the center of local activities.

The list of these functions is almost endless. It includes the
following: alien address reporting; sale of U.S. savings bonds;
issuance of civil service information; sale of documentary and
migratory-bird stamps; maintenance of "wanted" posters issued by the Federal Bureau of Investigation; provision of
notary public services; assisting the authorities to locate relatives of deceased servicemen; witnessing of the marking of
absentee ballots; receiving and transmitting funds for volun-
teer charities, such as the Heart and Cancer funds and the
March of Dimes. Whenever the federal government wants to
communicate with its citizens, it turns to the Post Office, which

* The Department did engage, on a temporary basis, an expert in Japanese
and another in Russian to look through a sampling of publications in those
languages sent through the mails. The two men were given relatively high
salaries and assigned to a cubbyhole in the old Post Office building, across
the street from the Department's present quarters. There they remained, and
there they were forgotten. After the war, whenever anyone entered (always
by mistake) their office, they would pick up their foreign-language papers,
and the intruder, thoroughly intimidated, would leave. In 1958, a management expert finally discovered that they had been collecting salaries but
performing absolutely no duties for thirteen peacetime years. The management expert told the author that he caught on only because their Japanese
and Russian newspapers had grown yellow with age. They had been too
lazy and too careless to replace them! They were finally declared "re-
dundant" and relieved of their nonexistent duties.

has become a kind of clearinghouse of American democracy.

The annual cost of these nonpostal functions cannot be accurately ascertained, and they are always a point of contention whenever the Postmaster General wants to increase postage rates. Since most people agree that the expense of performing these services should be borne by the taxpayer rather than by the users of the mails per se, the advocates of low postage rates are inclined to exaggerate the cost of nonpostal functions, while the Department is inclined to minimize it. In addition to the specific nonpostal functions already described, there are numerous others that the Department performs, such as providing free mail services for the blind and free-in-county delivery of newspapers. The large mail users once estimated the cost of these "welfare" functions to be as high as $392.4 million. The Department estimated the cost as low as $29 million. The answer, of course, lies somewhere between these two wildly disparate figures.

In the heat of the legislative battle over the interpretation of costs, the large users of the mails pointed to the fact that the Postmaster General is forbidden by law to contract for the transfer of mail from the railroads to other forms of transportation if rail service, no matter how inadequate, is available. This obsolete arrangement costs the Department a great amount of money and tends to impair the service. The large users of the mails maintained that the extra cost created by this restriction should be considered nonpostal expenditure, since it amounted to a hidden subsidy to the railroads. The Post Office Department did not agree. There were many other similar areas of total disagreement.

THE IMPORTANCE OF BUSINESS MAIL

The functions of the Post Office Department not only have grown considerably in number over the years but also have changed in character. The postal service, which was originally intended as a means of communication for the exchange of news, ideas, and information, has become the major channel through which American commerce flows. It is estimated that 80 per cent of all first-class mail today is business mail. More and more, because of the remarkable tradition of integrity and dependability that the postal service has developed, the mailman has become, in a very real sense, the paymaster of America. As Jerome J. Keating, president of the National Association of Letter Carriers, has pointed out:

More and more firms are centralizing and automating their financial operations and are sending their paychecks through the mails.

Old-age pensions are delivered through the mails.

More than 21 million people receive Social Security checks, totaling $19 billion a year, through the mails.

Almost 800,000 civil service annuitants receive $900 million in checks each year through the mails.

Almost 1.25 million veterans receive their pension checks, amounting to more than $2 billion a year, through the mails.

Almost all those receiving annuity checks from private industry, insurance companies, labor unions, and beneficial societies receive them through the mails.

Insurance premiums and insurance settlements are paid, for the most part, by mail.

Welfare checks are almost universally sent through the mails.

Most federal, state, and local income and other taxes are paid through the mails.

More and more, because of congested traffic conditions, Americans are banking by mail.

Most of America's bills are paid by mail.

And, of course, the financial community sends billions of dollars in the form of stocks, bonds, securities, and investment certificates through the mails.

In short, the Post Office Department estimates that trillions of dollars pass through the hands of its employees each year, and the postal service has altered its basic functions considerably. Instead of merely providing the principal means of communication between private citizens, it has also become the indispensable organ through which the financial, commercial, and mercantile communities of the nation conduct their business.

IX

Organization of the Department

When the Post Office Department began its operation under
the Constitution, the question of organization was a minor
matter indeed. The establishment was small and mail volume
insignificant. The problem was not structure but survival.
When Congress finally agreed that the Post Office should be
a permanent part of the government (1792), it placed the
service under the control of the Treasury Department. The
Postmaster General had an assistant and a few clerks. All
reports and, eventually, all funds due to the General Post
Office were forwarded to the national capital.

As this book has described earlier, the organization of the
postal service evolved in curious ways. John McLean, who
was Postmaster General from 1823 to 1829, was not the sort
of person on whom subservience sat easily, and he began the
practice (without either precedence or authority) of reporting not to the Secretary of the Treasury but directly to the
President. Nobody objected, and by the time of John Quincy
Adams, McLean's bold gambit had become a tradition. Then,
under Jackson, the Postmaster General became a cabinet officer, and in the eyes of the executive branch, if not the legislative, the Post Office was accepted as a department of government.

SECOND, THIRD, AND FOURTH ASSISTANTS ADDED

In the meanwhile, by the Act of April 30, 1810, Congress had created the office of second assistant postmaster general; the second assistant presided over the transportation of the mails, chiefly negotiating the Department's contracts with stagecoach companies and postriders. The first assistant postmaster general was concerned only with the actual operations of the establishment. When, under President Andrew Jackson, the Post Office Department became a political mechanism and the first assistant postmaster general found himself deeply involved in the hiring and firing of postmasters, much to the detriment of the efficiency of the service, a third assistant postmaster-generalship was created to take care of finances (Act of July 2, 1836). That, at least, was the official description of the function of the third assistant; in actuality, he had to take care of duties (loosely defined and overlapping) not being performed by the Postmaster General and the other two assistants.

Postmaster General John Wanamaker, both an innovator and a builder, envisaged the future growth of the postal service and argued strenuously for decentralization of its operations. He foresaw the problems that would ensue from strict centralization, with every postmaster in the country reporting back to one desk in Washington, and urged that a certain degree of autonomy be granted to responsible officials in the field. As in so many other instances, Wanamaker was decades ahead of his time, and his arguments were ignored by both Congress and the White House. However, he was able to develop the idea of building branches and stations in large cities so as to mitigate the overcrowding inevitable when all the mail for a given city was handled in one general post office.

He embarked on the first major building program that the Post Office Department had ever undertaken, and as the real estate problems of the establishment developed, it became apparent that a fourth assistant postmaster-generalship had to be created to take care of this new situation. Congress acceded to his request by the Act of March 3, 1891.

As the nineteenth century drew to a close, the top staff of the Department consisted of the Postmaster General, who usually was also the principal professional politician of the dominant party; the first assistant, who was charged with the responsibility of conducting the operations of the establishment (and of carrying out the political manipulations considered necessary for the welfare of the administration); the second assistant, who controlled the highly important transportation contracts; the third assistant, who busied himself with financial matters; and the fourth assistant, who was in charge of the building, acquisition, and maintenance of postal facilities and, later, of all postal property, including vehicles.

Although this arrangement seemed, on paper, straightforward enough, the overlapping of duties remained troublesome. In practice, the ranking of assistant postmaster-generalships in a numerical pecking order gave the first assistant's domain a degree of precedence over the other bureaus, often throwing the over-all operation of the establishment out of balance. (Since all functions of the Department could technically be classified as being part of postal "operations," there was some logic to this arrangement.)

Meanwhile, of course, the postal establishment was growing at a fantastic rate, and its operations were continually hampered by overcentralization. Postmasters were obliged to seek the permission of Washington for even the most minor deviations from the Procrustean regulations issued by the Department. And since the Department could not possibly evaluate individual requests intelligently, the answer to such requests was almost always negative.

In 1908, the Overstreet Commission, headed by Representative Jesse Overstreet of Indiana, recommended, in the strongest possible terms, that the Post Office Department decentralize and regionalize its operations. The recommendations were ignored, and the relationship between headquarters and the field continued to worsen, at great expense to the effectiveness of the service and to the American taxpayer.

After World War II, when the postal volume rose dramatically, the obsolete centralization of the postal establishment imposed a grotesque burden upon its efficiency. All 41,000 postmasters were reporting directly to Washington and had to await replies to their plaintive requests before they could purchase typewriters and adding machines, for example, or even repair a broken windowpane.

HOOVER COMMISSION RECOMMENDATIONS

In 1947 and 1948, the Hoover Commission (which, under the direction of former President Herbert Hoover, was making recommendations for the reorganization of the government at the request of President Truman) looked with considerable horror upon the administrative monstrosity of the Post Office Department and urged sweeping reforms, including, first and foremost, immediate decentralization of its operations.

Postmaster General Jesse M. Donaldson, a career man, a former postal inspector, and an extreme conservative in postal matters, accepted only a few of the Hoover Commission recommendations and those halfheartedly. He was most stubborn in his opposition to decentralization of authority. In fact, he insisted that almost everything affecting the service pass across his own desk and be subjected to his own personal scrutiny. The bottleneck in Washington became so bad that an intradepartmental memorandum was issued informing personnel that all unanswered correspondence that was more than two years old should be declared "dead" unless there had been a follow-up to the original letter. The postman, in short, had to knock at least twice before he could get an answer.

The typical reply was written in stilted language and based on the strictest and most conservative interpretation of postal regulations.* The letters were written and sent out by bureaucrats who did not have the slightest knowledge of or, often, interest in the local conditions that had prompted the request.

In preparing the departmental budget, it was common practice at headquarters automatically to cut all requests from postmasters by 10 per cent, without regard for the merits of the individual cases. Postmasters who were sophisticated enough to see through this system habitually padded their requests in anticipation of the reduction. They were able to run their offices competently. Those who were scrupulously honest in their budget requests were not so fortunate.

Donaldson did go along with one of the Hoover Commission recommendations. Embodied in the President's Reorganization Plan Number 3 (approved by the Congress in 1949), it created the position of deputy postmaster general and eliminated the numerical order of precedence of the four assistant postmasters general and, instead, designated them by their functions—operations, transportation, finance, and facilities. The idea was that the deputy should be a career man and would therefore survive the political mutations within the Department. (This system was followed in the British Empire and is followed today in most of the new nations that were formerly part of it.) The deputy postmaster general was to represent permanent career management in a constantly changing political milieu.

Of course, it did not work out that way. The political pressure on the Post Office was too strong. The first deputy postmaster general, an honorable and respected postal professional,

---

* Every office in the Post Office Department was provided with a "precedent" file, a huge book of letters covering every conceivable situation that could arise in the postal service. They were designed to discourage imaginative thinking and to eliminate any possibility of a feeling of warmth between the field service and headquarters. Like the old "Mother Hubbard" dresses, they covered everything and touched nothing.

Vincent C. Burke, took office on October 21, 1949, but was "retired" as soon as the Republicans recaptured the White House, in 1953. In the eighteen years that the office has been in existence, there have been eight deputy postmasters general. This was not the intention of the Hoover Commission. The deputy has been as changeable as the Postmaster General— and for the same political reasons.

The reclassification of the assistant postmasters general did nothing more than create a kind of formalization of the duties of the various offices. In theory, it made all assistant post-master-generalships equal in power, but since the assistant for operations controlled the distribution of approximately 90 per cent of the appropriations for the Department, all other assistants naturally yielded to him, at least tacitly.

During the Eisenhower Administration, Postmaster General Arthur E. Summerfield brought a new "business" concept into the postal establishment. The first Postmaster General since Wanamaker trained in the upper echelons of the market place, he found the recommendations of the Hoover Commission attractive, and he adopted most of them, with variations of his own. He was most successful in his wholehearted effort to decentralize postal operations. Summerfield, not without some justification, termed this effort the largest industrial reorganization program ever attempted, in or out of government, in the United States.

ATTEMPTED REORGANIZATION UNDER SUMMERFIELD

Summerfield hired an internationally known firm of management consultants to carry out the reorganization. This was a reasonable move, since the top echelon of the Post Office Department is so small (counting Presidential appointees, career executives, and key appointees from the civilian world, it amounts to fewer than thirty persons) that outside help is essential for any undertaking of this magnitude. The management consultants did an excellent job but either were almost totally unaware of the political implications in their work or thought them unimportant. They were, as a matter of fact, rather scornful and unmindful of politicians as they set about their massive task of reorganization. This attitude turned out to be a mistake.

The idea was to break down the postal service, eventually, into fifteen regions—with the regional directors having what amounted to autonomy in the areas under their control, subject to veto only by national headquarters—and to have experienced career men working in the field who would have the wit, will, and authority to correct errors on the spot and solve problems where they occurred. The regional directors would be chosen, for the most part, from the outside world, for it was felt that such men would bring to the Post Office Department the same degree of business know-how displayed by the new team that Summerfield had brought into the postal service.

It was a sound concept, but it did not work out. The Inspection Service, which had crept into management by the back door during Postmaster General Donaldson's administration, filling the vacuum of leadership in the field, opposed decentralization wholeheartedly. The inspectors did not want to have their newly assumed management prerogatives pre-empted. The high standards that the Civil Service Commission had set for the qualification of major regional officials made it hard to find executives to fill these jobs. Although the administration could induce any number of highly regarded business executives to spend some time in Washington, it could not attract people of comparable ability for jobs as regional directors in such places as Wichita or Memphis. But when Summerfield's assistants began to seek out the best talent within the postal career service to head up the regions, the Republican National Committee and the Republicans in Congress insisted that such high-paying jobs be given only to members of their own party. This restriction posed a serious problem, since few Republicans, after 1933, had risen to sufficient eminence in their local post offices to meet the requirements of the Civil Service Commission. Most of those still in the service who had held qualifying positions twenty years earlier were now old enough to anticipate retirement.

However, the postal inspectors were required by law to list their political affiliation when they joined the Inspection Service. The law says that a 50–50 balance must be maintained between Democrats and Republicans. When the Eisenhower Administration took over, the ratio was approximately 80–20 in favor of the Democrats. However, there were still approximately 200 certifiably Republican inspectors with executive experience in postal matters who could satisfy both the Civil Service Commission and the political "advisers." Thus, almost by default, the Inspection Service, which had originally opposed the entire program of decentralization, ended up by taking it over. Former inspectors soon dominated almost every region. In recent years, the situation has changed to a certain extent, as the Democratic administrations have been able to find enough Democratic postmasters and supervisors to staff the regional offices.

However, the hard core of executive leadership in the Post Office Department in Washington has resented almost every attempt by the regional officials to exercise the powers vested in them. It has been common practice for postmasters and postal employees to appeal regional decisions at the national level and win reversals. Prominent postmasters have ignored their regional officials almost entirely. The program did relieve the national headquarters of unnecessary paper work, and it did lead to quicker decisions in the field, but the overriding power remained right where it always had been—at Twelfth Street and Pennsylvania Avenue N.W., Washington, D.C.

When the Department first asked Congress for authority to decentralize its operations, the Democrats on Capitol Hill objected, charging that this was simply an attempt to build up a political machine in every section of the country. The Eisenhower Administration denied the charge, claiming that the staff at national headquarters would be greatly reduced and that there would be only small staffs in each region.

THE FIGURES TELL THE STORY OF WHAT HAS HAPPENED:

Year	Headquarters staff	Regional personnel
1952	1,851	—
1953	1,861	975
1954	1,789	1,104
1955	1,530	2,599
1956	1,343	4,418
1957	1,300	6,679
1958	1,329	6,277
1959	1,389	6,094
1960	1,481	6,491
1961	1,521	6,314
1962	1,626	6,309
1963	1,665	6,075[a]
1964	1,687	5,933
1965	1,849	5,505

[a] The sudden decline in regional personnel in 1963 can be attributed to the consolidation of a number of regional accounting offices at that time. Numerous accounting employees were transferred from the regional payrolls to the payrolls of local post offices.

It is obvious from the foregoing that a form of Parkinson's law has been at work. At first, the headquarters staff was steadily reduced as the regionalization program developed; but from 1958 on, there has been a steady increase in personnel in the Department, and today the level has returned to almost the exact point it was at before decentralization began. Meanwhile, the size of the regional staffs has grown steadily, since it was easier to superimpose functionaries of the "proper" political faith than it was to dismiss those of the "improper" political faith, many of whom had real, or at least arguable, civil service tenure.

Despite its obvious, almost comic shortcomings, the regionalization of the postal establishment has helped considerably to relieve the intolerable administrative bottleneck that had built up with the Department. Minor decisions are made more quickly in the field, and they make more sense than they did under the previous arrangement. However, the system falls far short of perfection, and major decisions are still made at the Washington level, often by people who have had no field experience and know nothing about the circumstances surrounding local problems. It is still difficult to get important policy decisions in the field, where the problems occur.

A FIFTH ASSISTANT IS ADDED

The organizational structure of the postal establishment was changed in another direction during Summerfield's administration, when permission was granted (Act of July 23, 1953) for the creation of a fifth postmaster-generalship, for personnel. It was high time for the Department, which employed more than 500,000 people and which spent more than 80 per cent of its appropriations on their wages, to add a bureau specifically occupied with the welfare of its employees. Unfortunately, the smothering hand of the Bureau of Operations has been upon the Bureau of Personnel, and despite the best intentions of its managers to date, it has remained a subservient and subsidiary function in the Department. (The usefulness of this bureau is almost irreparably impaired by the fact that it contains no experienced postal people.)

AND A SIXTH ASSISTANT

By the Act of July 5, 1966, the official "family" of the Post Office Department was again increased with the establishment of a sixth assistant postmaster-generalship, for construction and engineering. It is hoped that the added prestige given by this act to the research and development program of the Department will result in more realistic appropriations, to enable the postal establishment to keep abreast of the volume explosion that the American people have forced upon it.

In mid-1967, the organizational structure of the Post Office Department was as follows:

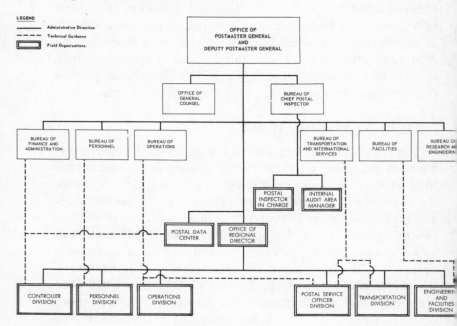

In addition to the six assistant postmasters general, whose separate duties have evolved as described above, a general counsel offers advisory opinions relating to laws prohibiting from the mails fraudulent, extortionate, or obscene matter, material pertaining to lotteries, subversive and propagandistic matter, and firearms. He may also initiate and prosecute cases involving infringement of any laws involving these issues. On the same administrative level is the chief postal inspector, who directs a force of about 1,100 men and advises the Postmaster General and his assistants on the condition and needs of the service and is responsible for the execution of policies, regulations, and procedures governing all investigations, operating inspections, and audits for the postal service. Another office of the postal service is that of the director of the Postal Data Center, who supervises the compilation of postal information and maintains, reviews, and verifies accounts, payrolls, taxes, and other operational aspects of the Department through modern data processing.

FOOTNOTE TO HISTORY

An interesting footnote to the organizational history and present status of the Post Office Department is revealed in the fact that, despite congressional reservations, the Postmaster General has always ranked fifth in seniority in the cabinet, behind the Secretary of State, the Secretary of the Treasury, the Secretary of War (now Defense), and the Attorney General. But old habits and old grudges die slowly on Capitol Hill, and Congress still includes Post Office appropriations in the same bill with Treasury appropriations legislation.

X

The Post Office and Congress

In the Constitution of the United States, signed on September 17, 1787, the seventh of the general powers delegated to Congress (Section 8) is to establish post offices and post roads. At the constitutional convention, the words "and post-roads" were added only after sharp discussion and by a close vote. There was considerable hesitancy about giving the new federal government too much power and thus endangering the chances of adoption of the new Constitution in the various states. After the Constitution was adopted, Congress decided that even though the form of the grant was limited, it was intended to authorize the legislative branch to create and regulate the entire postal system. The clause has been so interpreted ever since, and the Supreme Court has twice upheld that rather sweeping interpretation.

The peculiarly American system of checks and balances, as spelled out in the Constitution, serves the people well, but it also tends to create frictions between the legislative and executive branches of government. This has been particularly true for the Post Office Department, which became, over the years, the most political of American executive institutions.

During the first forty years of the life of the Republic, Congress concentrated on the building of post roads as a political contrivance. Almost every congressman's district needed roads, and the Post Office was the handiest means of fulfilling that need. The Post Office was used for opening up the wilderness, but it was also responsible for linking up some fairly improbable communities long before there was any hope of sufficient mail volume to justify the expense.

As described in Chapter III, after 1829, when Andrew Jackson made the Post Office an essentially political mechanism, and until the passage of the Ramspeck-O'Mahoney Act in 1938, the postmaster was the leading agent of the dominant political party in every city in the country. Before the passage of the Civil Service Act in 1883, all postal employees were also political appointees. Consequently, the postal work force became, in most instances, the hard core of the political machinery of the dominant party in every locality.

Since it was obviously impossible for the Postmaster General or the President to know the qualifications (political or professional) of the candidates for postmasterships in all the cities and villages throughout the country, it was natural for the administration to seek the advice of the local congressman (providing he was of the same party) before making a selection. If the congressman was of the opposition party, the local political leaders were consulted. The recommendations thus made were almost universally followed.

The Senate was not consulted in these matters. Senators were not directly elected by the people until ratification of the Seventeenth Amendment to the Constitution (1913) but were chosen by the legislatures of their respective states. Since they represented entire states rather than congressional districts, they were not expected to have the intimate knowledge of local conditions that congressmen had. The Senate, however, insisted on the right of confirming all Presidential appointees (1836) and thus managed to maintain a degree of control. If the Senate could not advise directly, it could—and still can—exert influence by withholding approval.

This system complicated the relationship between the Post Office Department and Congress, since it made minority congressmen hypercritical of the management of the postal establishment, particularly in their own districts, where their friends had been superseded by, or passed over for, their political enemies.

Unfortunately, even today, some congressmen (a minority) insist upon dictating who shall receive promotions within the post offices. If a congressman is sufficiently powerful so that his help is needed on legislation affecting the entire postal establishment, the Postmaster General has little choice but to accede to the request, often to the detriment of the service. A post office can survive an inefficient postmaster, but when an incapable person is placed in a key supervisory position, such as superintendent of mails, the service in that entire area can be in trouble.

THE POLITICAL CONSIDERATIONS

When, as often happens in off-year elections, the party in possession of the White House loses its majority in Congress, the difficulties of the Post Office Department intensify. At times, the obstructionism of a hostile Congress has made the management of the postal establishment almost a practical impossibility. There have been times when congressional leaders have tried to make the failure of the postal service a political embarrassment for the administration. (This was common during the nineteenth century, but there were also instances of it during the last two years of the Taft, Wilson, and Hoover administrations and during the last six years of Eisenhower's terms.) Obstructionism usually takes the form of inadequate appropriations, but it has also been manifested in the passage of crippling legislation contrary to the announced policies of the administration in power.

The Ramspeck-O'Mahoney Act of 1938 was the culmination of a continuing campaign, conducted over many years, to make the position of postmaster more professional than political. Woodrow Wilson, by an executive order (March 31, 1917), had made it necessary for candidates in first-, second-, or third-class postmasterships to pass an examination before appointment.* The examinations were not especially demanding, but they did determine whether a candidate could read, write, and do simple arithmetic. The President (upon the advice of the Postmaster General and also upon that of the local congressman) could then choose the most acceptable candidate from the top three who passed the examination. After the two world wars (especially after World War II), the system was seriously complicated by the veterans' preference laws, which made the political manipulation of postmasterships a far more delicate and hazardous business.

Congress has also devised means of circumventing the examination procedures. In the larger cities, it is possible for the Department (at the request of a congressman) to announce a "nonassembled" or "noncompetitive" examination. This arrangement is sensibly based on the premise that men of superior managerial talents are not going to compete for a postmastership by taking public examinations like schoolboys in a classroom. In these cases, a man is recommended and is privately examined by Civil Service Commission representatives to see whether his experience and managerial capacities measure up to the job. If he satisfies the questioners, he is appointed. He usually satisfies the questioners.

The Ramspeck-O'Mahoney Act brought postmasters under civil service. Today, technically, they are appointed for life (or, more accurately, until retirement), but there are still numerous loopholes in the law, and a vindictive administration, if it wishes, can get rid of any postmaster, in any city of consequence, any time it feels so inclined. Fortunately, during the two political turnovers since the passage of the act, both

---

* The President appoints postmasters to these offices. Fourth-class postmasters are appointed by the Postmaster General (upon the usual congressional advice) and are not subject to confirmation by the Senate.

the Republicans and the Democrats have generally had the common sense to resist the supplications of the spoilsmen.

During recent years, Congress has been more inclined than ever before to recommend career men for postmasterships, men who have come up through the ranks. In part, this change is due to the improved professional status of the postmaster, but it is also based on economic reasons. The position of postmaster, stripped by Ramspeck-O'Mahoney of its political prestige, today does not offer a salary sufficient to attract many men or women of outstanding talent from the civilian world, and so the talent search goes on more intensely among the ranks of the career employees. On the surface, this seems a healthy condition. However, there is serious doubt among career employees themselves about its over-all efficacy. Whether the postmaster is a career postal man or someone from the outside, his appointment remains inherently political. Often, the career man chosen is one who, over the years, has been more interested in carrying his precinct than in carrying the mails. A good career man can be a first-class postmaster, but, too often, his potential is blunted by inhibitions due to the long service and the allegiances he has accumulated within the Post Office during his long climb to the top.

In the Ninetieth Congress, early in 1967, Senator A. S. "Mike" Monroney, a Democrat from Oklahoma and chairman of the Senate Committee on Post Office and Civil Service, and Representative Ray J. Madden, a Democrat from Indiana, introduced legislation that, if passed, would take the appointment of postmasters and rural letter carriers completely out of the hands of Congress and out of the realm of politics. As these words are being written, the bill has passed the Senate with little opposition but is facing strong opposition in the House of Representatives, where, under the present system, the real power of patronage lies. The legislation is thoughtful and carries the sponsorship of the Civil Service League. There seems to be little chance for its acceptance at this time.

THE FISCAL CONSIDERATIONS

The most constant source of friction between the Post Office Department and Congress is appropriations. Until 1836, the Post Office Department operated on monies deposited, through revenues, in the Post Office Fund of the Treasury. When Postmaster General Barry, as described earlier in these pages, depleted that fund through overgenerous allowances to mail contractors, Congress became alarmed and moved to assume more direct control over postal finances. The Act of July 2, 1836, determined that: (1) all postal revenues would thereafter be paid directly into the U.S. Treasury instead of into the Post Office Fund; (2) the Postmaster General would thenceforth submit, in advance, an itemized budget estimate for the ensuing fiscal year, with the allocations divided into relatively "watertight" compartments, affording little opportunity for any juggling of accounts; and (3) Congress would thereafter appropriate monies for the Post Office Department each year out of Treasury funds. This unwieldy system, with minor modifications, is still in effect today and thus gives Congress the power of determining the direction and extent of postal operations.

From time to time, postmasters general have sought from Congress the right to operate the Department on a normal business budget. Such a system would undoubtedly make for more sensible administration, since it would permit the postal establishment to use its own revenues (supplemented by appropriations to cover the cost of the nonpostal or public service functions) and to engage in the long-range planning necessary for prudent management. The Hoover Commission suggested this change, and Postmasters General Summerfield and O'Brien also requested it. But so far, Congress has insisted on retaining its financial prerogatives.

The unwillingness of Congress to allocate postal funds more than a year in advance has severely crippled the mechanization program of the Department. The Post Office is, after all, a monopoly and is therefore the only customer for the types of machines it needs for the specialized and unique jobs it must perform. But the development of such machines costs a great deal of money, and industry is reluctant to gamble on developing highly specialized machines when the only possible customer for them might be unable to purchase them after they are developed. New leaders of an appropriations subcommittee might decide to curtail expenditures and make such purchases possible. Even when the Department has entered into contracts for the development of new machines, Congress is inclined to get suspicious of possible conflicts of interest between postal management and the industry involved. In such a political atmosphere, there is little incentive for private industry to risk its resources on the development of postal machinery.

THE DETERMINING COMMITTEES

The relationship between Congress and the Post Office Department is pretty much that of master and servant. Congress sets the rates of postage and determines how much the postal employees shall be paid. It determines what fringe benefits shall be allowed the employees and to what extent. It also insists upon the right of being consulted on all major policy changes. Since the public determines what the volume of mail shall be, this leaves the Postmaster General with little control over the fate of the huge enterprise he is supposed to direct.

The Department must deal, primarily, with two committees in each house of Congress. The Committee on Post Office and Civil Service concerns itself with rates, wages, policy, fringe benefits, and related matters. The Committee on Appropriations (or, to be more specific, the Subcommittee on Post Office and Treasury Appropriations) controls the purse strings and, in so doing, has more than a little to say about the formation of policy. The situation is further complicated by the fact that, especially in the House, the Post Office Committee is inclined to be more liberal in its approach to postal matters than is the Appropriations Subcommittee. Thus, the Committee on Post Office and Civil Service will upon occasion order improvements in service or in working conditions that the Appropriations Committee is unwilling to support with funds. This naturally leaves the management of the Post Office Department very much in the middle.

Congressional opinion has varied widely over the years on such issues as the extent and use of free mail, the treatment of the government employee force in comparison with workers in private industry, and the desirability of maintaining a federally operated postal establishment. Indeed, Congress has changed its mind on several occasions on the basic question of whether the postal establishment should be operated as a service, a business, or a public utility. In 1794, 1844, 1851, 1930, 1958, and 1962, Congress defined and supported the service concept of the Post Office. Intervening congresses permitted that policy to lapse or embraced the public utility concept. Whatever else is to be said on either side of this long-standing disagreement over what course the Post Office should follow, the lack of a consistent philosophy has certainly not been helpful to those who have had to manage the postal establishment.

On April 3, 1967, as noted in Chapter VII and elsewhere, Postmaster General Lawrence F. O'Brien startled Congress and the nation by recommending, in a speech to a gathering of magazine publishers, that the Post Office Department be abolished and replaced by a government-owned nonprofit corporation along the lines of the Tennessee Valley Authority or the Federal Deposit Insurance Corporation. He urged that Congress establish a firm policy on the kind of service the corporation should provide and then leave the management of the mails to a board of directors appointed by the President and a professional executive appointed by the directors. Because of the great respect in which O'Brien is held on Capitol Hill, the proposal was received courteously by the leadership of the Congress but with an almost total lack of enthusiasm. As yet, there is no indication that Congress is willing to relinquish one of its oldest, most troublesome, but also most intriguing prerogatives.

XI

Problems of Today and Tomorrow

Adam Smith once wrote that the Post Office as a public industry is the only mercantile project that somehow has been managed successfully by every sort of government. So far, history has proved him right—but sometimes by only the narrowest of margins. Besides, he was speaking of a type of postal service entirely different from that the United States has today.

Certainly, the Post Office in the United States has been the magnificent invalid. At times, its management has been brilliant, but it has survived many periods of gross mismanagement and flagrant, widespread corruption. It has endured the depradations of the spoilsmen and the most cynical and primitive political interference in its affairs. But the serious mail crisis of October, 1966, during which even first-class letters were delayed in the Midwest for as long as three weeks, proved that disaster can overtake the invalid at almost any time.

The principal problem of the postal establishment is its indispensability. Everybody depends on it. Everybody must use it, and the amount of use is dictated by the public, not by the management. Congress may control the volume somewhat by increasing the rates and the Post Office Department by making the service less attractive, but it is the citizenry, through its mailing habits, that determines what the volume is going to be. And the citizenry can be capricious. The figures on page 229 show that the mail volume has increased over the past twenty-five years out of all proportion to the increase in population.

On February 27, 1967, in hearings before the House Appropriations Subcommittee, postal officials estimated that the mail volume in fiscal year 1968 would reach 83 billion pieces, or 415 pieces per capita. They may have been conservative in their prognostication.

How to Handle Swelling Volume

The proliferating use of the mails leaves the Post Office Department with four choices:

1. To continue operating more or less as it has been for the past 190 years, increasing the work force to handle the swelling volume and depending on improved employee efficiency to keep the number of workers within reasonable bounds

2. To decrease the number and the quality of the services that the Post Office performs for its patrons, thereby obviating the need for a continually growing work force

3. To abolish the Post Office Department, as Postmaster General O'Brien has suggested, creating a federally owned corporation in its place and thereby permitting the government more or less to wash its hands of the whole problem

4. To develop and install, on a nationwide basis, more efficient and more sophisticated machines and techniques, thereby increasing production while making fewer demands on manpower

To Continue as Before?

The first possibility is unthinkable. The productivity of postal employees may improve slightly with each passing year, but not nearly in proportion to the expanding volume, which at present is increasing almost three times faster than the ability of the employees to handle it. If this trend were permitted to continue indefinitely, half the people in the United States

GROWTH OF THE MAIL SERVICE, 1940–65

Year	Population (millions)	Mail volume (millions)	Employees	Pieces per capita	Pieces per employee
1940	131.7	27,750	353,157	210	78,329
1950	150.7 (+14.4%)	45,064 (+62.4%)	500,578 (+41.7%)	298 (+41.2%)	89,948 (+14.8%)
1960	179.3 (+19.0%)	63,674 (+41.3%)	562,868 (+12.4%)	356 (+19.5%)	113,098 (+25.7%)
1965	192.0 (+ 7.1%)	71,873 (+12.9%)	595,512 (+ 5.7%)	374 (+ 5.1%)	120,795 (+ 6.8%)
Total increase	45.78%	159%	68.6%	78.1%	54.2%

would eventually be working in the postal establishment delivering mail to the other half.

Curtailment of Service?

The second course has been the one followed recently by postal management, at the insistence of the Bureau of the Budget and the appropriations committees of Congress. There has been a relentless diminution of postal services during the past quarter century. The number of deliveries has been drastically reduced, helpful operations have been abandoned, window hours in post offices have been curtailed, and users of the mails have been called upon to perform more and more functions for themselves.

This trend has given a distorted picture of the productivity of postal employees. Postmaster General O'Brien, for example, estimated that productivity had increased 400 per cent since 1890. The fact is that there is no way that one can measure productivity in a service organization. The Post Office Department has reduced the amount of service each employee can render to the individual patron to such an extent that, on paper, the productivity of the employee appears to have increased. Each employee handles more pieces of mail a year because he performs fewer services in doing so.

However, there is a point beyond which curtailment of services cannot go, especially in view of increased postage rates. The public has been remarkably patient, but it is possible that the conduct of the U.S. mails could make the postal service a serious political issue in a national election—as it was in 1876, 1884, and 1920. Also, further curtailments might have a deleterious effect upon the national economy.

The Corporate Approach

A corporation such as Postmaster General O'Brien has proposed would be a government agency, with a budget subject to annual review, and would provide many protections for the user of the mails. But the plan poses many questions. For example, what would be the attitude of a corporation (even a government-owned nonprofit one) toward unremunerative postal services? Would the money-losing rural delivery service be abandoned or curtailed? Would unprofitable third- and fourth-class post offices be closed? Would city delivery be maintained and extended according to community needs?

Postal employees are puzzled as to what their status would be if a corporation were their employer. Would they still have the protection of civil service status? What would happen to the hard-won benefits they have gained over the years? What would happen to their salaries? If their right of appeal to Congress were taken away from them, they reason, they would, of course, demand the right to strike, and that would open up a new world of problems.

The large users of the mails also have their doubts. What would happen to postage rates under a corporate setup? Would they skyrocket to a point where only the most affluent users of the mails can stay in business? Would first-class postage be increased so that the Post Office would be less accessible to the average citizen?

Moreover, no experienced observer really believes that Congress will ever be persuaded to keep its hands entirely off the postal establishment, especially since it would be called upon to make annual appropriations to cover the public service costs of the corporation. Corporation or no corporation, no congressman worth his salt is going to stand mute if the postal service in his district is inadequate or the postage rates too expensive for his constituents.

It should be noted that the O'Brien proposal is not a new one. It has been suggested seriously in the United States on at least three previous occasions, and a similar plan is now being tried in Great Britain. In any case, the question is academic. Congress shows no inclination to follow the O'Brien proposal at this time.

Mechanization?

The fourth choice, that of developing new machines and new techniques, is, in this writer's opinion, the one on which postal management must principally depend if the postal service is not to collapse under its own weight. Much has been attempted along this line, and much is planned. It may be a case of too little and too late, but a start has to be made somewhere. Unfortunately, until 1953, almost no sustained effort was made to mechanize and improve the techniques of handling mail. Sorting and distribution processes were almost the same as they had been half a century previously. Worse still, many important postal facilities were too small and too old to permit the installation of modern machinery.

Arthur E. Summerfield, during his administration, did make a beginning on mechanization. It was not as successful as he— or the public—had hoped it would be. Some of the machines imported from postal systems abroad (such as the "Transorma" from Holland) proved to be impractical in the United States. Other experiments, such as the highly mechanized (and publicized) postal facility in Providence, Rhode Island ("Operation Turnkey"), developed so many operational bugs that they had to be extensively rebuilt and redesigned.

Summerfield never was able to get from Congress the money necessary to implement his program of modernization. Many of the machines he felt he needed had not even been invented, and he was accused by the appropriations committees of being too visionary and flamboyant in his approach to the problem. The failure of some of his early experiments helped to discourage further investment of public funds. But he did focus attention on the need for mechanization, and he was able to establish in the Post Office Department, for the first time, a respectable research and engineering division (1958) to make plans for coping with the problem.

The three postmasters general since Summerfield have had

somewhat better success with mechanization. They have received more sympathetic attention from Congress and have been able to develop a program that—given the money, the imagination, and the opportunity—will reduce the number of individual handlings given each unit of mail as well as the manpower demands within the postal establishment. The raising of the Division of Research and Engineering to the status of a full-fledged departmental bureau, with a Presidentially appointed assistant postmaster general in charge (as was done in 1966), may give it the impetus and the prestige necessary for success.

In the decade 1957–67, the Post Office Department spent approximately $100 million on mechanization—a substantial sum, but nowhere near the amount that private industries of comparable size have spent in the same area. (In 1963, the sum expended was only $224,000.) Consequently, the mechanization of the postal establishment is still in its infancy.

As this is being written, postal management is confident that optical scanners and automatic sorting machines (which will be able to "read" addresses without the aid of the human eye) will eventually eliminate the need for postal clerks to perform these services.* It is estimated that these mechanical devices, working in concert (with the assistance of the ZIP Code system), will be able to sort letters for 1,000 different cities at a rate of 36,000 units an hour.

Postal management also estimates that, eventually, 80 per cent of all first-class mail will be handled in post offices by automatic devices requiring minimal attention from human beings. (This figure is based primarily on the rough estimate

* Such devices, however, have been promised for many years. During Summerfield's administration, an automated scanner could do a reasonably good job of "reading" certain typewritten addresses. Unfortunately, it could not distinguish between a postage stamp and such nonnegotiable substitutes as Easter seals and was ultimately rejected. The sorting devices currently in use still show an 8 per cent factor of error. This is far below the acceptable standard of accuracy demanded of a human postal clerk.

that 80 per cent of all first-class mail is business mail and is therefore typewritten. No one has suggested a machine that could deal with the vagaries of human chirography.)

By 1965, 204 automatic facer-canceling machines had been installed in seventy-two post offices throughout the country, yielding (according to Department estimates) a return of 46.8 per cent a year on their original investment. The Department also hopes to increase the efficiency of these machines by 14 per cent by treating airmail stamps with a luminescent coating that will activate the mechanism and separate such letters from ordinary first-class letters. Some of the new devices are incredibly complicated. One of them has 400,000 separate parts as compared with only about 4,000 parts for the average automobile. The specifications for the machine consume 300 pages of text and are supplemented by 1,900 drawings. Automatic devices will also be used for sorting parcel post packages.

These are all significant developments—or could be, if they turn out to be as practical as postal management hopes. But, of course, they must be widely installed throughout the country if the over-all service is to benefit.

The chairman of the Post Office Subcommittee of the House Committee on Appropriations, Representative Thomas Jefferson Steed, a Democrat from Oklahoma, has blamed the political power of the postal unions for the reluctance of Congress to approve massive mechanization of postal facilities. He has claimed that the postal unions resent and resist any program of mechanization that would cut down their potential membership.

There is little evidence to support this contention. On the contrary, there is much evidence to refute it. The problems of mechanization and automation do not seriously concern the letter carriers, for example. After all, none of the proposed improvements foresees the replacement of the human being who walks the city sidewalks delivering letters to the houses along his route. It is true that postal clerks will be affected by the growth of automation. They represent the area where savings in manpower and expense can and must be made if the postal work force is going to be kept within reasonable limits in the face of mushrooming growth in mail volume. But E. C. Hallbeck, president of the United Federation of Postal Clerks, a responsible leader with more than forty-six years' postal experience, takes a reasoned approach to the problem, asking that "technology not be permitted to outrun . . . ethics" in the rush toward mechanization and that "the enormous power of the cybernetic world . . . be the handmaiden of society, not its master." His concern is for the postal clerks now on the rolls or who will be on the rolls when the automation program reaches fruition. He is, in short, devoted to protecting the rights and the welfare of those whom he has been elected to represent and is not attempting to stand in the way of progress.

The indication is that it is not the unions but Congress that is opposing or neglecting the modernization of postal facilities and the installation of advanced machines throughout the system. But postal management is also to blame, for it lacks the boldness to seek sufficient appropriations for the "industrial revolution" it delights in predicting. For fiscal year 1966, for example, the Department asked for only $16.1 million for research and development, less than three-tenths of 1 per cent of its total expenditures. At the same time, the Department asked only $17.8 million for constructing, leasing, or refurbishing new facilities (down from $70 million in 1961). Despite a volume increase of more than 150 per cent, up to 1966, not one major postal facility had been built in a large Eastern city since before World War II.* The postal plant in Chicago, which became choked with piled-up mail during the crisis in the autumn of 1966, was built in 1933. Mail volume

* A new postal facility is now under construction on Third Avenue in New York City.

in that city has increased by about 400 per cent since that time.

PROBLEMS WITH OTHER AGENCIES

The operation of the postal establishment has been complicated in recent years by the emergence of the Bureau of the Budget and the Civil Service Commission as policy-making agencies. Both have consistently shown more interest in cutting down postal expenses than in improving and developing postal services.

The Bureau of the Budget, which came into being as a result of the Budget and Accounting Act of June 10, 1921, had a humble beginning. Its function was not to participate in policy-making but merely to approve or disapprove appropriation requests before they were sent to Congress. As late as 1930, the Bureau of the Budget had only forty employees. But under Franklin D. Roosevelt and his Budget Bureau director, Lewis W. Douglas, all that was changed. The Budget Bureau was expanded, and Douglas was invited to attend cabinet meetings and participate in some cabinet decisions.

Roosevelt became "quite horrified" (his own words) by the zeal of some of his agency heads in asking legislation without first getting proper clearance from the White House. On December 13, 1934, upon instructions from the President, Donald Richberg, executive director of the National Emergency Council, issued a memorandum to all agency heads reminding them that all legislation "carrying appropriation measures" had to be cleared first by the Bureau of the Budget and that all "other proposed legislation" must be first cleared through the Council.

This arrangement proved unsatisfactory, so on December 21, 1935, Budget Circular 336, issued "by direction of the President," ordered that all agency proposals for legislation and all reports on pending legislation, including all oral testimony before committees, should be cleared through the Bud-

get Bureau "for consideration by the President" before sub-
mission to Congress. The circular enlarged the influence of the
Bureau of the Budget far beyond the area of appropriation requests. Ever since, the Bureau of the Budget has played a
dominant part in the definition of federal policies, including,
of course, those of the Post Office Department.

The Bureau of the Budget has forced upon the Department
a succession of "economies" that have eroded the service. It
has also consistently opposed granting postal employees a
wage structure comparable to that of private industry. Since
good postal service depends to a large extent upon the recruit-
ment and the retention of capable and dependable employees,
this insistence upon sterile economy has made it almost impossible for the Department to operate at desirable levels of
efficiency.

The Civil Service Commission is a more recent entry in the
policy-making field. Its original function was to administer the
Pendleton Civil Service Act of 1883, to ensure the job security of career postal and federal workers, to protect them
from political interference, and to administer the pay and em-
ployee-benefit programs authorized by Congress. It, too, has
changed in many ways. Since the accession of the Kennedy-
Johnson administrations, the chairman of the Civil Service
Commission has joined the director of the Bureau of the Budget as official spokesman for the President in attempting to
discourage legislation that would improve postal services or
raise postal wages.

When the conservative policies of the Civil Service Commission made it difficult for postmasters to recruit competent employees into the service, the Commission's answer was to lower
the entrance requirements so that less competent applicants
could be hired. Postmasters in communities where the cost of
living is high have publicly complained that they have to rely
upon "warm bodies" for the operation of their offices. Serious
service impairment is inevitable under such circumstances.

Postal work demands intelligence and experience if it is to be performed adequately. It cannot be performed adequately by incompetents or by casual laborers.

The situation of the post office employee vis-à-vis the Civil Service Commission has taken an ironic turn as a result of these developments. Postal employees once considered the Civil Service Commission their shield and ally. The Commission does continue to perform many useful services essential to the welfare of the employees. But on fiscal policy matters, postal employees today consider the Civil Service Commission one of their natural enemies.

On October 2, 1967, while testifying before the Senate Committee on Post Office and Civil Service, John W. Macy, Jr., Chairman of the Civil Service Commission for six years, and before that a ranking executive of the Commission, admitted, under questioning, that he had no idea that postal employees have to begin their careers as substitutes and remain in that capacity for several years, on the average, before achieving status as regular employees. Postal employees can be excused for believing that ignorance of their basic conditions of work indicates a lack of interest in their welfare.

These developments have placed the management of the Post Office Department in a delicate and uncomfortable position. The Bureau of the Budget and the Civil Service Commission have more influence in the federal government in setting the fiscal policies of the Post Office Department than do the officials of the Department. Under such conditions, the Postmaster General has no choice but to go along with the official policies of these two agencies. This compliance is inescapable, but it has made the efficient operation of the Post Office Department almost impossible.

THE PROBLEM OF POSTAGE RATES

One continuing problem of the Post Office Department is how much the government should charge for the services that the postal establishment performs. Should the Post Office pay its own way? Or should it be regarded as a service to all the people of the United States and be subsidized as other such federal services to the general public are subsidized? Are postage rates intended to defray the expenses of the Department? Are they a form of taxation? Or are they merely intended to keep the postal volume within reasonable limits?

Congress has repeatedly approved legislation enunciating the service concept as the policy of the government—most notably in 1851, 1930, 1958, and 1962. Many postmasters general, the Bureau of the Budget, and, in recent years, the Civil Service Commission have generally favored the public utility, or "break-even," principle.

In 1967, the federal government was once again making a determined attempt to raise postage rates in all categories in order to keep the postal deficit within reasonable limits. Almost everyone, including the largest users of the mails, agrees that some increase is necessary and even desirable. But how much of an increase can the traffic bear? The difficulty with raising postage rates is that first class (i.e., letters) is where the volume is and therefore where the money is. It is also where the voters are, and Congress is habitually reluctant to increase the rates in this category.

It is common belief that the way to end the continuing financial crisis of the Post Office Department is to increase the postage rates on second- and third-class mail to a point where these categories will be able to operate on a break-even basis. Unfortunately, the problem is far more complex. It even includes almost complete disagreement as to where the break-even point lies.

Resistance to postage rate increases often centers around the fact that first-class mail, according to the Post Office Department's Cost Ascertainment Division, usually makes money— or, to be more accurate technically, produces revenues in excess of its allocated costs. The Cost Ascertainment Division estimates that first-class mail is now paying 103 per cent of its costs. Historically, it has averaged about 113 per cent. However, most objective critics of the Post Office Department discount the Cost Ascertainment figures to a considerable extent, since the methods employed in evaluating volume and costs in post offices are too haphazard to provide an adequate base for detailed statistical conclusions.

The arguments on this subject are endless. However, it should be pointed out that the entire mechanism of the postal establishment was set up primarily to handle first-class mail. The hundreds of thousands of letter boxes throughout the country are maintained and serviced by postal personnel solely for the deposit and collection of first-class mail. First-class and most second-class mail is given immediate and preferential treatment in post offices, while the other classes of mail are deferred and handled during periods when postal employees have no other pressing duties to perform.

It must be remembered that the principle of differential pricing applies to the postal service as it does to every other form of merchandising. First-class mail receives many time-consuming and expensive services that are not given other classes of mail and should therefore cost more per unit than other classes. This is the principle that applies to air transportation (first class versus coach), to the telegraph and telephone industries (day versus night rates), to selling time on radio and television (Class "A" time versus Class "B"), and so on.

Second-class mail contributes only 3 per cent of the total postal revenues but accounts for approximately 11 per cent of the total postal volume. The Department's accountants claim that this class of mail pays about 35 per cent of its allocated costs. Second class, which is mostly newspapers and magazines, receives preferential "red tag" treatment, often superior to the treatment afforded first class. It has been estimated that, in the case of *The Wall Street Journal* alone, red tag treatment costs the Department as much as $20 million a year. However, publishers are called upon to perform many of the services that post offices might perform. Magazines are presorted according to ZIP Code specifications. They are bundled and tied and often deposited directly on trains without even passing through a post office. Some large publishers even arrange for their own truck transportation between cities and leave to the local post office only the job of delivering their product after its arrival.

The tradition of permitting newspapers and magazines to go through the mails at rates below cost is older than the Republic itself. Benjamin Franklin, it will be remembered, sought and accepted the position of postmaster of Philadelphia because this would permit him to send his own newspaper through the mails on his personal frank. When he became deputy postmaster general for the colonies, he extended the right to the use of the mails at below-cost rates to all papers and periodicals.

The practice was encouraged during the nineteenth and early twentieth centuries. The United States was still fundamentally a frontier country. Public education was by no means universal. The newspapers and journals performed a vital social function in keeping the public informed. When Abraham Lincoln was postmaster at Salem, Illinois, in 1833, he considered one of the major attractions of the position the fact that he could better his education by reading the newspapers and journals before delivering them to his patrons.

Today, the proponents of higher second-class rates insist, the importance of the social and educational functions of newspapers and magazines has diminished, since citizens depend on their television and radio sets for the news as much as they do on the printed word. Is it logical, these critics ask, to subsidize the publishers and not the manufacturers of radio and television sets?*

---

* The publishers maintain that below-cost postage rates permit them to sell their product more cheaply to their subscribers. The subsidy is therefore not to the publishers but to the American people. When this argument

The revenues from second-class mail in fiscal year 1966 came to only $126 million, out of a total of $4.4 billion. If an attempt were made to force second-class mail to meet all its allocated costs, the rates would have to be raised approximately 300 per cent. This step would force all but the most prosperous of the publishing enterprises out of business, so that little or nothing would be added to postal revenues. Even if the rates were raised by that amount and if all the publishers were somehow able to remain in business, the total revenues accruing to the Treasury from this class of mail would be increased by only 350 million, or less than 8 per cent of the total revenue. Clearly, a too drastic increase in second-class rates would harm the publishing industry far more than it would help the Post Office Department and would also price the surviving publications beyond the reach of many Americans.

Third-class mail, which returns to the Treasury approximately 70 per cent of its allocated costs, is, for the most part, advertising matter. In fiscal year 1966, it was responsible for 26.7 per cent of the volume and 15.3 per cent of the revenues of the Department. Such mail is given such deferred treatment that it often takes as long as twenty-eight days to travel from coast to coast.

Third-class-mail users, like magazine and newspaper publishers, must perform many postal functions. Bulk mail, for example, must be presorted at the mailer's expense, not only according to city and state, but by 551 postal sectional offices and by 6,000 zones prescribed by the Department's ZIP Code system. When the Post Office Department ordered all bulk mailers to adopt modern electronic techniques for ZIP Coding

---

was presented during Summerfield's administration, an assistant to the Postmaster General replied: "That is like saying that the loss we sustain on the sale of migratory-bird stamps is a subsidy, not for the hunters, but for the birds."

their products, the cost of this to industry was estimated at $250 million.

The whole problem of the economics of postage rates is a complicated and difficult one. Too drastic an increase in rates will discourage the users and will result in a decrease not only in volume but also in revenues. If Congress were to increase third-class rates to a point where they were competitive with first-class rates, then the largest users of the mails would feel justified in sending their material first class and insisting that the post offices give it the same meticulous, expensive treatment that all other first-class mail receives. This would create chaotic conditions in the postal service and could make the serious breakdown that occurred in the Middle West in the autumn of 1966 look relatively insignificant. The establishment does not have and cannot get enough competent help to handle such a load.

Postmaster General Summerfield recommended to Congress that it set a formula by which each class of mail would be able to pay a predetermined percentage of its allocated costs and that the rates thereafter be adjusted by a Presidential commission in accordance with the formula. The scheme fell through because there was no hope of reaching an agreement on what the percentages for each class of mail should be or on what the allocated costs for each class actually were.

The picture has been further confused by the growth of the third-class mail industry into the second-largest advertising medium in the United States. The industry (which for all practical purposes came into being in 1928, when Congress, at the request of the Post Office Department, created bulk third-class mail) now employs approximately 5 million persons on a full- or part-time basis and, according to the U.S. Department of Commerce, generates $35 billion in sales each year.

This development has drawn the competitive fire of certain newspaper and magazine publishers envious of the advertising dollars being poured into third-class mail. Congressional thinking, understandably, has been greatly affected by this editorial barrage against third-class mail, which has come under attack as worthless junk, a nuisance, an invasion of privacy, and even a menace to the morals of the nation and the economy of the postal service.* During the postage rate controversy of 1967, the campaign of second-class-mail users against third-class-mail users fell below any recognizable standards of fair play.

There is rarely any objectivity in evidence when Congress takes up the subject of adjusting postage rates. Even the newspapers that advocate an across-the-board rate increase, including second class, are usually those with little or no out-of-town circulation and are not dependent upon the post offices. A rate increase would hurt their competitors without injuring their own position.

There is no magic formula for creating a postage rate structure that will be fair to the taxpayer and the users of the mails. The problem of rate adjustment will remain one of the thorniest that postal management faces as long as the postal service exists. Certainly, as the 1967 round of rate increases once more proves, Congress shows no indication of increasing the rates on first-class mail without raising rates on second- and third-class mail. Anyone who proposed or supported legislation to this end would be risking political oblivion.

The question that has persisted over the years is: Should a matter as technical and as complicated as this, vital to the economy and the social welfare of the nation, be settled by persons who are admittedly not experts in the field, in a political atmosphere? If not, what means would achieve more satisfactory results and still safeguard the interests of the citizenry?

---

* Ironically, many of the publishers who attack third-class mail employ it when they embark on programs to promote circulation.

Parcel Post Rates

One category of mail that does not have its rates set in a political atmosphere is parcel post (fourth-class mail)—and it is in perennial trouble. When parcel post was instituted, in 1913, Congress was concerned about the competition it would give privately owned express companies. It decreed that the Postmaster General must set the rates for parcel post through petitioning the Interstate Commerce Commission but that this class of mail must operate within 4 per cent of its break-even point. Today, whenever parcel post fails to meet this criterion, its rates must be raised. Congress, over the years, has also encumbered parcel post with fussy and confusing regulations that make it unattractive to the average potential patron. Whenever parcel post starts losing volume to the privately owned express companies and the revenues decline, the rates must be increased, thus causing further reductions in volume and revenues. Congress, over strong objections from the express companies, has relaxed the rules somewhat in recent years, but not nearly enough to ensure the survival of this useful class of mail. Parcel post remains the "sick man" of the postal service. Unless significant remedial steps are taken, it will wither away.

Speed Versus Consistency

It may also be true that the Post Office Department would do better if it were to concentrate less on the *speed* of the mails and more on the *consistency* of the mails. Speed has little benefit to the user of the mails unless he can depend upon it. As this is being written, the transmission time for a letter between, for example, New York City and Washington, D.C., is very uncertain. Half the time, the letter will arrive the next day; the other half, it may take two or even three days.

This inconsistency, which is widespread throughout the

service, causes serious embarrassment to many business users of the mails. Merchants who depend upon a profit on discounts through prompt payment, stockbrokers, bankers, businessmen who are paying interest on substantial loans, and many others who must consider the time factor in their business operations are often victimized by the unreliability of the service. The average user of the mails—and certainly the average businessman—could tolerate a little less haste in exchange for a great deal more dependability.

As This Is Written . . .

The Post Office Department is suffering from the "economies" and the delays in necessary spending that have been forced on it over the years. The problem grows worse with each year of neglect, and its solution becomes potentially more and more expensive. Its present ills can be cured only if the executive and legislative branches of the government, as well as the American people themselves, give priority to the allocation of funds for the restoration of its well-being. The Post Office returns to the Treasury approximately 85 per cent of its appropriation; the remaining 15 per cent is, in effect, a sound investment in the economy of the country. Although the postal deficit has become a major target for public criticism, few declaim against the much larger deficits of other agencies of government.

There are several basic ways in which a nation is judged and evaluated by its peers. Is its currency sound? Are its banks safe? Is its civil service honest and dependable? Is its transportation prompt and trustworthy? Is its mail service swift and reliable? In this last regard, the United States has failed to maintain the norms of other nations of comparable importance. Even allowing for the problems peculiar to the U.S. postal establishment, such as the distances to be traversed, the exploding and shifting population, and the enormous volume to be handled, the over-all performance of the postal service falls short of what the citizens have every right to expect.

The handful of really great postmasters general in U.S. history—Hazard, McLean, Kendall, Blair, Wanamaker, Hays, Farley, and perhaps one or two others—dared to break the inhibiting patterns of the past and thereby extended and improved the service. Postmaster General O'Brien has shown the determination to follow that same pattern of achievement, despite the frustrating influence of the more conservative elements in the executive and legislative branches of the government. In the face of suppressive budgetary restrictions, he has been imaginative in his planning for today and tomorrow.

O'Brien has announced that it will take a minimum capital investment of $1 billion a year for five years to put the postal establishment on a modern basis. This amount may seem high, but the Postmaster General's estimate of the fiscal needs of the future are, if anything, modest—if the wage scale of the postal service is to be made competitive with that of private enterprise in the race for competent talent; if the machines for electronic processing of mail are to be developed, produced, and installed; and if the physical plant is to be reorganized and, in many cases, rebuilt or relocated.*

In addition, more attention needs to be paid to the problem of training a competent supervisory postal force. Supervision in the postal establishment is very weak compared with the standards maintained in the private sector, and the Department has no program for training its supervisors.†

The postal establishment today is enmeshed in paper work.

---

* Many members of Congress have been much to blame for misplacement of post offices. They have too often insisted on civic monuments in the heart of a community rather than working mail factories strategically located far from the strangulating crush of urban traffic.

† In fiscal year 1966, the Department asked for (and was refused) an appropriation of $2 million to train supervisors in procedures for negotiating local labor-management contracts with employees under their direction. There was no request for money to train supervisors in procedures for moving and delivering the mails more efficiently.

There are more than 13,000 different forms in use throughout the service. The average postal supervisor or employee finds himself filling out these interminable pieces of paper instead of working at the basic task of moving the mail from point A to point B. Far too much time, money, and energy are spent counting the mail, measuring it, weighing it, evaluating employee performance with stop watches, determining employee attitudes, evaluating employee skills in irrelevant areas of activity, and accumulating unnecessary statistics. Far too little time, money, and energy are spent getting the mail delivered as quickly, consistently, and efficiently as possible. Thousands of people are employed in relatively useless jobs instead of in performing the functions for which the postal service exists: the collection, transportation, and delivery of the nation's mail.

In the opinion of this writer, Postmaster General O'Brien's proposal that the Post Office be turned into a government-owned corporation is not the answer to the problem. The Post Office is so much the people's business that it always should be immediately supervised by the people's elected representatives. But Congress must learn to distinguish more clearly between supervision and interference, and it should permit the best practices of the private sector to prevail in the postal establishment.

There is no reason why a vast and essential government service cannot be operated as efficiently as a privately owned public utility. Just because it is a service is no reason for it to be managed in a slovenly fashion—as a patronage-dispensing machine first, a bureaucratic organism second, a whipping boy for unimaginative government accountants third, and only incidentally as the essential element it is in the social and economic life of the American people.

Appendix A
Summary of the Most Important
Laws Concerning Postage Rates
(1789–1967)

Act of February 20, 1792 (1 Stat. 232). Effective June 1, 1792, this was the first postage rate law enacted under the Constitution. It fixed the base rates as follows: single letter (one sheet of paper, folded), not exceeding 30 miles, six cents; from 30 to 60 miles, eight cents; from 60 to 100 miles, ten cents; from 100 to 150 miles, twelve and a half cents; from 150 to 200 miles, fifteen cents; from 200 to 250 miles, seventeen cents; from 250 to 350 miles, twenty cents; from 350 to 450 miles, twenty-two cents; more than 450 miles, twenty-five cents. Double letters cost double; triple letters, triple. Every packet weighing one ounce was paid for at the rate of four single letters going the same distance. (The packet rates went up in proportion per ounce.) Letters transported by packet ship, either overseas or to other U.S. ports: eight cents single, sixteen cents double, twenty-four cents triple. All newspapers: one cent up to 100 miles; one and a half cents for more than 100 miles.

Act of May 8, 1794 (1 Stat. 359–66). Authorized for the first time the use of letter carriers, imposing a two-cent surcharge on all letters delivered. (The two cents went to the carrier.) Liberalized newspaper rates made it possible to send a paper anywhere within a given state for one cent.

Act of March 2, 1799 (1 Stat. 734, 738–40). This law raised postage rates as follows: single letters, up to 40 miles, eight cents; from 40 miles to 90 miles, ten cents; from 90 miles to 150 miles, twelve and a half cents; from 150 miles to 300 miles, seventeen cents; from 300 miles to 500 miles, twenty cents; more than 500 miles, twenty-five cents. Packets were paid for at quadruple rates

249

up to one ounce and in that proportion for any greater weights. Packets weighing more than three pounds were not mailable.

Act of December 23, 1814 (3 Stat. 159). Effective February 1, 1815. This act increased all rates of postage by fifty cents to help pay for the war with England.

Act of February 1, 1816 (3 Stat. 252). Effective March 31, 1816. Repealed the rate increases of December 23, 1814.

Act of April 9, 1816 (3 Stat. 264). Increased postage rates: single letters, up to 30 miles, six cents; between 30 and 80 miles, ten cents; between 80 miles and 150 miles, twelve and a half cents; between 150 miles and 400 miles, eighteen and a half cents; more than 400 miles, twenty-five cents.

Act of March 3, 1825 (4 Stat. 105, 111, 112, 114). Renewed rates of 1816 (with minor changes) and regularized the rate structure.

Act of March 3, 1845 (5 Stat. 733, 737). Effective July 1, 1845. This act significantly simplified the zone system of postage rates. Single letters, under 300 miles, cost five cents; more than 300 miles, ten cents. Double letters cost double. Parcels of a half ounce or less cost the same as a single letter. Rates increased with each half ounce. Newspapers of not more than 1,900 square inches in size were transported free of charge up to 30 miles; larger newspapers, two and a half cents up to one ounce, any distance; one cent extra for every additional ounce. Pamphlets, magazines: two and a half cents a copy up to one ounce and one cent for every additional ounce, regardless of distance. Packets weighing more than three pounds were not mailable.

Act of March 3, 1847 (9 Stat. 200–202). Authorized the use of adhesive stamps for the prepayment of postage. It also subjected all newspapers to postage except those sent as exchanges or sent out under an authorized frank.

Act of March 3, 1851 (9 Stat. 587–89). Effective June 30, 1851. Simplified the rate structure by virtually doing away with the zone system of postage charges. Single letters, up to 3,000 miles, three cents prepaid, five cents not prepaid; more than 3,000 miles, double rates. Weekly newspapers: free within county where published; out of county, up to 50 miles, five cents per quarter. The newspaper rates went gradually upward to thirty cents per quarter for a distance exceeding 4,000 miles. Bound books were declared mailable, for the first time, by this act. Newspaper rates were also regularized.

APPENDIXES 251

Act of March 3, 1855 (10 Stat. 641). Effective April 1, 1855. Single letters, up to 3,000 miles, three cents; more than 3,000 miles, ten cents. This act made prepayment of postage compulsory. It also established registered mail, for a fee of five cents per letter.

Act of February 27, 1861 (12 Stat. 168, 169). Modified previous act, making the rate ten cents per half ounce on any single letter crossing the Rocky Mountains in either direction. This act also authorized the introduction of merchandise into the mails.

Act of March 3, 1863 (12 Stat. 704–7). This act eliminated the single-letter factor in determining postage and substituted the half-ounce factor. It divided mail into three classes: first class, letters; second class, publications issued at stated periods; third class, all other mailable matter. All letters, regardless of distance, three cents for the first half ounce and two cents for every additional half ounce. It eliminated the collection of the additional two cents for delivery by letter carriers, thus establishing (in certain cities) the principle of free city delivery. The weight limitation on packets was raised to four pounds. The rate for newspapers was set at five cents per quarter for weekly newspapers and went up progressively to thirty-five cents per quarter for dailies.

Act of June 8, 1872 (17 Stat. 296, 300–304, 308). Slightly rearranged the three classes of mail. Postage on newspapers of less than two ounces in weight was set uniformly at one cent per paper, except for weeklies, which retained the rate set in the previous act.

Act of March 3, 1879 (20 Stat. 358–61). Repealed all former laws regarding classification of mail. It divided mail matter into four classes: first class, letters, postal cards; second, newspapers and other periodicals; third, circulars, books, transient newspapers; fourth, all other matter, principally merchandise. First-class letters were to be prepaid at the rate of three cents per half ounce; postal cards, one cent. Second-class matter retained basically the same postage. Third-class matter cost one cent for each two ounces. Fourth-class matter cost one cent per ounce.

Act of March 3, 1883 (22 Stat. 455). Effective October 1, 1883. Reduced postage on first-class matter to two cents per half ounce.

Act of March 3, 1885 (23 Stat. 387). Effective July 1, 1885. Reduced the rate on first-class letters to two cents per ounce instead of per half ounce; reduced rate to one cent per ounce in communities where free city delivery did not exist. Special delivery was instituted by this law, with an added rate of ten cents per letter.

Act of July 16, 1894 (28 Stat. 105). Gave to publications issued by benevolent, fraternal, educational, or professional groups the same privileges as those given to other second-class mail.

Act of May 19, 1898 (30 Stat. 419). Permitted the use of private mailing cards, with postage of one cent apiece.

Act of August 24, 1912 (37 Stat. 550, 551, 553, 557). Effective January 1, 1913. Established the parcel post system, with an elaborate rate structure, and gave the Postmaster General authorization (subject to the consent of the Interstate Commerce Commission) to reform the rates in order to ensure that the revenues paid the cost of the service. The act also included regulations concerning the amount of advertising that second-class matter could carry and still retain its right to preferential rates.

Act of May 18, 1916 (39 Stat. 159 and 162). Made the weight limitation of first-class mail the same as that applicable to fourth-class mail. (It had previously been limited to four pounds.)

Act of October 3, 1917 (40 Stat. 327, 328). Effective thirty days after passage. This act increased the rate on first-class letters from two cents to three cents and on postal and post cards from one cent to two cents. (*Postal* cards are stamped cards issued by the Post Office. *Post* cards are commercially produced and sold.) It also raised and complicated the second-class rate structure and gave preferential treatment to religious, fraternal, etc., publications.

Act of May 10, 1918 (40 Stat. 548). Authorized the Postmaster General, at his discretion, to require the payment of postage on mail carried by airplane at a rate not exceeding twenty-four cents per ounce. (The Postmaster General, later in 1918, used his discretion to reduce the maximum rate from twenty-four cents to sixteen cents and, finally, to six cents, effective December 15. On July 18, 1919, the rate was dropped to two cents per ounce.)

Act of February 24, 1919 (40 Stat. 1150). Returned letter rates to two cents per ounce and the rate on postal and post cards to one cent.

Act of February 2, 1925 (43 Stat. 805). Provided for transportation of mail under contract, the rate of postage being not less than ten cents an ounce.

Act of February 28, 1925 (43 Stat. 1066–69). Effective April 15, 1925. Increased the rate on private mailing cards to two cents each, while retaining the one-cent rate on postal cards. This act also changed the basic law regarding the rates on second- and third-class matter and redefined each class of mail.

Act of May 17, 1928 (45 Stat. 594). Provided that airmail postage should be not less than five cents per ounce.

Act of May 29, 1928 (45 Stat. 940–44). Reduced the rate on private mailing cards to one cent each. Provided for the acceptance, without prepayment of postage, of business reply cards and envelopes, the postage to be paid by the original sender upon delivery. It also made sweeping changes in the second- and third-class rate structures. For the first time, special rates for bulk third-class mailing were provided in this act.

Act of June 6, 1932 (47 Stat. 285). Effective thirty days after enactment (to remain in effect until July 1, 1934). First-class letters were raised to three cents per ounce. Advertising matter in second-class publications was also given higher rates.

Act of June 16, 1933 (48 Stat. 254). In sections 2 and 3(a) of this act, the President was authorized to proclaim such modifications of postage rates on mail matter as might seem advisable by reason of an increase in business or the interests of the public. The President was not permitted, however, to lower first-class letter rates below two cents an ounce or to modify the rates on post cards and postal cards. This act also amended the Act of June 6, 1932, by returning the rate on local first-class letters to two cents (effective July 1, 1933).

Act of May 10, 1934 (48 Stat. 760). Continued the three-cent rate on first-class nonlocal mail as well as the President's authority to modify rates until July 1, 1935 (renewed subsequently June 28, 1935; June 29, 1937; June 29, 1939; May 28, 1941; June 17, 1943).

Act of June 12, 1934 (48 Stat. 933). Effective July 1, 1934. The rate of postage for airmail was set at six cents per ounce.

Act of February 25, 1944 (PL 72-235). Effective March 26, 1944 (to remain in effect until roughly six months after termination of hostilities). Local first-class mail increased from two cents to three cents, airmail increased from six cents to eight cents per ounce.

Act of August 14, 1946 (60 Stat. 1062). Effective October 1, 1946. Established airmail rate of five cents per ounce.

H.J. Resolution 221 of June 30, 1947 (61 Stat. 213). Provided permanent rate of three cents per ounce on all first-class letter mail.

Act of June 29, 1948 (62 Stat. 1097–98). Established air parcel post service with appropriate rates, based on zone system.

Act of July 3, 1948 (62 Stat. 1260–67). Increased airmail rate to six cents per ounce and made sizable increases in third-class rates.

Act of October 30, 1951 (65 Stat. 672–77). Increased rate on post cards and postal cards from one cent to two cents. Also significantly increased the rate for third-class bulk mailings.

Act of May 27, 1958 (72 Stat. 134). The Postal Policy Act raised the rate on first-class letters to four cents, on post cards and postal cards to three cents, and on airmail letters to seven cents an ounce. It also raised all other classes of mail.

Act of October 11, 1962 (76 Stat. 832). Increased postage on first-class letters to five cents, post cards and postal cards to four cents, and airmail letters to eight cents per ounce. All other classes of mail also increased.

Appendix B
Summary of the Most Important Laws Concerning Free Mail (1789–1967)

Acts of September 22, 1789 (1 Stat. 70), *August 4, 1790* (1 Stat. 178), and *March 3, 1791* (1 Stat. 218). Continued in effect the ordinance enacted by the Continental Congress on October 18, 1782. This ordinance permitted free mail to and from members of Congress (during sessions), to and from the heads of the departments of Finance, War, and Foreign Affairs, and to and from the principal officers of the U.S. Army.

Act of February 20, 1792 (1 Stat. 237, 238). Extended the frank to the President, the Vice-President, the Postmaster General, and their assistants, but limited the franking privilege of members of Congress to packets of two ounces or less. It also permitted every newspaper publisher to send, free of postage, one copy of his paper to every other publisher of a paper.

Act of March 3, 1797 (1 Stat. 512). Extended the frank to George Washington, after he left the Presidency, for the rest of his life. (This set a precedent that has been followed ever since.)

Act of March 2, 1799 (1 Stat. 737). Extended the frank to postmasters and certain other designated officials.

Act of April 3, 1800 (2 Stat. 19). Extended the frank to Martha Washington, widow of the late President. (This custom has also been followed ever since.)

Act of February 27, 1813 (2 Stat. 806). Permitted vaccine matter or printed material relating to the subject of vaccination to travel free through the mails.

Act of April 9, 1816 (3 Stat. 265). Extended the time during which congressmen might enjoy the franking privilege to thirty days before and after each session.

Act of March 3, 1825 (4 Stat. 110). Limited postmasters to free postage on letters not exceeding one-half ounce and to the receipt of one free newspaper a day. Extended the franking privilege of members of Congress to sixty days before and after each session. Those specifically granted the franking privilege included the President, the Vice-President, the secretaries of State, Treasury, War, and Navy, the Attorney General, the Postmaster General, the assistant postmasters general, the comptrollers of the Treasury, auditors, and the register and commissioner of the General Land Office.

Act of July 30, 1834 (4 Stat. 740). Permitted governors to transmit documents to governors of other states free of postage.

Act of July 2, 1836 (5 Stat. 88). Forbade postmasters to send or receive under the frank any packet containing anything other than paper or money.

Act of March 3, 1845 (5 Stat. 732–35, 739). Repealed all former acts on the subject. Tightened up the regulations and reduced the number of persons permitted the frank. Officers in the executive branch of the federal government were instructed to keep an account of all postage they had paid on official letters directed to them or emanating from them so that they could be reimbursed at the end of each quarter from the contingency fund of their own bureaus. The Post Office Department was given the right of reimbursement by the Treasury of all funds it would have collected if franked material had been charged postage.

Act of March 2, 1847 (9 Stat. 153). Permitted all postmasters whose compensation did not exceed $200 per year to send and receive personal letters (up to half an ounce each) free of postage.

Act of March 3, 1847 (9 Stat. 200–202). Repealed the provision of the Act of March 3, 1845, requiring the Post Office Department to keep accounts of all free mail and provided that the Treasury pay the Department $200,000 a year to cover the cost of this service.

Act of March 3, 1851 (9 Stat. 588, 591). Provided for free-in-county mailing of weekly newspapers. Raised the annual payment to the Post Office Department for the transmission of free government mail to $500,000 a year, payable quarterly.

Act of May 15, 1862 (12 Stat. 388). Permitted the Commissioner of Agriculture to send and receive free of postage all matter relating to the business of his department not exceeding thirty-two ounces in weight.

Act of March 3, 1863 (12 Stat. 708). Limited the privilege of franking mail matter to the President; the Vice-President; the heads of all executive departments; other functionaries in executive departments prescribed by the Postmaster General; members of Congress; postmasters, when writing officially to other postmasters; and petitions to Congress. A limit of four ounces was placed on all packages except petitions to Congress and seeds, roots, and the like. This act still permitted congressmen to receive and send mail free of charge, but limited all others within its purview only to *send* mail free of charge.

Act of March 16, 1864 (13 Stat. 30). Restored to the President and Vice-President the privilege of receiving, without charge, all mail matter directed to them.

Act of June 1, 1872 (17 Stat. 202). Repealed the provision of the Act of March 3, 1851, that provided for a specific appropriation to cover the expense of free mail. The Post Office Department was directed to cover the expense thereafter out of its annual appropriation.

Act of June 8, 1872 (17 Stat. 306, 307). Once again limited the franking privilege and redesignated those to whom it should apply. Permitted heads of executive departments to receive mail free of postage.

Act of January 31, 1873 (17 Stat. 421). Effective July 1, 1873. Abolished the franking privilege altogether. The act did not provide any compensation whatsoever to members of Congress or heads of executive departments for their postage costs.

Act of March 3, 1873 (17 Stat. 559). Repealed all laws and parts of laws permitting the transmission by mail of any free matter whatsoever.

Act of June 23, 1874 (18 Stat. 233). Re-established free-in-county delivery of weekly newspapers.

Act of March 3, 1875 (18 Stat. 343). Permitted congressmen to send speeches and reports through the mails free. Also re-established the privilege of the Commissioner of Agriculture to send seeds, cuttings, and the like free.

Act of March 3, 1877 (19 Stat. 335, 336). Permitted official communications from executive departments to go through the mails free, with the stipulation that anyone using this privilege for personal or private business would be subject to a fine of $300. (Thus "penalty mail" as differentiated from "franked mail" was created.)

Act of December 15, 1877 (20 Stat. 10). Permitted all elected officers of the federal government to send or receive free all public documents printed by order of Congress.

Act of March 3, 1891 (26 Stat. 1081). Permitted members of Congress to send official mail under their frank to any officer of the government.

Act of January 12, 1895 (28 Stat. 611, 617, 620, 622). Restored to members of Congress the right of sending letters free to private individuals as well as to officers of the government.

Act of April 27, 1904 (33 Stat. 313). Permitted the free transmission of material printed in raised characters for use by the blind.

Act of October 3, 1917 (40 Stat. 327). Extended to military personnel stationed overseas and engaged in the fighting of the war the privilege of sending letters through the mails free of postage.

Act of June 30, 1939 (53 Stat. 989). Clarified existing laws concerning free postage.

Act of March 27, 1942 (Sec. 901, PL 77-507). For the duration of hostilities, granted free postage privileges to all members of the armed forces on active duty.

Act of June 28, 1944 (58 Stat. 394–95). Effective July 1, 1944. Ordered all agencies of the federal government to include in their appropriation requests sufficient monies to cover the anticipated cost of their penalty mail and to deposit in the Treasury a sum sufficient to meet such costs. All penalty matter (except books and documents and stamped paper and supplies used by the Post Office Department) had a weight limit of four pounds.

Act of June 25, 1948 (62 Stat. 1048–49). Repealed the provisions of the Act of June 28, 1944, that required government agencies to pay the Treasury anticipated cost of their penalty mail.

Act of August 15, 1953 (67 Stat. 614). Provided that all departments, agencies, and establishments using the penalty privilege pay to the Post Office Department an amount equivalent to postage due for transmission of official matter. It also provided that the Post Office Department be paid by lump-sum appropriation for postage sent under the franking privilege by the President, the Vice-President, and members and members-elect of Congress.

Appendix C
Career Opportunities

The Post Office Department is a mammoth business operation, and its problems are at least equal to its size. In recent years, mail volume has been rapidly increasing, labor costs rising, and rail service, the principal means of moving the mails, steadily decreasing. This has left the Post Office with management and operational problems on all levels.

Well-trained, intelligent individuals with a variety of backgrounds —business, engineering, law, liberal arts—are needed to bring new managerial talent to the Post Office. Those qualified will be chosen from the Management Intern Examination, administered by the Civil Service Commission. There is opportunity—and challenge.

For additional information and specific details concerning this program as well as other areas of postal work, anyone interested should write the Bureau of Personnel, the Post Office Department, Washington, D.C. 20260.

Bibliography

The basic sources of information for this work include: (1) the annual reports of the Postmaster General (the first report, for the year 1789, was reproduced as Senate Executive Document 40, 48th Cong., 2d Sess., Vol. I, Part 1; the reports were then issued annually, beginning in 1823); (2) the *Congressional Globe,* 1835–73; (3) the *Congressional Record,* 1873–1967; (4) miscellaneous orders of the Postmaster General, published by the Post Office Department annually, beginning with Vol. I, 1897; (5) the various publications of postal employee organizations (principally, *The Postal Record, The Union Postal Clerk, The National Rural Letter Carrier,* the *Postal Supervisor,* the *Postal Transport Journal,* the *Postmasters' Advocate,* and the *Postmasters' Gazette*).

BOOKS, PAMPHLETS, AND PERIODICALS

BAYLES, W. HARRISON. "Postal Service in the Thirteen Colonies," *Journal of American History,* Vol. V, No. 3, 1911.

BEVERIDGE, ALBERT J. *Abraham Lincoln* (2 vols.). Boston: Houghton Mifflin, 1928.

Biographical Directory of the American Congress, 1774–1961. Washington, D.C.: Government Printing Office, 1961.

BLAINE, JAMES G. *Twenty Years of Congress* (2 vols.). Norwich, Conn.: Henry Bill Co., 1884–86.

BOWERS, CLAUDE G. *The Tragic Era.* Boston: Houghton Mifflin, 1929.

BRETZ, J. P. *Some Aspects of Postal Extension into the West.* New York: American Historical Association, 1900.

BRYCE, JAMES. *The American Commonwealth* (2 vols.). New York: Macmillan, 1891.

BUTLER, RUTH LAPHAM. *Doctor Franklin: Postmaster General.* New York: Doubleday, 1928.

CHU, PAO-HSUN. *The Post Office of the United States*. New York: Columbia University Press, 1932.

CONWELL, RUSSELL H. *The Romantic Rise of a Great American: John Wanamaker*. New York: Harper & Brothers, 1924.

CORDTZ, DAN. "It's Now or Never for the Post Office," *Fortune Magazine*, Vol. LXXV, No. 3, March, 1967, p. 134.

COX, WILLIAM VAN ZANDT. *The Life of Samuel Sullivan Cox*. Syracuse, N.Y.: H. M. Northrup, 1899.

"Crisis Coming in the Mails," *U.S. News and World Report*, Vol. LXII, No. 17, April 24, 1967.

CULBERTSON, WILLIAM S. *Alexander Hamilton*. New Haven, Conn.: Yale University Press, 1916.

CUSHING, M. H. *The Story of Our Post Office*. Boston: A. M. Thayer & Co., 1897.

DANIEL, EDWARD G. *United States Postal Service and Postal Policy 1789–1860*. Cambridge, Mass.: Harvard University Press, 1941.

DAVIS, MADISON. *The Public Career of Montgomery Blair*, Vol. XII. New York: Columbia Historical Society, 1910.

DAY, J. EDWARD. *My Appointed Round*. New York: Holt, Rinehart & Winston, 1965.

Dictionary of American Biography (20 vols.). New York: Scribner, n.d.

DOHERTY, WILLIAM C. *Mailman U.S.A.* New York: David McKay & Co., 1960.

DONALDSON, J. M. *A Wartime History of the Post Office Department*. Washington, D.C.: Government Printing Office, 1951.

DUNBAR, SEYMOUR. *A History of Travel in America* (4 vols.). Indianapolis: Bobbs-Merrill, 1915.

DYER, BRAINERD. *Zachary Taylor*. Baton Rouge, La.: Louisiana State University Press, 1946.

ECKENRODE, H. J. *Rutherford B. Hayes*. New York: Dodd, Mead, 1930.

FARLEY, JAMES A. *Behind the Ballots: The Personal History of a Politician*. New York: Harcourt, Brace, 1938.

———. *Jim Farley's Story*. New York: McGraw-Hill, 1948.

FENNO, RICHARD F. *The Power of the Purse: Appropriations Politics in Congress*. Boston: Little, Brown, 1966.

———. *The President's Cabinet*. Cambridge, Mass.: Harvard University Press, 1959.

FINLAY, HUGH. *Journal (1773–1774)*. Brooklyn, N.Y.: Frank H. Norton, 1867.

FIELDE, A. M. *A Political Primer of New York State and City*. New York: Macmillan, 1897.

FISH, C. R. *The Civil Service and the Patronage*, Vol. II. New York: Harvard Historical Studies, 1905.

FOWLER, DOROTHY GANFIELD. *The Cabinet Politician: The Postmaster General 1829–1909*. New York: Columbia University Press, 1943.

HAFEN, LEROY E. *The Overland Mail*. Cleveland: Arthur E. Clark Co., 1926.

HARLOW, ALVIN F. *Old Post Bags*. New York: D. Appleton & Co., 1928.

HARRIS, JOSEPH P. *Congressional Control of Administration*. Washington, D.C.: The Brookings Institution, 1964.

HENRY, LAURIN L. *Presidential Transitions*. Washington, D.C.: The Brookings Institution, 1960.

HOOGENBOOM, ARI. *Outlawing the Spoils: History of Civil Service Reform 1865–1883*. Urbana, Ill.: University of Illinois Press, 1961.

HOWE, M. A. DE WOLFE. *George von Lengerke Meyer: His Life and Works*. New York: Dodd, Mead, 1920.

HOLBROOK, STEWART H. *The Old Post Road*. New York: McGraw-Hill, 1962.

JAMES, MARQUIS. *Andrew Jackson: Patriot and President*. New York: Grosset & Dunlap, 1937.

JONES, W. B. *The Story of the Post Office*. Burlington, Vt.: Wells Richardson Co., 1889.

JOSEPHSON, MATTHEW. *The Politicos (1865–1896)*. New York: Harcourt, Brace, 1938.

KELLY, CLYDE. *United States Postal Policy*. New York: D. Appleton Co., 1932.

KLEIN, PHILIP SHRIVER. *President James Buchanan*. University Park, Pa.: Pennsylvania State University Press, 1962.

KONWISER, HARRY MYRON. *Colonial and Revolutionary Posts*. Richmond, Va.: Dietz, 1931.

LEARNED, HENRY BARRETT. *The President's Cabinet*. New Haven, Conn.: Yale University Press, 1912.

LEECH, D. D. T., and W. L. NICHOLSON. *History of the Post Office Department, 1789–1879*. Washington, D.C.: Judd & Detweiler, 1879.

LEECH, MARGARET. *In the Days of McKinley*. New York: Harper & Brothers, 1959.

LINDSEY, DAVID. *"Sunset" Cox: Irrepressible Democrat*. Detroit: Wayne State University Press, 1959.

LOMASK, MILTON. *Andrew Johnson: President on Trial*. New York: Farrar, Straus & Cudahy, 1960.

LYNCH, DENIS T. *The Wild Seventies*. New York: Appleton-Century, 1941.

MANN, DEAN E., and JAMESON W. DOIG. *The Assistant Secretaries: Problems and Processes of Appointment*. Washington, D.C.: The Brookings Institution, 1965.

McCORMAC, EUGENE IRVING. *James K. Polk: A Political Biography.* Berkeley, Calif.: University of California Press, 1922.

McREYNOLDS, ROSS ALLAN. *History of the United States Post Office 1607–1933.* Chicago: University of Chicago Press, 1935.

MERRILL, HORACE SAMUEL. *William Freeman Vilas: Doctrinaire Democrat.* Madison, Wis.: The State Historical Society of Wisconsin, 1954.

MINER, WARD L. *William Goddard: Newspaperman.* Durham, N.C.: Duke University Press, 1962.

MORONEY, RITA LLOYD. *Montgomery Blair: Postmaster General.* Washington, D.C.: Government Printing Office, 1963.

NEUSTADT, RICHARD E. "The Presidency and Legislation: The Growth of Central Clearance," *The American Political Science Review,* Vol. XLVIII, No. 3, September, 1954, p. 641.

NEWCOMB, H. T. *The Postal Deficit.* Washington, D.C.: William Ballantyne & Sons, 1900.

OBERHALTZER, ELLIS P. *A History of the United States Since the Civil War* (5 vols). New York: Macmillan, 1917–30.

POORE, BEN: PERLEY. *Reminiscences of Sixty Years in the National Metropolis.* Philadelphia: Hubbard, 1886.

"The Progress and Present Condition of the General Post Office," *United States Magazine and Democratic Review,* Vol. VI, No. XXI, September, 1839.

REES, JAMES. *Foot-Prints of a Letter Carrier.* Philadelphia: J. B. Lippincott & Co., 1866.

RICH, WESLEY EVERETT. *The History of the United States Post Office to the Year 1829.* Cambridge: Harvard University Press, 1924.

RICHARDSON, J. D. (ed.). *Messages and Papers of the Presidents,* rev. ed. New York: Bureau of National Literature, Inc., 1923.

ROGERS, LINDSAY. *The Postal Power of Congress.* Baltimore, Md.: Johns Hopkins University Press, 1916.

ROPER, DANIEL C. *The United States Post Office.* New York: Funk & Wagnalls, 1917.

SANDBURG, CARL. *Abraham Lincoln: The War Years* (4 vols.). New York: Harcourt, Brace, 1939.

SCHURZ, CARL. *The Reminiscences of Carl Schurz* (3 vols.). New York: McClure, 1908.

SMITH, ADAM. *The Wealth of Nations.* New York: Modern Library, n.d.

SMITH, THEODORE C. *The Life and Letters of James Abram Garfield* (2 vols.). New Haven, Conn.: Yale University Press, 1925.

SPERO, STERLING DENHARD. *Labor Movement in a Government Industry.* New York: Doran, 1924.

SUMMERFIELD, ARTHUR E. *U.S. Mail.* New York: Holt, Rinehart & Winston, 1960.

UNITED STATES POST OFFICE DEPARTMENT. *Financial Policy for the Post Office Department* (published 1954).

————. *The Impact of Postal Rate Increases* (published 1960).

————. *Postage Rates 1789–1930* (published 1930).

————. *Postage Rates 1930–1944* (published 1944).

————. *Survey of Postal Rates* (published 1960).

————. *United States Domestic Postage Rates 1789–1956* (published 1956).

WERNER, M. R. *Tammany Hall.* New York: Doubleday, Doran, 1928.

WIGHT, WILLIAM WARD. *Henry Clay Payne: A Life.* Milwaukee: Burdick & Allen, 1907.

WILLIAMS, N. B. *The American Post Office.* Fayetteville, Ark.: University of Arkansas Press, 1909.

WOOLLEY, MARY EMMA. *The Early History of the Colonial Post-Office.* Providence, R.I.: Rhode Island Historical Society, 1894.

Index